ANTIOQUEÑO COLONIZATION IN WESTERN COLOMBIA

ANTIOQUEÑO COLONIZATION IN WESTERN COLOMBIA

BY

JAMES J. PARSONS

Revised Edition

UNIVERSITY OF CALIFORNIA PRESS
BERKELEY AND LOS ANGELES
1968

First Edition, 1949
University of California Publications in
Ibero-Americana, Vol. 32
Second Edition, Revised, 1968

Spanish-language editions (translated and annotated by Emilio Robledo)
Medellín, 1950, and Bogota, 1961

University of California Press
Berkeley and Los Angeles
California

◆

Cambridge University Press
London, England

Library of Congress Catalog Card No.: 68-58002

copyright © 1968 by the
regents of the university
of california

PREFACE TO THE REVISED EDITION

THE FIELD WORK on which the original version of this study was based was carried out during a seven-months sojourn in Colombia in 1946, with headquarters in Medellín. I would here reiterate my deep sense of gratitude and affection to Professor Carl O. Sauer, my mentor for half a lifetime, who originally directed my interests towards Antioquia as a distinctive culture area, and who has been a continuing source of intellectual stimulation and guidance ever since. Among many genial Antioqueño hosts I would again single out Luis Ospina Vásquez and the late Dr. Emilio Robledo and Gabriel Arango Mejía, all Medellinenses, whose kind counsel and assistance is reflected throughout these pages.

Since the appearance of the first edition of this work (University of California: Ibero-Americana, vol. 32, 1949), and the later Spanish-language versions, so generously translated and annotated by Dr. Robledo (*La Colonización Antioqueña en el Occidente de Colombia*, Medellín, 1950; revised, Bogotá, 1961), great change has come to the Antioqueño countryside. The extent and pace of this change perhaps comes even more forcibly to the attention of the returning visitor than it does to the permanent resident. In the last two decades Medellín has evolved from an isolated provincial capital to a metropolitan conurbation of more than a million persons. Indeed, it has recently occurred to me that more than half of the present population of Antioquia and Caldas had not yet been born at the time I took my first stroll across the Parque Berrío in 1946. But notwithstanding the very rapid rate of population increase, so characteristic of most of Latin America, the level of living and literacy in Antioquia has continued to climb at a pace substantially above the average.

The reception given the original version of this work by Colombians has encouraged me to prepare a second English-language edition. Several visits to Colombia over the intervening years have provided the bases for many of the revisions and alterations in the original text, but I have drawn equally upon the considerable literature on the regional geography and social history of western Colombia that has appeared since 1949. Especially noteworthy have been the works of Ernesto Gühl, Everett E. Hegen, Luis Ospina Vásquez, and

Robert C. West. These and other important contributions of direct relevance to the subject of this study that have appeared since the first edition, are listed in the supplementary bibliography, pp. 000. Colombia's 1964 Census of Population and the 1964 Census of Manufactures, although not yet available in final form, have been used to update much of the statistical data. My recent monograph on *Antioquia's Corridor to the Sea: An Historical Geography of the Settlement of Urabá* (University of California: Ibero-Americana, vol. 49, 1967) further expands on some of the themes originally developed in this volume.

The principal substantive changes and additions in this second edition will be found in the sections on population growth, transportation, and industrial development (chapters 8, 11, and 12). Parts of chapters 4, 6, and 10 have also been revised, and the text throughout has been brought up-to-date wherever possible. A few notes and a somewhat larger number of bibliographic citations also have been added. Maps 8, 9, and 13 have been redrawn and several of the photographic plates at the back have been replaced by others. These changes have not significantly altered the sense of the original thesis, essentially a delineation in historical perspective of the distinctive Antioqueño culture and economy and the extent and character of its geographic spread.

J. J. P.

August, 1967

CONTENTS

CHAPTER	PAGE
I. The People	1
II. The Natural Setting	10
III. Original Indian Inhabitants	29
IV. Spanish Mines and the Labor Supply	36
V. Colonial Agricultural Settlement	60
VI. Modern Antioqueño Colonization	69
VII. Public Land Policies	96
VIII. Population Growth	102
IX. The Agricultural Basis of Occupance	109
X. Coffee	137
XI. Transportation	154
XII. The New Industrial Era	174
Notes	191
Bibliography	214
Index	227
Plates	236

MAPS

1. Antioqueño Colonization (circa 1950)	Frontis
2. Physiographic Regions of Central Colombia	12
3. Climatic Zones	18
4. Principal Indian Provinces at the Time of the Conquest	32
5. Administrative Divisions of Colonial Antioquia	40
6. Nineteenth-Century Land Grants on the Southern Frontier	68
7. The Department of Caldas, 1907	88
8. The Coffeegrowing Areas of Colombia	143
9. Movement of Colombian Coffee from the Interior to Maritime Ports (circa 1960)	146
10. Major Pack Trails (*Caminos de Herradura*)	156
11. Railroad Construction in Central Colombia	164
12. Highway Construction in Central Colombia	168
13. Major Industrial Establishments in the Valley of Aburrá, 1966	177
14. The Antioqueño Country: Orientation Map	foldout

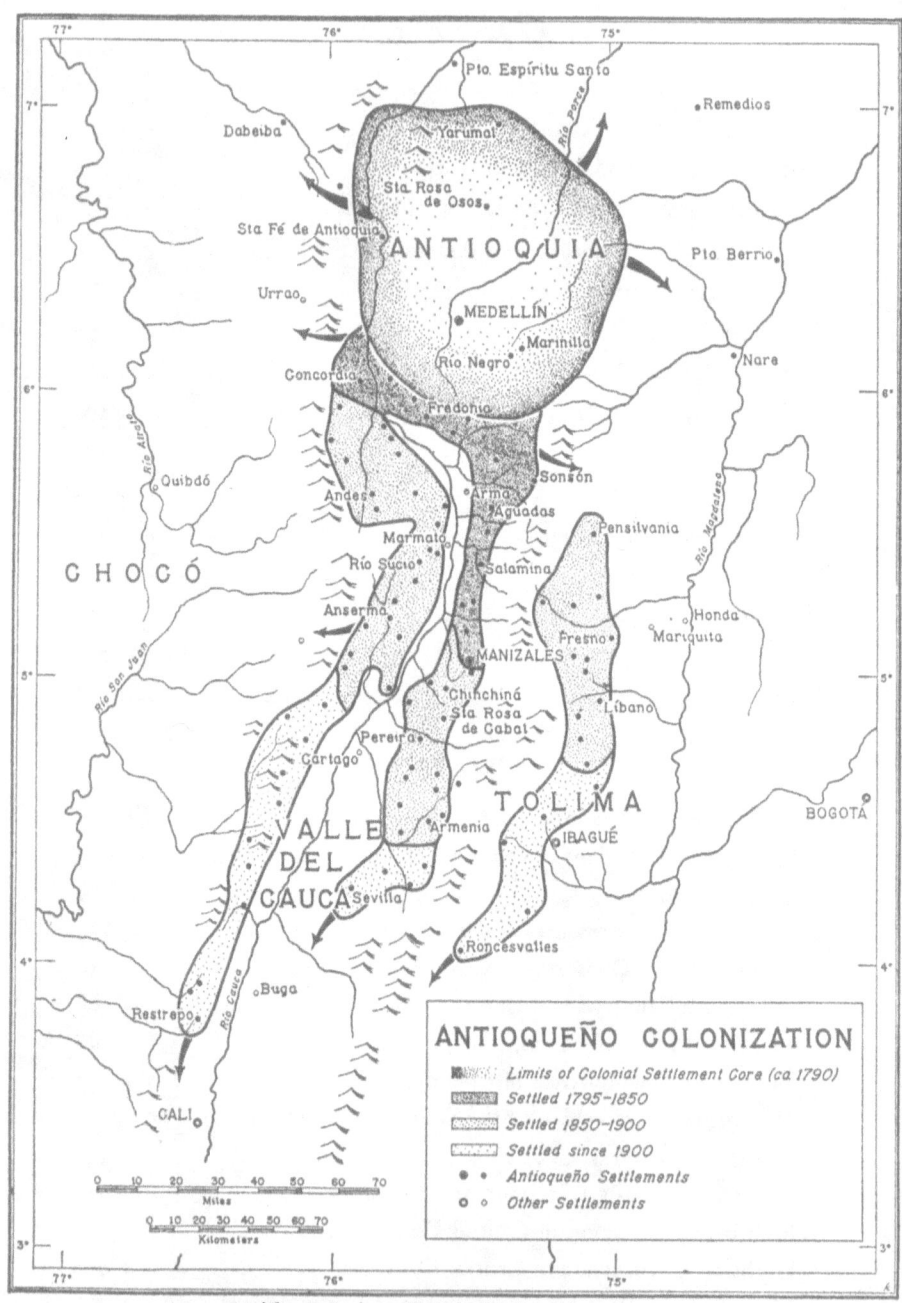

Map 1. Antioqueño Colonization (circa 1950).

I. THE PEOPLE

THE TEMPERATE uplands of the northernmost Andes of western Colombia are the home of the energetic and thrifty Antioqueños, the self-styled "Yankees of South America." They are shrewd, aggressive individualists whose extraordinary colonizing genius and vigor have made them the dominant and most clearly defined population element of the republic. Their long and effective geographical isolation in the interior highlands of Colombia is reflected in a determined conservatism and a marked cultural particularism. Being Antioqueño means more to them than being Colombian.

In a surge of colonizing fervor which began a century and a half ago, before the Viceroyalty of New Granada became Colombia, they have pushed their frontier southward along the rugged Andean slopes until today they occupy a zone some 400 kilometers long by 160 kilometers wide between the Magdalena Valley and the rain forest of the Chocó. The heart of the settlement area is bisected by a belt of darker-skinned peoples living in the hot lowlands along the Río Cauca, which cuts a furrow through the western Colombian highlands (maps 1, 14).

The "Antioqueño country" includes much more than the old Province of Antioquia, within which lives only half of the four million Colombians who call themselves Antioqueños. Besides the coffee-rich department of Caldas, "proudest achievement of the Antioqueños," and its recent offshoots, Risaralda and Quindío, the area of settlement includes the coffee lands of northern Tolima and Valle del Cauca, extending southward along the slopes of the Central Cordillera and Western Cordillera to the new Antioqueño *municipios* of Roncesvalles and Restrepo, and beyond. Despite this geographical expansion all the cultural ties and allegiances of these people lead back to the old heartland of highland Antioquia and to the beautiful, mile-high valley of Medellín. The rural society of Antioquia is composed of small landholders and homesteaders and is in sharp contrast to most of latifundian Latin America. Notwithstanding dependence on coffee as the single cash crop, Antioqueño agriculture has shown a reasonably healthy diversity; cattle raising is an important subsidiary undertaking. The economy has remained aloof from the speculative rushes into tobacco, quinine, indigo, and cotton which characterized much of nineteenth-century Colombian economic history.[1]

The quest for gold was the immediate cause of the sixteenth-century Spanish settlement of the Province of Antioquia. Drawn by legends of fabulous hidden riches and by news of actual strikes, the first conquistadores were soon followed by the more numerous Basque and Asturian immigrants. The hill of Buriticá, in the Western Cordillera behind the old capital of Santa Fé de Antioquia, was the place of greatest interest to the early gold seekers, the source of much of the Indian gold from the Quindío and Sinú graves. However, most of the lodes and placers, worked by primitive, hand-washing methods, left little surplus beyond that needed to pay for foodstuffs brought in on the backs of Indian carriers over trails often made difficult by tropical rains. Moreover, the Indian labor supply was rapidly reduced by virulent diseases introduced by the Spaniards, and capital necessary for the importation of Negroes from the Cartagena slave market was seldom available. While the richer settlers exploited the gravels and quartz ore bodies with their slave gangs, others went with pan and pickax as independent prospectors (*mazamorreros*). Many of the Spaniards, as well as their mestizo offspring, were thus forced into productive labor for their own account. This situation gave an early impetus to Antioquia's democratic tradition of work, which has contrasted sharply with the class structure to the south and west where the Indian element has remained more numerous.

There is a curious quality to the Antioqueño picture, reminiscent of French Canada. The notably small number of surnames suggests the selection imposed by geography on the very few hundreds of Spanish immigrants from which the present-day families have sprung. Such names as Restrepo, Uribe, Mejía, Londoño, Jaramillo, and Arango are recognized as typically Antioqueño throughout Colombia. The credentials which the great majority of these settlers brought with them from their home parishes on the Peninsula indicate that they were "Old Christians" (*cristianos viejos, limpios de toda mala raza*).[2] Yet the fable still persists that early Antioquia was settled by Sephardic Jews. It has been nurtured by the Antioqueños' reputation as am-

[1] For notes to chap. i, see p. 191.

bitious, hard-headed businessmen with a superior aptitude for trade and commerce. In 1720, when the Crown ordered all foreigners expelled from the colonies, only two were found in the Province of Antioquia, both Italians. The descendants of one, Juan Botero, are so numerous today that the surname is as characteristically Antioqueño as Restrepo or Uribe.

The arduous river journey up the Río Magdalena and Río Cauca to the head of navigation at Zaragoza or Puerto Espíritu Santo, and then ten or more hard days over mountain mule trails, could hardly have enhanced the attractions of Antioquia to new arrivals in Cartagena. The alluvial valley lands around Medellín and Santa Fé de Antioquia had been granted to conquistadores and their mestizo descendants, and the deeply weathered crystalline uplands were of value only for their mining rights, so that the opportunities for a landed gentry were restricted. Among the immigrants there were no courtiers and probably fewer Spanish women than the patrilineal genealogists of Antioquia would admit. But women did come, especially in the surge of settlement in the seventeenth century which brought a shift from the old, hot-country capital at Santa Fé to the new *villa* of Medellín. The conquistador Jorge Robledo had earlier set the precedent by returning from a visit to Spain with a new wife and a party of sixteen ladies-in-waiting. One of these, Doña Mencia de Carvajal, is said to have lived in the province to the ripe old age of one hundred and ten years, personally directing the operations of her mine and ranch interests. Although several of the more aristocratic branches of the early families have kept their blood lines "pure," the basic tri-ethnic quality of the Antioqueño stock is clearly evident in the rural areas, as well as in the working-class suburbs of Medellín and Manizales.

From the early mixture of the Spanish, and Indian and Negro slave elements there evolved the people who today, in ethnological heresy, call themselves *la raza antioqueña*. Although this misapplication of the term "race" to cover a cultural concept has been criticized by local scholars, it is firmly entrenched in popular usage. Indeed, a regional magazine recently established in Medellín carried the title *La Raza*. The characteristic Antioqueño physical type has been described as tall, dark, with large and piercing eyes, an aquiline nose, high forehead, and hair and beard abundant, but it is their cultural cohesion rather than any physical similarities which distinguishes them. The social and economic distinction between whites (*blancos*) and half-castes (*gente de color*), precisely marked in an earlier day, has become increasingly obscured. Until 1918 the national census regularly included a breakdown according to "color" which, of course, merely reflected the social attitudes of the interrogator and interrogated. Yet

TABLE 1
RACIAL COMPOSITION OF ANTIOQUIA

Race	Census of 1808[a]	Census of 1912	Census of 1918
	per cent	per cent	per cent
Mestizo and mulatto.................	57.7[b]	45.0	52.4
White.............................	25.6	34.6	31.1
Negro.............................	12.2[c]	18.2	15.3
Indian............................	4.5	2.2	1.2
Total population...................	106,856	735,470	823,226

[a] Computed from statistics in Filipe Pérez, *Jeografía Física i Política del Estado de Antioquia* (Bogotá, 1863), p. 3.
[b] Includes free Negroes.
[c] Slaves only.

the preponderance of mixed blood, indicated in table 1, is in striking contradiction to the frequent assertion that Antioquia is a white province. In the new Antioqueño department of Caldas both the 1912 and 1918 censuses showed a similar preponderance of mestizos and mulattoes. In the populous Quindío region, for instance, the mixed bloods (*mezclados*) outnumbered the whites by nearly four to one.

During colonial times the whites constituted an honored if unpolished aristocracy whose position was unquestioningly accepted by the lower classes. The governor reported to the Crown in 1776:

> They have a great enthusiasm for nobility and are so inordinately proud that all are immersed in the study of their titles and their relationships with the first conquistadores and settlers. They ordinarily contract marriage with very immediate relatives within their own family (in my judgment with no little gain in privilege) because each is reputed among themselves as better than the others.

They dearly love tedious and ceremonious formalities in public functions, perpetuating tenaciously the customs of the times of the conquistadores.... Their luxury and fashion have a very limited sphere, for all vanity is reduced to wishing to be people of quality and position. Their dress styles are the most out-moded and strange. Some newly arrived Spaniards and other patricians who have had business with the outside or go abroad to study occasionally introduce new dress, but within a few days they all return to the old.[ ]

Until the end of the colonial period most observers were struck by the general backwardness, illiteracy, and poverty of the province. Agriculture was almost completely neglected for the mines, and commerce was undeveloped. For want of iron the land continued to be cleared by flint-headed Indian axes (*macanas*). Most of the tillable valleys, as well as the granitic uplands, were held by a few wealthy grantees like Antonio de Quintana, whose immense domain included the present municipios of Carolina, Angostura, and parts of Yarumal and Santa Rosa de Osos.

The cultural and economic renaissance which transformed this tranquil but impoverished backwoods province into a virile, literate, and relatively wealthy state was initiated under the energetic leadership of the royal inspector (*oidor*) appointed by the Crown in 1784 at the request of Governor Francisco Silvestre, whose detailed and thoughtful reports on the province had been one of the first products of the new period of French enlightenment in New Granada. The Oidor Juan Antonio Mon y Velarde, although in the province only three years, has been called "The Regenerator of Antioquia."[ ] His far-reaching social, economic, and juridical reforms stirred the lethargic community to activity. New towns, the first truly agricultural settlements in the province, were established in the cooler, malaria-free uplands, and bounties were offered for the introduction of new crops. Vagrancy laws were enforced and the idle sent to help people the new towns and till the new fields. His was the discipline of work under which the Antioqueño economy and culture was to flower in the following century, and he wrote:

> We are all born to work and it is necessary to consider as delinquents of human society those who are not useful to their country and who do not employ their energies and talents in providing at least their own subsistence.[ ]

In his last report to the King he predicted that "this Province of Antioquia, today the most backward in all the New Kingdom of Granada, will one day be the most opulent."

By the late eighteenth century both gold production and immigration had fallen off sharply. The scattered nature of the mineral deposits had encouraged a gradual expansion of settlement into the cooler uplands, so that for a time Ríonegro (elev., 2,120 m.) challenged Medellín (elev., 1,540 m.) as the first city of the province. Early marriage and large families favored a rapid increase in the population which, in turn, brought increasing pressure on available food supplies. The new emphasis on agriculture which followed Mon y Velarde's *visita* and the termination of the prolonged litigation between Ríonegro and the old villa of Santa Fé de Antioquia for ownership of the Río Negro meadowlands brought the first significant spilling over of Antioqueño settlers into the empty, forested slopes to the south and southwest at the beginning of the nineteenth century. Here the unproductive, red surfaces of the Antioquia highlands gave way to the deep, fertile volcanic soils of the Mellizos and Ruiz-Tolima areas. Here, too, was the principal break in the girdle of tropical rain forest which hemmed in Antioquia to the north, east, and west.

Sonsón and Abejorral in the south, and, later, Fredonia to the west, became general headquarters for pioneers advancing into the present Caldas and Tolima and westward across the Río Cauca into the *Occidente* of Antioquia. For nearly a century and a half this homesteading frontier has pressed steadily southward along the middle slopes of the cordillera in three separate lobes (map 1) until today there are outliers of Antioqueño colonies even beyond Popayán, in the volcanic lands of Moscopán in Huila, on the slopes of the Bogotá Cordillera, in the Florencia area of Caquetá, and even in northernmost Ecuador. More recent colonization has taken place on the northern fringes of the Antioqueño country and toward the Magdalena valley, but the traditional Antioqueño frontier has remained in the mountains to the south.

The frequent litigation over land titles is reminiscent of early California. Most of these unoccupied mountainsides were claimed *in absentia* under Spanish land grants, but the squatters won out in the end. In Colombia, too, possession has always been nine-tenths of the law. Between 1847 and 1914 the Congress of the Republic attempted to regularize and encourage settlement. Land grants, usually of 12,000 hectares (29,640 acres), were made to more than twenty new towns in Caldas and Tolima, either voiding or disregarding colonial claims. The consequent insecure position of landholders, together with almost constant political unrest, seems to have operated as an impetus to push the frontier ahead.

As the empty lands to the south have filled in and the "growing edge" of Antioqueño settlement has moved farther from Medellín and Manizales, the pace of colonization has slackened. Agrarianism is today being challenged by an explosive new industrial urbanism which, in considerable measure, is an outgrowth of a revolution in transportation. Almost overnight greater Medellín, with a population of one million persons, has become one of the most important manufacturing centers of Latin America. Within the memory of many adults the city was dependent on pack trains or human carriers for its links with the outside world. Today it is a road hub, and its airport handles some fifty scheduled passenger flights a day. The other major Antioqueño cities, Manizales (pop. 190,000 in 1964), Pereira (150,000), and Armenia (125,000), have experienced an almost equally explosive growth.

Once the objects of pity and concern, the frugal, hard-working Antioqueños today boast the highest standard of living in Colombia. Amongst them tradesmen and small proprietors have achieved a dignity and economic opportunity not common in other parts of Latin America. Even before coffee and textiles had begun to pour new wealth into the department a German traveler had observed:

> There are probably few places of similar size in South America where as many important fortunes are concentrated as in Medellín. The number of families considered as rich is considerable, but with few exceptions they appear so unassuming that their wealth, won mostly by trade and mining, and less commonly through farming and stock-raising, is not apparent. Even the middle classes or artisans are well situated.[8]

There has been a certain reorientation of Antioqueño colonizing energies in the past fifteen years toward the rainier tropical lowlands of Urabá, the Sinú country, the lower Cauca (Bajo Cauca), and the middle Magdalena valleys. Facilitated by revolutionary improvements in highway and air transport, it has been of a character quite different from the traditional Antioqueño settlement on the southern frontier. Here capitalists and merchants tend to replace the colonist. Antioqueño economic and cultural penetration involves no moving frontier but rather a leapfrogging to favored nuclei of settlement, often far removed from the mountainous heartland. The community cohesiveness of an earlier period is replaced by a looser set of ties, for now the hard labor of felling the forest and establishing maize plantings and pasture is largely in the hands of day laborers from the coast or the Magdalena lowlands. The Antioqueño is the entrepreneur, not the settler. In place of individual initiative in establishing the frontier infrastructure, dependence is increasingly on such government agencies as the Land Reform Institute (INCORA), which provides supervised credit, confirmed land titles, access roads, and technical assistance.

From a colonial mining-camp society there developed in Antioquia a kind of Latin puritanism which still prevails throughout the rural areas and which survives in only slightly modified form in the strict social and moral codes of modern Medellín and Manizales. In piety and devoutness the Antioqueños are far ahead of other Colombian ethnic groups, for they embrace Catholicism with the conscientious passion of their forefathers. The frequent occurrence of Biblical place names, such as Belén, Betulia, Betania, Jericó, Líbano, Palestina, and even Antioquia itself, further attests to this.

The strong regional characer of Antioqueño diet, dress, and speech is being stubbornly and proudly preserved. The extensive local poetry and literature continues to extoll the simple virtues of the traditional subsistence agricultural economy (*la vida maicera*) of these mountains. In dress it is still the inevitable *carriel,* a fur-covered side bag of countless hidden pockets, that is the surest mark of the true Antioqueño (*de pura cepa*), whether it is worn under a white cotton *poncho* or its dark woolen counterpart, the *ruana*. Outside of his native habitat the Antioqueño can usually be identified by his accent and his loquacity—of both he is extraordinarily proud. Although it is often held that the Spanish spoken around Medellín is the purest to be found in the Americas, a large number of provincialisms of Carib and Quechua origin have crept into the direct and graphic speech. An acute consciousness of this penetration is reflected by the poet Gregorio Gutiérrez González when he says, in the prologue to his beloved *Memoria Sobre el Cultivo del Maíz*, "I write not Spanish but Antioqueño."

Although elsewhere in the republic the down-slope migration of agriculture and settlement has been a persistent theme for more than a century, the Antioqueño countryman (*campesino*) has retained his mountaineer's attitude. The introduction of coffee as a major cash crop after 1880 simply reinforced the pattern of small mountainside holdings which characterized the earlier homestead frontier. Wherever the settler has gone he has transplanted his unique cultural heritage. Thus Caldas has become a second Antioqueño department "more Antioqueño than Antioquia." This cultural cohesiveness has its roots deep in the past, in the time before the limited opportunities of an impoverished homeland sent the Antioqueño searching for new lands to the south and west.

II. THE NATURAL SETTING

TOPOGRAPHY

THE TWO GREAT river valleys of Colombia, the Magdalena and the Cauca, provide avenues from the Caribbean plains into the heart of the Andean ranges where the snowy crests of Ruiz and Tolima tower directly above the hot lowlands both on the east and on the west. Like the prongs of a fork, the three cordilleras flare out northward from the massive Pasto Knot where the two parallel Andean ranges of Ecuador merge just north of the international boundary. The middle prong of the fork is the high Central Cordillera, an imposing volcanic range culminating in the 5,400-meter Nevado del Ruiz. North of the Caldas-Antioquia border volcanic slopes give way to the older, stable crystalline highland of Antioquia (map 2), whose rolling upland surface gives clear evidence of former peneplanation. This old plateau (*meseta*) is diagonally pierced by the deep canyon of the Río Porce which, in its upper reaches, widens out into the U-shaped valley of Medellín or Aburrá[1] (pl. 1). To the east of the Central Cordillera, beyond the Magdalena lowlands, lies the massive Bogotá or Eastern Cordillera, with its high, treeless *páramos* of Cundinamarca, Boyacá, and Santander, traditional centers of Chibcha, Spanish, and Colombian culture and government. The third north–south trending Andean spur, the lower Western Cordillera, blocks off the Cauca Valley[2] from the Pacific Ocean and the hot, rain-drenched Chocó.

The upper Río Cauca is a placid stream in its 150-kilometer course across the level floor of "El Valle" above Cartago, but through the heart of the Antioqueño country it is deeply entrenched and areas of level land along or near it are very limited. It enters the rapids-filled box canyon of Caldas north of Cartago and continues through the spectacular lower gorge beyond Santa Fé de Antioquia before emerging onto the flood plain of the lower Río Cauca. In this middle, 215-kilometer stretch the turbulent river has an average gradient of 3.6 per cent as compared with the 0.3 per cent gradient between Puerto Valdivia and the Río Magdalena.

[1] For notes to chap. ii, see pp. 191–193.

The Natural Setting

The morphology of the Caldas and Antioquia mountains is little known. Hettner's 1893 account, based on existing literature and his own brief trip from Bogotá to the Marmato mines, termed Antioquia a *terra incognita*.[3] His references were principally to the observations of a few mining engineers and travelers who had visited the mines of Antioquia, Cauca, or the Chocó—Boussingault, Degenhardt, Pashke, Regel, White, Karsten, and Stübel. The first attempted delineation of the topography was De Greiff's map of 1857, which provided the base for the maps accompanying Schenck's 1880 and 1883 reports in *Petermanns Mitteilungen,* but the first contoured map was the handsome Bogotá sheet of the American Geographical Society's 1:1,000,000 series, published in 1945. Grosse has mapped in detail a belt, 25 kilometers wide, along the Cauca between the Río Arma and Sopetrán in connection with his studies of the Amagá coal seams.[4] Topographic maps (1:50,000) are being prepared from air photos by the Instituto Geográfico.

The structural and geographical relationships of the Central Cordillera of Colombia show that it is clearly a continuation of the majestic, volcano-topped Eastern Cordillera of Ecuador. Geologically it comprises ancient granites, gneisses, and crystalline schists, mother rocks to the gold and silver enrichments of the Caldas and Tolima flanks and the auriferous highlands of Antioquia, overlain locally by folded early Tertiary sandstones and shales. From Pasto north to the Antioquia border the older range has been crowned by ash and lava beds derived from a chain of still-active volcanoes. Several of these peaks reach well above the permanent snow line (4,500–4,800 m.), including the Puracé-Coconucos cluster behind Popayán, the Nevado de Huila southeast of Cali, and the Ruiz-Tolima or Quindío cluster between Manizales and Ibagué. Nowhere between Pasto and Sonsón is there a break in this mountain wall, and the high, cloud-ridden passes (e.g., Guanacas, 3,130 m.; Yerbabuena, 2,980 m.; Calarcá, 3,280 m.; Quindío, 3,485 m.; La Elvira, 3,684 m.; Herveo, 3,650 m.) provide no easy route between the Valle del Cauca and eastern Colombia.

At least two post-Conquest falls of ash and one catastrophic mud flow are known to have taken place. The eruption of Ruiz, on March 12, 1595, which Fray Pedro Simón reported,[5] left three inches of ash and pumice over the town of Cartago and did great damage to corn-

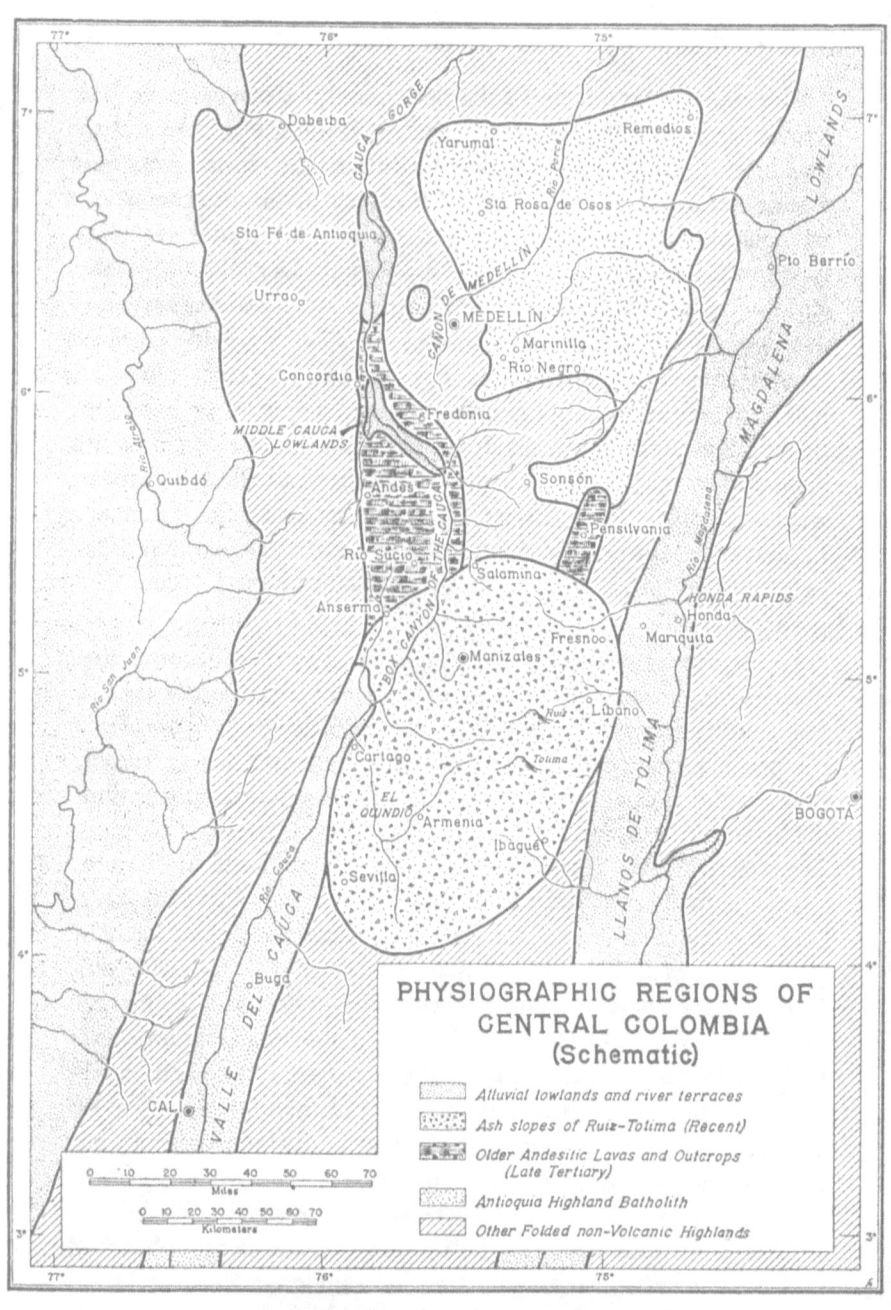

Map 2. Physiographic Regions of Central Colombia.

The Natural Setting

fields as far west as Toro Viejo, in the Río San Juan (Chocó) drainage, 28 leagues west of Cartago. A second rain of ashes "from the east" fell over Cartago and the Chocó, on March 14, 1805, covering plants with a black ash at Anserma.[6] The mud flow of February 19, 1845, supposedly caused by a sudden melting of the snow and ice cap on Ruiz, inundated the valley of the Río Lagunilla and the town of Armero on the Tolima flank of the volcano.[7] Such eruptions have built a deep mantle of ash, cinders, and lava on both flanks of the central range and this material has weathered into the productive soils on which much of the Antioqueño colonization has been based.

There are at least seven distinct crater cones in the Quindío cluster (Ruiz, Olleta, Cisne, Santa Isabel, Quindío, Tolima, and Machín) which give evidence of activity in the recent geologic past. Their relative heights and even identity are, however, badly confused.[8] All these craters, except Machín, extend into the zone of permanent snow. The exposure of andesitic lavas under thick ash deposits in the canyon of the Río Roble northwest of Circasia (Caldas) suggests that lavas from earlier fissures and vents may underlie the great modern cones.

The Antioquia highland is an extensive Mesozoic batholith which covers an area of at least 8,000 square kilometers.[9] Its deeply weathered quartz-diorites and grano-diorites display a gently rolling relief which contrasts strongly with the higher, comblike volcanic range which stretches south from the Caldas border. Although its southern boundary has been mapped as the Caldas-Antioquia line, these same older rocks appear along the lower flanks of the Central Cordillera at least as far south as Manizales and Mariquita. Everywhere they are laced with gold-bearing quartz and calcite veins. The deep, transverse cleft of the Río Porce (Río Medellín) divides the acid igneous area into two almost equal parts. The batholith is tilted asymmetrically and drainage is from its high western rim toward the Río Magdalena. In their upper courses the streams are typically sluggish and swamp-bordered, but further eastward they plunge turbulently from the highlands through steep-walled ravines. Near Entrerríos, Peñol, and Sonsón there are striking exfoliation domes which were once misinterpreted as glacial erratics.[10]

The granitic area is flanked on its margins by more resistant pre-Cambrian and Paleozoic metamorphics and associated basic intrusives. On its western edge amphibolites and serpentines predominate, from La Unión northward to San Andrés and Yarumal. Around Medellín the serpentines are represented by the barren red lands (*los parches*) which form both slopes of the valley of Medellín between the city and Copacabana. South of La Unión and along the eastern margin of the batholith they are replaced by schists, quartzites, and marbles. The margins of the batholith have not been mapped in detail but are currently under investigation by the Escuela de Minas and Planta Metalúrgica in Medellín. They are of economic importance because of the localization here of mineralized fissures.

On some of the highest parts of the granitic highlands, in the vicinity of Santa Rosa de Osos, Amalfi, and Guarne, overburdens of stratified gravels of uncertain origin reach depths of more than sixty feet.[11] Both these gravels and the deeply rotted bedrock of the batholith have been extensively worked by gold miners for more than three centuries. At Santa Rosa, which stands on a high knoll overlooking the bleak uplands of much of northern Antioquia, mining activities have caused them to be ripped with deep gulleys which seriously interfere with access to the city.

The north-south parallelism of the topography, absent in the Antioquia highlands, is recognizable in the lower and more broken, folded Tertiary zone, 20 kilometers wide, which follows the axis of the Río Cauca trough from northernmost Caldas to beyond the city of Antioquia. Here are found the coal-bearing early Tertiary strata studied by Grosse. They comprise the two compactly parallel, synclinal axes of Ebéjico-Titiribí and Heliconia-Amagá-Poblanco, their straight borders represented by overthrust folds. In the broadest sense of the word the middle Cauca lowland below the Río San Juan has been interpreted by Grosse as of similar origin (*eine solche Überschiebungsenke*).[12] Within this zone the more resistant uplands are commonly blocks of pre-Cambrian schists or slates. At Amagá, where the Ferrocarril de Antioquia obtains its supplies, the coal horizons average 10 meters in exploitable depth. In Caldas the formation has been mostly buried under ash and lavas, but exposed seams have been less extensively worked at Quinchía, Aranzazu, and Chinchiná. Further south, in southern Valle, the more important Cali and Yumbo mines may represent an extension of the same geologic formation.

This intensively folded and overthrust Tertiary hill belt, tucked between the batholith and the Río Cauca lowlands, has been widely disturbed by vulcanism and laccolithic intrusions which have profoundly influenced Antioqueño colonization and settlement in the last century. The landscape of this eruptive belt which rent the middle of the Cauca trough from Marsella to Titiribí (in the Pliocene?) is characterized by volcanic sheet flows and numerous andesitic necks or intrusions, their tuff and lava mantle worn away to expose them as sharp pinnacles. In Fredonia and Venecia they are especially numerous, including the conspicuous, triangular-faceted Cerro Tusa (Corncob Hill) and the massive Cerro Bravo, the fertile slopes of which became the forcing bed of western Colombia's modern coffee economy. Other prominent plugs to the south are the twin spires of La Pintada, the Faroles de Valparaíso, and the curious sugar loaves which give the Ríosucio-Quinchía district of Caldas its unique, jumbled appearance. The center of this volcanic activity was probably the massive Alto de los Mellizos, a 3,000-meter high laccolithic (?) dome on the Antioquia-Caldas border west of the Río Cauca, linked to the Western Cordillera by an arm of high land which forms the watershed between the north-flowing Río San Juan and the south-flowing Río Risaralda. It is built up by broad sheet flows, broken with andesitic plugs and dikes. The Río Cauca has cut into these tremendous deposits of lava, breccia, ash, and pumice and separates the Altiplano de Jericó from the geologically identical Fredonia-Venecia area. Other laccolithic intrusions, still retaining a part of their sedimentary roofs, are in Titiribí and Amagá. Along the margins of these intrusions and in fissure veins gold and silver mineralization occurs, as at Marmato and Titiribí.

These late Tertiary disturbances, reinforced by the later activity of the Quindío volcanic cluster, must have caused the great Cauca Lake which filled the inter-Andean trough for almost 200 kilometers south of Cartago, forming the level, productive floor of the Valle del Cauca. The Río Risaralda–Río San Juan alignment seems to represent the original course of the Río Cauca, but the ponded river found its way through the ash and lava of the Mellizos and Quindío complexes by way of the great convex bend through the box canyon of Caldas.

On the eastern flanks of the Central Cordillera, in the Caldas municipios of Manzanares, Pensilvania, and Samaná, there is apparently a second, more restricted area of late Tertiary eruptives which have been the basis of the prosperous coffee farms (*fincas*) of this zone. It is delineated by a row of at least four extinct andesitic plugs extending northeastward from Cerro Guadalupe (elev., 2,530 m.), behind the town of Manzanares. They are probably of an age similar to the Mellizos–Cerro Bravo volcanics.[13]

The Western Cordillera of Colombia is one of the last frontiers of Andean exploration and settlement. Its deeply folded and overthrust metamorphic and sedimentary series are intruded by massive batholiths of uncertain age which are associated along their margins with mineral enrichment (Frontino, Buriticá). Vulcanism has been practically absent.[14] In parts of the departments of Caldas and Valle del Cauca, however, the cordillera ribs have been mantled with ash and lavas from the Quindío and Mellizos clusters so that its agricultural potential has been significantly enhanced. Like the Central Cordillera, it forms an unbroken mountain barrier from the Río Patía gorge northward to the Paramillo, but its passes average at least 1,000 meters lower than those of the central sierra. The lowest are the two 1,600-meter saddles which lie west of the Valle and connect it with the Buenaventura coast. Northward, in Caldas and Antioquia, there is a series of passes from 2,000 to 2,600 meters elevation, which have been used since colonial times as trade routes to the Chocó. The northernmost of these, the Boquerón de Toyo, route of the highway from Medellín to the Gulf of Urabá, apparently follows a unique transverse fault zone extending north-northwest along the Río Tonusco–Cañasgordas–Río Sucio axis from Santa Fé de Antioquia. South of it lies the Páramo Frontino (elev., 4,080 m.) and to the north the little-known Paramillo (elev., 3,960 m.) on the slopes of which lies the famous Indian and colonial mining camp of Buriticá. Beyond, toward the Caribbean, the cordillera fingers out into the three distinct but little explored ranges (*serranías*) of Ayapel, San Jerónimo, and Abibe which eventually lose themselves under the coastal savannas.

CLIMATE

In the Colombian Andes the seasons are delimited by rainfall. The annual march of temperature at all stations in Caldas and Antioquia is minimal. Long term records for Medellín show a difference in temperature of only 1.1° C (2° F) between the warmest and the coldest month. Such a markedly isothermal condition, together with a moderate, well-distributed annual rainfall and the brilliant translucence of the Andean air, rightly qualifies these mountains as "a land of perpetual spring." Medellín's average temperature is very close to 22° C (71.5° F), the average diurnal range 6° C (10.8° F). Nights are cool enough for a light blanket; the average minimum is 19° C (66° F). Temperatures below 16° C (60° F) or, in the daytime, above 28° C (82° F) are rare.[15] A light but steady breeze blows constantly up the valley during the daytime, and the blueness of the sky is usually broken by a few fleecy, white cumulus clouds.

The tropical rainfall regime of double maximums and minimums is typical throughout the Antioqueño country. The dry periods are known as the *veranos* (summers) and the wet months are the *inviernos* (winters). The first of the two rainy seasons usually extends from late March to mid-June, the second from September through the first days of December. The rainiest months are most commonly May and October, but occasionally they may fall outside the inviernos entirely, as occurred in 1938 when August was the wettest month of the year in Manizales, Sonsón, and Medellín.

The Western Cordillera acts as a partial barrier to the penetration of moisture-laden Pacific air masses, so that in no part of the Antioqueño lands is the rainfall excessive, as in the Chocó littoral. Average annual rainfall for most of the upland area is between 1,500 and 3,000 mm., but toward the north, on the low Cauca plains, an average of 4,399 mm. (173.19 in.) has been recorded at Pato. In the vicinity of Santa Fé de Antioquia there is a rain-shadow pocket extending along the Río Cauca for some 50 kilometers where savanna-steppe conditions prevail. Average annual rainfall at Santa Fé de Antioquia, based on records for four nonconsecutive years, is 895 mm. (35.24 in.), but the xerophytic character of the vegetation may, in part, be attributable

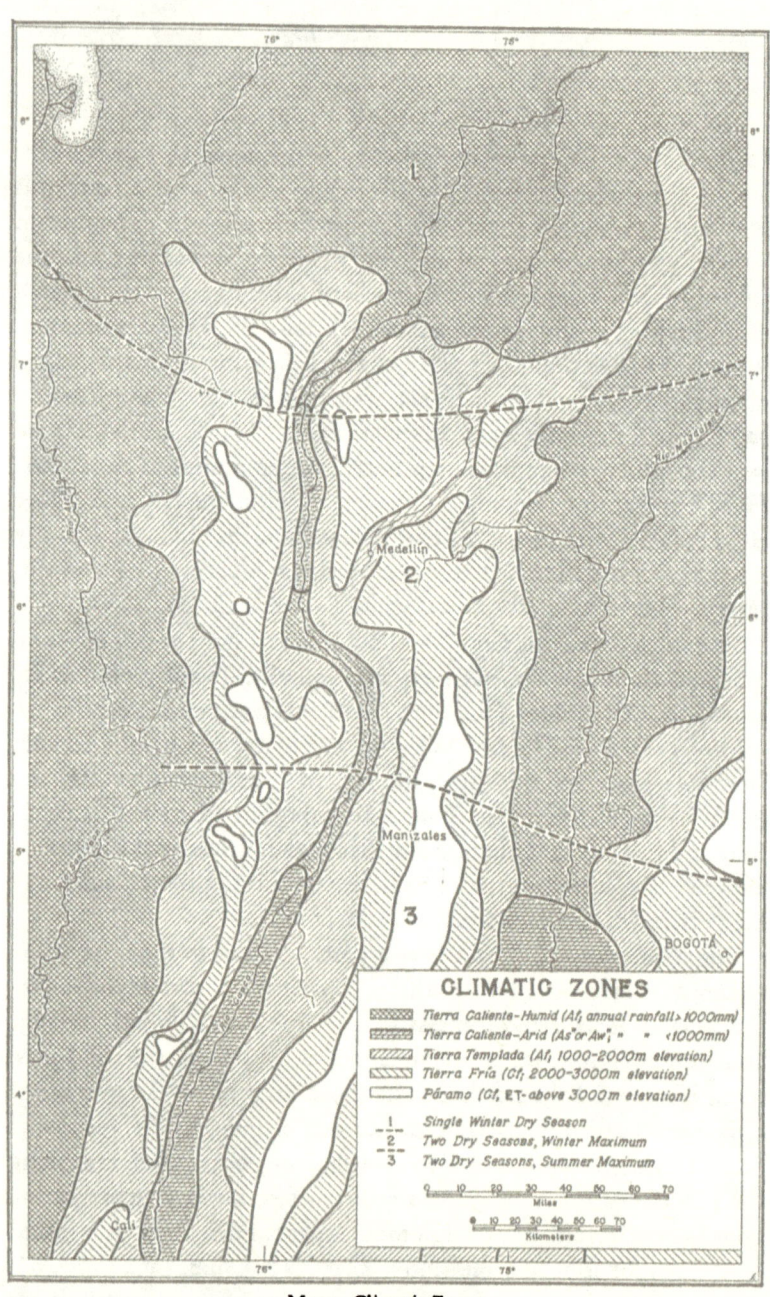

Map 3. Climatic Zones.

to the long occupance by stock-raising Europeans. Medellín (1,446.2 mm. [56.94 in.]) is also in a rain-shadow position in the deep canyon of the upper Río Porce. The broad, level floor of the Valle del Cauca south of Cartago constitutes another relatively dry area, with annual rainfall averaging 900 to 1,200 mm.

Extreme climatic years rather than averages are commonly the limiting factors on life. At Medellín the driest year on record (1923) recorded 714.5 mm. (28.12 in.), while the all-time high of 2,177.5 mm. (85.68 in.) fell the following year. For Manizales similar extremes have been a 1941 minimum of 1,004.4 mm. (39.54 in.) and a maximum of 3,651.3 mm. (147.68 in.) in 1938.

In the inner tropics of the northern hemisphere the longer of the two dry seasons normally follows the winter solstice, whereas the secondary and less severe *veranillo* comes in July and August. It is these veranos, not the wet seasons, which are critical for man's habitation of these mountains. For nearly four hundred years their length and severity has determined the amounts of gold which could be washed from the rich gravel bars of Antioquia's streams, for only at times of low water are the richest gravels exposed or made accessible to the gold washers. Further, the veranos have a direct relationship to crop yields, being especially critical for the second (February) harvest of maize and beans in the warmer zones where two crops a year are expected. Domestic water supplies for growing Antioqueño cities such as Medellín and Manizales have had to be rationed stringently in recent years during the dry months, but completion of new and larger aqueducts has recently relieved the situation.[16] Finally, as with recent Antioqueño settlement on the slopes of the Western Cordillera within the department of Valle del Càuca, distribution of the land among numerous small holders or *minifundistas* has been encouraged by the lack of water supplies adequate for the operation of large-scale coffee beneficiation plants.[17]

Throughout the department of Antioquia and north to the Caribbean the driest months are January and February; December and March are also months of scant rainfall.[18] The secondary dry season in July and August is apparent at all stations in Antioquia south of 7° north latitude,[19] but in Medellín, for example, it is neither so severe nor so dependable as the winter dry period. Occasionally July or August may be wet months but never January or February.

South of the Antioquia-Caldas boundary within the Río Cauca drainage and south of Ambalema in the upper Magdalena Valley an anomalous condition exists. Here the driest month is either July or August; January and February constitute the secondary verano. These regions of "maximum summer drought" and "maximum winter drought" (map 3) correspond to the *s″* and *w″* suffixes of Köppen.[20] They may provide the explanation for the contrasted coffee-ripening seasons of Antioquia and the lands to the south. In Antioquia and northern Caldas the main harvest falls between October and December. In the Quindío, Tolima, and Valle del Cauca the principal harvest is between March and May. Since approximately eight and a half months elapse between the fertilization of the ovary and the ripening of the coffee berry the relationship of these contrasting harvest seasons and rainfall regimes strongly suggests that maximum flower setting occurs during periods of moderate but not extreme dryness, that is, during the secondary dry season. In both areas there is a secondary harvest, known as the *atraviesa* or *mitaca*, which occurs during the other half of the year and which occasionally surpasses the main harvest.

Rainfall intensities are not uncommonly high. A three-year (1936–1939) record for Medellín[21] gives a record fall of 19.4 mm. (0.76 in.) in a five-minute period on October 26, 1936; 53.2 mm. (2.09 in.) fell in one hour during the same storm. These intensities were far in excess of the next heaviest storm that has been recorded, the unusually late rain of January 7, 1939, when 7.8 mm. (0.30 in.) of rain fell in a period of five minutes. Such extremes, nevertheless, greatly increase the hazards of soil erosion on the steep, clean-tilled slopes which are characteristic of much of the area of Antioqueño occupance.

Most of the precipitation falls at night or in the late afternoon and is frequently associated with thunder and lightning. High winds are rare but not unknown as accompaniments of rainfall.[22] Long periods of drizzle are encountered only on the highlands above 2,000 meters where damp, clammy weather, with low-hanging clouds, may linger for several days during the rainy seasons. Everywhere, except along

TABLE 2

AVERAGE MONTHLY RAINFALL FIGURES FOR SELECTED COLOMBIAN STATIONS[a]
(in millimeters)

Antioquia	Medellín 1908–1944	Cisneros 1935–1944	Frontino 1936–1944	Pato Mines 1912–1940	Sonsón 1935–1944	Yarumal 1935–1944
Jan.	54.5	166.3	180.4	121.9	97.3	65.5
Feb.	69.0	83.5	54.7	66.0	76.4	20.1
Mar.	90.7	202.5	191.1	109.2	116.1	99.5
Apr.	147.6	249.0	352.6	322.5	238.4	256.1
May	184.4	398.2	340.5	475.0	287.9	310.7
June	139.6	324.6	278.2	525.8	161.1	287.2
July	96.6	236.7	196.3	436.9	120.9	256.3
Aug.	127.9	231.6	254.1	548.6	125.9	252.9
Sept.	149.7	182.5	271.9	518.2	210.2	239.5
Oct.	172.8	217.7	356.9	515.6	294.1	260.4
Nov.	141.2	186.4	364.4	492.8	218.8	204.9
Dec.	71.7	161.6	194.0	264.2	181.6	109.0
Year	1,446.2	3,080.0	2,625.8	4,399.3	2,053.8	2,018.7

Other departments	Manizales 1927–1944	Chinchiná 1941–1946	Armenia 1938–1944	Riosucio 1936–1944	Ibagué 1934–1944	La Manuelita 1904–1944
Jan.	68.2	171.3	230.8	158.6	116.0	68.2
Feb.	84.1	186.1	112.4	151.8	128.3	84.1
Mar.	110.3	199.4	157.1	197.9	177.1	110.3
Apr.	142.1	283.0	171.9	192.0	222.6	142.1
May	133.4	311.7	250.1	308.8	277.6	133.4
June	73.2	200.8	147.2	174.4	219.1	73.2
July	36.5	128.6	69.7	93.3	69.0	36.5
Aug.	43.7	119.4	63.5	258.9	112.9	43.7
Sept.	77.0	156.2	100.4	209.9	152.7	77.0
Oct.	138.9	335.6	336.9	362.8	275.8	138.9
Nov.	125.8	301.4	424.0	280.3	238.7	125.8
Dec.	88.5	186.4	280.1	410.3	123.8	88.5
Year	2,171.3	2,579.9	1,811.9	2,110.8	2,068.9	1,103.6

[a] Sources: Medellín: Facultad Nacional de Agronomía; Pato Mines: Company records; Manizales: Colegio de Cristo; Chinchiná: Central de Investigaciones Nacional de Café; all others from unpublished compilations of Sección Meteorología, Contraloría General de la República, Bogotá. (La Manuelita is a sugar hacienda on the floor of the Valle near Palmira.)

NOTE: For the longer, 57-year record, 1908–1965, Medellín has recorded an average annual precipitation of 1,421 mm. (55.95 in.). The slight decrease this represents from the 1908–1944 average reflects the subnormal precipitation of recent years. Thus, in the decade 1957–1966 the annual rainfall did not once reach the long-term average. (Since 1950 Medellín records have been kept by Empresas Públicas in the center of the city.) A similar decline in annual precipitation is evidenced in the Pato Mines record. Since 1953, when the gauge was moved some 20 km. down the Río Nechí, from Pato to the new El Bagre camp, recorded rainfall in only one year, 1956, has exceeded the 1912–1940 average. Tomas Feininger, in a letter to *Science* (April 5, 1968, "Less Rain in Latin America"), has called attention to this singular decline in rainfall at these two Antioquia stations. He suggests that "it may have been produced by widespread felling of rain forests in Colombia and neighboring countries, although this remains unproven. On the other hand it may be cyclical and unrelated to the rain forest."

the more arid stretches of the Cauca lowlands, there is adequate precipitation to keep the hills green twelve months of the year and yet the marked nighttime incidence of the unobtrusive rainfall makes the climate particularly attractive.

For all of the Antioqueño country the best temperature map is the topographical map, for every contour line may also serve as an isotherm. The decrease in temperature with increasing altitude approximates very closely 0.6° C. for each 100 meters. In the space of a few hours on foot or in the saddle a traveler can experience the same change of seasons which in more northerly latitudes would require several months. From the hot country of the Cauca lowlands in the vicinity of Santa Fé de Antioquia, with an average annual temperature of 27° C. (80.6° F.), to Santa Rosa de Osos, with an average temperature of 15° C. (59° F.), it is only twenty miles as the crow flies or one long day in the saddle. "This condition," a local scholar early observed, "provides us with an unusual opportunity for the preservation of our health and is moreover an excellent basis for the development of an almost infinite variety of plant and animal products among us."[22]

The life zones of equatorial mountains have a more direct influence on human occupance than those of more northerly latitudes. The rapid succession of life forms deeply impresses an observer traveling through any part of the Colombian Andes. It was here that the science of plant geography received its first great impetus with the observations of Humboldt and Bonpland on the altitudinal distribution of plant life.[24] Their contemporary and host, the little-known Colombian naturalist and geographer, Francisco José de Caldas, had even earlier reported on the relationship between altitude and the distribution of economic plants in New Granada.[25] Later writers, especially Führmann and Mayor,[26] with their excellent charts of the vertical distribution of plant and animal life, and Bürger,[27] have refined the observations without challenging the classical presentations.

The limits and definitions of the conventionalized temperature zones of tropical America have varied with peoples and with latitudes. In Colombia usage is far from standardized, but the 1,000- and 2,000-meter isohypses, with annual average temperatures of 18° C.

(64.4° F.) and 24° C. (75.2° F.) are the limits of the *tierra templada* as most commonly understood. Below this temperate zone lies the *tierra caliente,* above it the cool uplands of the *tierra fría* (map 3). Occasionally in the Antioqueño country settlements as low as 1,800 meters may be referred to as within the tierra fría, especially outside the coffee-growing districts, but each term is employed in a relative sense with no specific temperature or elevation limits implied. For the biologists, who have most concerned themselves with the relationship of life to these zones, logic is probably on the side of a simple two-way breakdown into "tropical" and "temperate" zone flora and fauna, in which case the 1,800-meter contour has generally been accepted, as by Wolf[28] and Chapman.[29]

A fourth zone, the *páramo,* generally above the tree line and delimited especially by the lower limits of the giant Compositae, *Espeletia,* is recognized in common usage throughout the Andes. In Antioquia, where there is little true páramo, the term is loosely applied to the upper lands above 3,000 meters, even though they are wooded and the *Espeletia* unimportant (e.g., Páramo de Sonsón). On the other hand the páramos of Herveo and Paramillo are true, treeless páramos, standing like mountainous brown islands in a sea of green.

The malarial tierras calientes of the Magdalena and Cauca lowlands have been predominately areas of Negro and mulatto occupance, of large cattle fincas, of planted Pará and India grass pastures, and of cacao. Its upper limits have generally been taken as the lower limits of coffee cultivation, which in most places is a little above the 1,000-meter contour. Coffee has become the accepted indicator of the tierra templada or subtropical zone. In the Antioqueño country this belt, extending to 2,000 meters, is also referred to as the *tierra del café.*[30] Here, at the middle elevations, Antioqueño settlement has been most active. Besides coffee it has also been characterized by precipitous slopes, the white creole cattle and, more recently, the African molasses grass (*yaraguá gordura*) which has turned many worn out Antioquia and Caldas hillsides into productive pasture. Above this belt are the high and healthy tierras frías which have supplied a large proportion of the colonists who have spread southward toward Caldas, Tolima, and Valle during the past century. Their agricultural utility has been

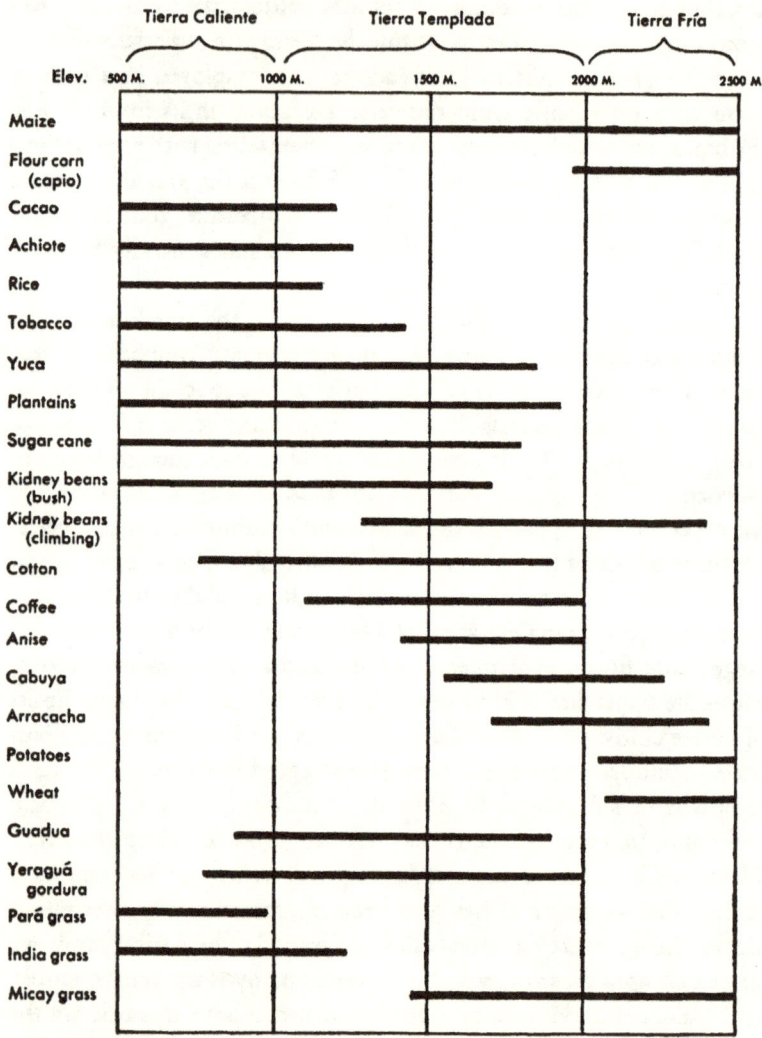

Fig. 1. Vertical Distribution of Economic Plants in Antioquia and Caldas.

limited by the extensive areas of heavy, reddish clay soils which support only a meager vegetative cover of bracken and scrub.

NATURAL VEGETATION

Wherever Antioqueño settlement has extended, clearing of the forests has been one of the first undertakings. The result has been both an increasing threat of watershed destruction and a growing scarcity of charcoal, fuel wood, and lumber, especially in the cities. Forests are now limited to the least accessible regions, to the peaks and highest ridges and to the humid tierra caliente of the Magdalena, Atrato, and lower Cauca. Elsewhere pasturelands, maize fields, and shaded coffee plantations have replaced the original cover of broadleaf trees.

Clearing activities began early. By 1788 Mon y Velarde could write that "bad management and many owners" at the salt wells of Heliconia had destroyed the forests, making firewood scarce and costly." In 1826 the commissioner of the La Estrella Indian reservation, south of Medellín, reported that the highly valued timbers of *comino* (*Aniba* spp.), which had been rafted down the river to Medellín for frames and trusses, were giving out, and the *cedros* (*Cedrela*), *caobas* (*Swietenia*, *quimulás* (*Laplacea*) and *barcinos* (*Callophyllum*) were gone." The woods remaining were on the highest cordilleras from which it was not profitable to bring them to the riverbank. Later, Antioquia boasted that the ties of the railroad, which was pressing in toward the interior from Puerto Berrío, were of this same durable comino, which has been referred to as "the classical wood of the Antioqueños." But soon its extreme scarcity was again being lamented.

The aborigines had practiced a shifting, fire agriculture which involved the continuous rotation of crop and forest land. J. E. White, Antioqueño pioneer of English stock who knew the Dabeiba-Frontino region on the far slopes of the Western Cordillera probably better than anyone, believed that this activity was so intense that most of the forests existing today in this area should be interpreted as second growth rather than as undisturbed virgin cover." The vast canebrakes (*cañaverales*) of bamboo-like guadua which so impressed the early chroniclers in the Quimbaya country of southern Caldas were apparently the result of man's disturbance of the original cover. This adventive species is extremely widespread up to 2,000 meters elevation throughout the southern two-thirds of Caldas, from Salamina southward. In Antioquia it is often replaced by the *cañabrava* (*Gynerium*), a more frail but tall bamboo-like grass which is restricted to the river courses and which is also cultivated near Medellín as a construction material.

The earliest areas of Spanish settlement in interior Antioquia were unforested. Cieza de León wrote that the road out of Antioquia La Vieja to Anserma was "very rough, with naked hills and few trees" as far as the Caramanta country (Río San Juan), but that from there on the route was through dense forests."[24] Around the old capital of Antioquia Acacia, Mimosa, Caesalpinia, and cacti are dominant forms, and on the coarser sands and gravels of the higher terraces these are more commonly separated by barren ground than by grass. Mining and grazing activities over four centuries have brought with them extensive soil destruction. Deeply gullied badlands flank the old city on both the north and east, and the entire structural pocket, which includes Sopetrán and San Jerónimo, now supports only a few browsing, ill-fed cattle.

The Sabanas de Aburrá, which by the end of the sixteenth century were supplying cattle to the mining camps of Zaragoza and Remedios, were the verdant natural meadows (*vegas*) along the flood plain of the upper Río Porce around Medellín. On the steeper slopes above, the red, impoverished serpentine soils which extend northward some twelve kilometers on both sides of the valley as far as Copacabana, supported only a meager brush cover of scrub oak, *noro* (*Byrsonima*), *chagualo* (*Clusia*) and *sietecuero* (*Tibouchina*). The last, with particularly handsome, multicolored flowers, is a close relative of the showy pleroma of California gardens. These barren slopes within sight of the modern capital still lie unused and empty, except where they have been encroached upon by new urban subdivisions on the northeast side of town.

Similar geological conditions are apparently responsible in part for the extension of this chaparral-like vegetation into the high plateaus on both sides of the valley of Medellín. On the sticky primary soils of these higher lands the original cover was apparently a low stand of evergreen oak (*Quercus Humboldtiana*) which has since been destroyed by miners and charcoal burners. During the last century the red and yellow cinchonas and the wax myrtle (*Myrica*) were also of commercial importance here. The latter is a laurel, the seeds of which yielded a wax used for illumination, as well as in house construction.³⁵ Both of these species have also been greatly reduced. Today various types of ferns comprise the dominant element in the vegetation. From Santa Rosa de Osos, which overlooks a desolate expanse of impoverished bracken cover, scarcely a tree is visible in any direction.

Local areas of grass were encountered by the early Spaniards along the flood plains of many highland streams in Antioquia. The most extensive of these were the meadows of the three valleys which come together at the city of Ríonegro. On the other side of the Cañon de Medellín similar but smaller areas of grassland occupied the Llanos de Ovejas (on the Medellín–San Pedro road), the upper valley of the Río Chico, and the Llanos de Cuibá, north of Santa Rosa.

Eastward, on the lower lands toward the Magdalena, stretched the damp, luxuriant rain forest with its lianas, bromelias, and giant ceibas. Its economic members include several latex-bearing Sapotaceae, of which chicle and balata are the most important products today, ivory-nut or tagua palm (*Phytelephas*), and the *platanillo* (*Heliconia bihai*), the leaves of which are used extensively for covering lean-tos, houses, and for wrapping food. The Castilla rubber tree, which was the basis for an early rubber excitement in Caldas, occurs here as well as in the higher subtropical mossy forests of the tierra templada into which the rain forest imperceptibly blends. It is these damp subtropical forests that are the classical home of the gorgeous orchids which grew throughout Antioquia in tremendous profusion and variety until recent years.

A single island of natural grassland interrupted these monotonous forests at the time of the Spaniards' arrival. This was the beautiful, rolling Lomas de Cancán on the Yolombó-Remedios road between the Río Volcán and Quebrada de la Cruz, site of a now-forgotten colonial settlement. Local inhabitants interpret them as the result of Indian burning. Today the rank stand of dried grass is still fired annually by stockmen to improve pasturage. From earliest colonial times Cancán was an important stock region, supplying the mining camps of the lower Nechí and Remedios as well as providing the only good grazing for pack animals on the alternate route from Medellín to the Magdalena by way of Yolombó.

The newer volcanic soils of southwestern Antioquia, Caldas, and Tolima were clothed with forests almost down to the margins of the Río Cauca and the dry *llanos* of Tolima. For three hundred years they resisted settlement, remaining unknown and unoccupied woodland until cleared during the last century by Antioqueño colonists.[26] Forests were lacking only on the low hills which hem in the Río Cauca through Caldas and here Indian clearings and fires probably had been responsible for their destruction. Cieza de León described the settlement of Arma as being surrounded by unforested ridges,[27] as it is today, but it was also here that the chronicler described a dense and prosperous native population.

Among the original forest trees of these slopes the leguminous *guamo* (*Inga* spp.) was perhaps the most common. It is still a dominant genus here today, not as a component of the natural forest but as a planted shade tree in the hillside coffee plantations. The conspicuous, silverleafed *yarumo* (*Cecropia*), visible for miles away, occurs here as elsewhere as a succession plant.

When clearings have been made the fire-resistant palms have generally been allowed to remain, valued for their majestic beauty, fibrous leaves, tough wood, and their nutritious nuts, eaten by cattle and occasionally by man. The most common of these palms are the *corozo grande* (*Acrocomia*), *corozo chiquito* (*Martinezia*), *chontaduro* (*Guilielma*), and *cuesco* (*Scheelea*), all of the tierra caliente and the lower tierra templada. West of Santa Bárbara, in the Río Poblanco drainage, the spiney-trunked corozo grande stand in extensive groves in the planted Pará and India grass pastures. Here the red Ayapel cattle are fattened for the Medellín market. The magnificent wax palm (*Ceroxylon*), which is a forest dominant on the Tolima side of the old Quindío Pass, is not important in Antioquia.

III. ORIGINAL INDIAN INHABITANTS

POPULATION ESTIMATES for aboriginal Colombia have generally been unrealistically low. Even Rosenblatt's extremely conservative figure of 850,000 has been termed excessive by at least one recent investigator,[1] impressed by the absence of large permanent village sites. Yet the overwhelming evidence of the early chronicles, the incredibly numerous Indian graves (*guacas*), and the extensive old fields all point to a very dense peopling of the Antioqueño country. The population on the optimum agricultural soils of the Quindío basin, indeed, must have been one of the most dense in all of pre-Columbian South America. In the light of the evidence at hand, Tulio Ospina's[2] estimate of an aboriginal population of 600,000 for Antioquia at the time of the Conquest, the equivalent of 120,000 working Indians (*de macana* and *de mina*), does not seem unreasonable. With the addition of the thickly peopled Quindío the figure may be advanced at least to the million mark for all of the Antioqueño country, something less than half the population it supports today.

Cieza de León's excellent account is replete with notes on the exceptionally large numbers of natives encountered by Robledo's men. The Province of Arma alone had 20,000 *indios de guerra*, not counting women and children. There was convincing evidence of an even larger population in an earlier time. Of the Valley of Nore, second site of the city of Antioquia, he wrote: "In ancient times there was a large population in these valleys, as we judged from the edifices and burial places of which many are well worth seeing, being so large as to appear like small hills."[3] Similar suggestions of an earlier, more populous civilization were found in the Quindío, the valley of Aburrá, the territory of the Zenufanáes, and the Valle del Cauca.[4]

Beyond the drainage basin of the Río Cauca populations seem to have been equally dense. In 1551, for instance, the Pedroso party met more than 2,000 armed natives in the valley of the Río Guatapé.[5] Twenty years later a detailed census of the natives within a twenty-five mile radius of Remedios (then in the vicinity of modern Yolombó) showed 4,030 dwellings, the equivalent of at least 20,000

---
[1]For notes to chap. iii, see pp. 193–194.

Indians, and many already had fled or fallen in earlier epidemics.[5] In the Province of Urabá on the western slopes of the Western Cordillera (municipios of Dabeiba, Frontino, Cañasgordas) White has estimated that there were at least 300,000 inhabitants at the time of the Conquest, or many more than today, observing that ". . . the major portion of the existing forests must be considered to have been clearings three centuries ago, for whenever two or more trees are felled old road embankments and habitation sites are revealed."[7]

For the high tierras frías, however, there is a scantiness of reports of Indian occupance which is in striking contrast to the picture elsewhere in Colombia where the highest lands, even the páramos, were traditional centers of Indian life and culture.

For few parts of the Americas is our knowledge of the native peoples and culture so meager and uncertain as it is for western Colombia.[8] Within a very few years after the Conquest the aborigines of Antioquia had been so reduced in numbers either by disease, starvation, or retreat into the anonymity of the Chocó rain forests that those who remained formed an amorphous and disordered group which lost its cultural identity with amazing rapidity. The subjugation of these remnants was a frequent activity of the captains of Antioquia for two centuries; expeditions against the Chocóes were recruited in the capital on at least a dozen occasions until the Indians began to weary of the game and yielded themselves up to the missionaries of the Cañasgordas and Urrao missions. In the Ríosucio area of Caldas, where demand for mine labor at Marmato was high, a small remnant group of Indians has survived to the present day.

Early Spanish accounts employed special tribal designations for the native inhabitants of almost every valley, but there are only broad hints of linguistic and cultural differentiation. Most of them have been placed within the great Carib linguistic family by Rivet. Commonly they were independent tribal units, to each of which was applied the name of the ruling cacique at the time of the Spaniards' arrival. The *entradas* of César and Badillo first encountered the formidable Catíos in the Western Cordillera and it was they, under their famous chief Nutibara, who offered the most spirited and prolonged opposition to the intruders. East of the Río Cauca were the

Nutabes, and the land between the Río Porce and the Río Magdalena was occupied by the Tahamíes (map 4). Each of these groups consisted of several subgroups or tribes, each with discernible differences in language and culture. Interior Antioquia seems to have been known to the Indians and early chroniclers as the Province of Zenufaná. The name Panzenú was applied to the country between the Cauca and the Río San Jorge; Finzenú was the Alto Sinú. To the south, in modern Caldas, there were many other independent tribes, including the Armas, Pozos, Carrapas, Ansermas, Picaras, and Paucaras and the enigmatic Quimbayas and Quindíos.[9] Lacking completely the centralized control of the organized states in México, Perú, and in the area of Chibcha dominance, they proved easy prey to the invaders, who soon learned to play off rival groups one against the other. Thus, following Cortés' celebrated example, Robledo obtained an alliance with the Carrapa to attack the neighboring Picara and with both of them to fight the Pozo. Once the caciques and their sons were gone, organized resistance disappeared.

Cannibalism seems to have been extraordinarily developed among the Indians of the Cauca drainage.[10] Early Spanish chronicles are filled with reports of mass slaughters, including women and children, who were consumed in ritualistic orgies. Its undoubted ritual importance was never recognized by the Spaniards, who saw in it simply an act of cruel and barbarous heathens who "spoke with the devil." Yet, even allowing for the manifest exaggerations of some of the chroniclers, this area is clearly established as one of the major centers of cannibalism in the Americas.

The Indians were talented agriculturalists, and some early accounts even suggest that they employed irrigation to a limited extent. Their habitations were most commonly beehive-shaped, built of cane or straw. In many regions today houses or hilltop cattle corrals (*siestadores*) occupy the small platforms leveled by prehistoric Indians. Some of these habitation sites, like those near Darién and Restrepo (Valle), are described as extensive artificial terraces, each from 6 to 7 meters wide.[11] Stonemasonry seems never to have been used, so that archeological evidence of occupance has been chiefly limited to the extensive burial grounds, and yet the extremely high population

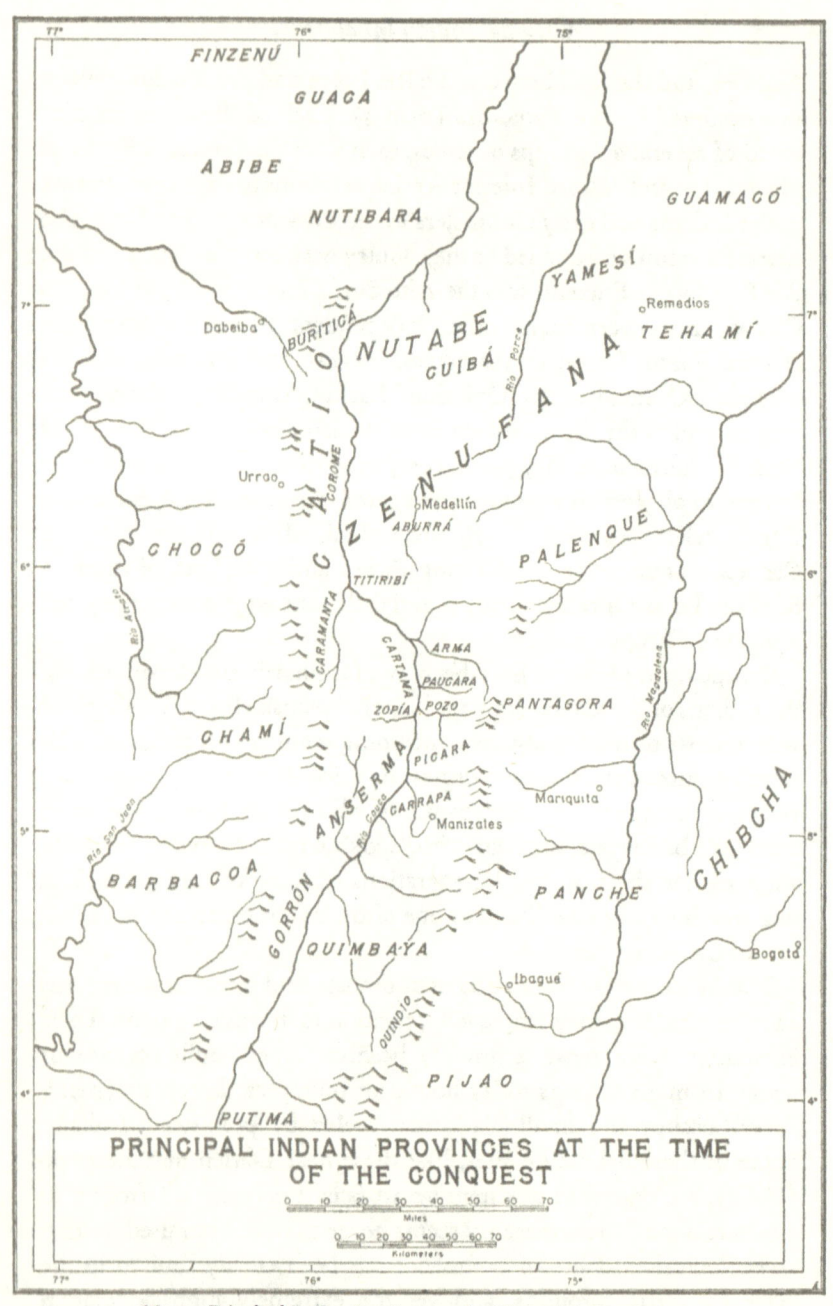

Map 4. Principal Indian Provinces at the Time of the Conquest.

density indicated by burials and old fields in such areas as the Quindío is incontrovertible evidence of an advanced social structure. In spite of the persistent grave robbing by local inhabitants the archeology of the Caldas-Antioquia region is very poorly known and has been the subject of almost no scientific field work.

Among the aborigines of the New World those of western Colombia were outstanding especially for their work in gold and the high development of the culture trait of prizing gold. Their metallurgical techniques included smelting, casting, plating, soldering, and the making of gold-copper alloys (*tumbaga, muchimba*) which could be worked into implements of fairly fine cutting edges. Much of the gold was hammered into thin, flat sheets and decorated with repoussé design. Cast or hollow figurines, scepters, vases, bowls, nose rings, breastplates, and other items of personal adornment were common.

All of the Colombian gold work which we possess today has been taken from the graves of the chiefs, for their lifetime collection of gifts and tributes were customarily buried with them. Much of the best of this art has been lost to the rapaciousness of generations of grave robbers, but the Banco de la República has recently performed a lasting service to science and to Colombia by assembling a fine representative collection of these materials in Bogotá.

It was the legends of Dabeybe, Cuyr-Cuyr, Panzenú, and Arbi that brought the first Spaniards into the Antioqueño country. The entire pattern of the Conquest and early occupance hinged on the wheedling or stealing of as much gold as possible from the chiefs or from their sepulchers. More than two centuries later they were again the lure which set off the wave of Antioqueño colonization south and westward toward the Occidente of Antioquia and Caldas, Tolima, and Valle. For many years almost all of the inhabitants of the Quindío took an active part in the business of *guaquería* or grave plundering. Today it is still a very real factor in the expansion of Antioqueño settlement southward along the flanks of the Western Cordillera in Valle del Cauca. In August, 1946, discoveries near Restrepo (Calima) by Antioqueño *guaqueros* were reported in the press to have yielded one and a half million pesos ($850,000, U.S.); a single grave contained fourteen pounds of gold.[12]

There were virtually no commanding eminences in the tierras templadas of Antioquia and Caldas that did not contain burials. Some of them were cemeteries containing hundreds of graves. In the Quindío the most famous of these were Pueblo de la Muerte, Soledad, and Montenegro, all lying close to the 20° C. (68° F.) isotherm, the thermal belt of densest Indian population here.[13] On a single high knoll behind the Catholic cemetery at Montenegro there are scars of more than a thousand pits abandoned by guaqueros after they had ransacked the area for gold more than fifty years ago. The commonest type of grave consisted of a deep shaft (*cajón*) and a lateral recess (*bóveda*) or interment chamber, but there were many variations. In the Quindío and the valley of the upper Río Calima, near Restrepo, some of these deep-level graves have been described as much as 25 meters below the surface.[14] The great depth from the surface might be accounted for by a recently deposited volcanic ash overburden in the Quindío, but such an overburden does not appear as far south as Restrepo.

Additional impressive evidence for a dense native population in earlier times is the extensive, ridged, and furrowed Indian old fields (*surcos de los indios*) which modern Antioqueño colonists encountered in the guadua-covered Quindío. Cieza de León apparently had noticed them, for he wrote that "all the dense canebrakes seem once to have been peopled and tilled."[15] Their conspicuous, corduroy patterns, which seem to have covered virtually all of the Quindío between 1,400 and 2,400 meters, are presumed locally to have been old maize fields, but in modern Colombia this system of cultivation is used only with root crops and sugar cane. The rows in the old fields do not follow contours but instead go up and down slope, suggesting a concern for drainage. Excessively steep lands seem to have been avoided, however, and on the cordillera flanks above the rolling Quindío basin on the Armenia-Ibagué road only the small mesetas or terraces give evidence of former cultivation. The ridges, about 12 inches high, have remained remarkably well preserved wherever the land has been left in natural pasture after clearing. Their wide spacing, almost 5 feet from crest to crest, seems also to argue against maize cultivation. The land must have been worked very deeply, judging from the depth at which potsherds are found. If pre-Colombian agriculture in this region was oriented around a root-crop complex, as their present-day variety and numbers hint, then both arracacha and sweet manioc (*yuca*) at once suggest themselves. Today the latter is the most important tuber grown in this area, cultivated almost to 2,000 meters in elevation; the arracacha comes down from the tierra fría to perhaps 1,600 meters. Potatoes are not grown much below 2,100 meters in Colombia today, although some of the lesser known varieties might have been adaptable in these fertile Quindío soils. The ulluco was possibly another root crop here; it is little known today in the Quindío, yet is common above Popayán and has varieties which thrive at 1,400 meters in the upper Magdalena drainage (Huila).

These remarkable old fields reach their greatest development in the undulating, newly cleared pasture lands of the Quindío, just above the coffee zone, between 1,800 and 2,200 meters. They may be seen today particularly in the environs of the settlements of Sevilla (Valle) and Circasia (Caldas), but according to early settlers "virtually all of the land not in roads" showed evidence of prior Indian cultivation. This, together with the tremendous numbers of Indian burials uncovered in the Quindío, has led some observers resident in the region to believe that the population in Indian times must have been even greater than it is today in this, the most densely settled rural agricultural area of modern Colombia.

Landscapes rippled with these ridged old fields are absent in Antioquia and northern Caldas. Their distribution seems to be closely correlated with areas of recent volcanic ash soil such as characterizes the Quindío. Other old fields within the Río Cauca drainage, may be seen for several miles along the Cali-Popayán railroad immediately north of Piendamó (Department of Cauca) on similar rolling ashland topography and again at an elevation of 1,800 to 2,200 meters. Here, too, they cover virtually all available land in this favored zone.

Other pre-Columbian ridged fields and raised planting beds of impressive extent may be seen in the lower Cauca and San Jorge river floodplains in the vicinity of Ayapel and San Marcos.[16] Here they are confined to areas that are seasonally inundated. They represent a major engineering achievement by a once numerous and sophisticated population.

IV. SPANISH MINES AND THE LABOR SUPPLY

THE POSITION of Antioquia made it a natural zone of contention between rival factions of Spanish gold seekers pushing southward from Cartagena and northward from Perú in the sixteenth century. As a disputed frontier area, accessible only by tedious overland marches across excessively broken terrain, it did not fit particularly well into the designs of Heredia or Pizarro. The activities of the first conquistadores, here far removed from their superiors and their bases of operations, were characterized by a marked freedom and independence of action—forerunner of the movement for political separatism which was to be one of the most persistent themes of later Antioqueño history.

It was two expeditions from Pedro de Heredia's territory on the Caribbean which carried out the first *entradas* into the region. Searches for the fabled treasures of Dabeybe and Sinú had led to the dispatching of an overland expedition from San Sebastián de Urabá in 1537 under Francisco César, who had formerly accompanied Sebastián Cabot on his voyage to the mouth of the Río de la Plata. Crossing the precipitous Serranía de Abibe and descending the valley of Guaca,[1] they routed the cacique Nutibara and plundered the gold from the local sepulchers.

Returning to the Caribbean nine months later, César joined a second party under the leadership of the Oidor Juan de Badillo. Retracing the route to the valley of Guaca, they continued southward to discover the Río Grande de Santa Marta (Río Cauca), which they followed upstream at some distance from its left bank through the provinces of Buriticá (where were "the best and largest mines of Tierra Firme"), Caramanta, and Anserma, arriving at Cali on December 24, 1538, after much suffering. It was with this party that the observant and reliable chronicler, Pedro de Cieza de León, then in his nineteenth year, made his first acquaintance with the Antioqueño country, in which he was to remain for eight years and which he described in the first part of his remarkable *Chronicle of Perú*.[2]

---

[1] For notes to chap. iv, see pp. 194–198.

At Cali the Badillo party encountered the vanguard of a Peruvian force under Sebastián de Belalcázar which, pushing northward through Quito, Pasto, and Popayán, had founded Cali in 1536. The newcomers not only bolstered the garrison's spirits but brought incentive for new conquests. To Jorge Robledo, a nobleman of Úbeda in Andalucía, who had first come to the New World in 1528, fell the assignment of subduing the tribes to the north and of founding a town in the province of Anserma.

From Santa Ana de los Caballeros (later Anserma), founded August 15, 1539, Robledo sent scouting parties northward as far as Buriticá and the country of the Titiribíes and westward to the Chocó. To protect the right flank against the Quimbaya, the Picaras, the Carrapas, and the Pozos, the city of Cartago, named in honor of the Carthaginians in the party, was formally founded on August 9, 1540, across the Río Cauca at the site of modern Pereira.

In the following year Robledo pushed northward into Antioquia, desirous of establishing another base of operations against the gold-rich aborigines. In the territory of the Zenufanáes, above modern Bolombolo, extensive ruins of earthworks and stone irrigation ditches suggested that perhaps the legendary land of riches for which they were searching might not be far away, but the Indians, playing an old game, capitalized on their credulity and greediness by assuring the Spaniards that a little farther on they would find the golden valley which they were seeking. Robledo later wrote:

> From Cenufaná to Aburrá it is six leagues and along this road are extensive ruins of former settlements, large buildings, and of very wide, hand-laid roads across both the mountains and gentler slopes, which are not surpassed by those of Cuzco. And all this has been lost and destroyed and there is no Indian who can say what their origins were or why they have been abandoned.[2]

After passing the important salines of Heliconia (Guaca), known to the Indians as Murgia, the party reached the valley of Aburrá (Medellín) on August 24, 1541, naming it the Valle de San Bartolomé. Here again were evidences of an earlier, richer civilization which:

> ... had all the roads and other characteristics which should be expected of the Valley of Arbi [Herveo?], great highways and aqueducts, all made

by hand, and great old buildings which the Indians say have been destroyed in wars amongst themselves...'

Seemingly unmoved by the natural attractions of this temperate valley, which was later to become the center of Antioqueño culture and site of the capital city, and disillusioned by their failure to find the elusive Arbi, the party turned again toward the Río Cauca lowlands. Crossing the river near modern Olaya they continued downstream against strong Indian opposition to the populous valley of Ebéjico, approximately 7 kilometers south of Peque on a small tributary of the Río Cauca in the parish known today as Santa Agueda. Here was founded La Ciudad de Antiochia (Antioquia), named for the great city in Syria, so important in the early history of the Christian Church. Like Anserma and Cartago before it, it was to be a fortified military base, conveniently situated in the shadow of the famous hill of Buriticá, from whence already had come great riches.

Soon thereafter, en route to Cali to report to Belalcázar, Robledo was apprehended and placed in chains on orders from Heredia. He was sent to Spain for trial, charged with having encroached on the jurisdiction of Cartagena.

Meanwhile the province was foundering in dissensions and rivalries between the followers of Belalcázar and of Heredia who both claimed authority over the region. Pedro de Heredia himself traveled overland from San Sebastián to skirmish briefly for command of the garrison of Antioquia. He may have been responsible for its removal, late in 1542, to a more open site "in the valley of Nore, between two small rivers" where the Indians were numerous and better disposed. This was in the Western Cordillera in the vicinity of modern Frontino (elevation, 1,500 meters) on one of the tributaries of the Río Sucio draining westward towards the Atrato.[5]

Jorge Robledo remained in Spain three years, cleared of all charges brought against him by the Royal Council of the Indies and granted the title of Mariscal de Antioquia. Incessant conflict with the Indians, together with the boundary dispute with Heredia, must have suggested, meanwhile, the prudence of reëstablishing a base in the Cauca drainage. On Robledo's return in 1546 the new villa of Santa Fé de Antioquia was founded at the site of the present city of Antioquia on

Spanish Mines and the Labor Supply 39

the Río Tonusco, 5 kilometers above its junction with the Río Cauca. Its geographical and administrative importance led to its formal proclamation as a city (*ciudad*) in 1590-1592.⁶ The settlement in the valley of Nore (Antioquia la Vieja) survived in a reduced state until about 1573 when Indian uprisings forced its complete abandonment.

By virtue of the formal acts of establishment carried out by Robledo, acting as lieutenant of Belalcázar, Antioquia remained under the secular jurisdiction of the Province of Popayán and the Audiencia of Quito during its first years. Its detachment from Popayán came in 1569 with the appointment of Andrés de Valdivia, like Robledo a native of Úbeda, as first governor and captain general of "the Provinces of Antioquia, Ituango, Nive, Breruno, the Land Between the Two Rivers and the Province of Urabá to the Sea of the North."⁷ The villa of Santa Fé itself was excepted, remaining under Popayán for ten additional years, the subject of much conflict. After Valdivia had established the city of Úbeda on the forested, knifelike Loma de Nohava (Moava) near the site of the present town of Valdivia, he met a violent death as a result of a mutiny and subsequent native insurrection. He was followed in the governorship by Gaspar de Rodas, early resident of the region and a vigorous personality. Rodas had been largely responsible for the rapid development of the villa of Santa Fé on the Río Tonusco, which Robledo had left as an insignificant mining camp, moving the town corporation members (*vecinos*) with their encomiendas of Indians there from Antioquia la Vieja. He founded Cáceres on the site of Valdivia's Úbeda in 1576,⁸ Zaragoza in 1581, and led several expeditions against the recalcitrant Indians of the Chocó and Mariquita before his death in 1607.

Rodas seems to have played a very important role in stabilizing the remote *gobernación* of Antioquia as an independent entity, now completely severed from the Province of Popayán and under the jurisdiction of the Audiencia at Bogotá, which had been established in 1550. The boundaries, never clearly defined, remained a subject of much dispute throughout the colonial period and even into the twentieth century, but its core was always the Río Tonusco settlement and the valley of Aburrá (map 5). Cartagena and Mompox bordered Antioquia on the north and Arma and Anserma, in the Province of

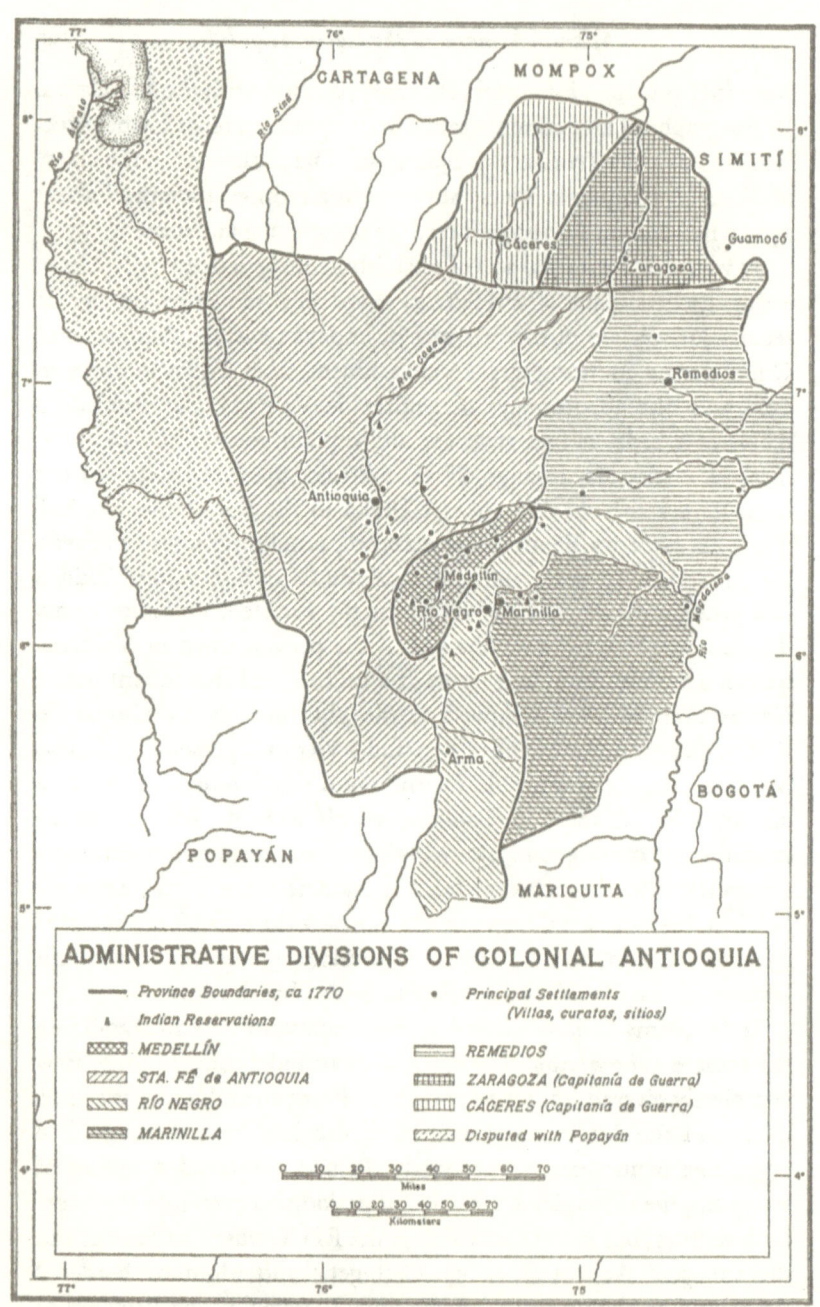

Map 5. Administrative Divisions of Colonial Antioquia.

Popayán, on the south. Arma, for the most part an unoccupied wilderness on the right bank of the Río Cauca, was separated from Popayán and added to Antioquia about 1750. The *corregimiento* of Mariquita included all of a vast area south of the upper Río Negro and eastward from Cancán to the Magdalena, including Remedios and Marinilla, until the middle of the seventeenth century, when it came under the administration of the Province of Antioquia.

In ecclesiastical jurisdiction, equally as important as temporal government in colonial times, most of Antioquia remained in the bishopric of Popayán, which in turn was in the archdiocese of Bogotá. Remedios, however, was subject to the bishop of Bogotá, whereas Zaragoza, Cáceres and later the new *real de minas* of Guamacó fell within the jurisdiction of the diocese of Cartagena.[9]

EARLY MINING CAMPS

There were other sixteenth-century gold-mining centers in the New World, as at Zaruma, Ecuador, and Comayagua, Honduras, but the Antioquia mines were probably the best known and the most extensive. The hill of Buriticá and the placers of the lower Río Nechí were believed by the early Spaniards to have been the source of the gold treasure taken from the Sinú, from whence came the early wealth of Cartagena. These mines, together with the gravels of the middle Cauca and its tributaries near Arma and Marmato, were discovered and exploited by the conquistadores. After a brief period of high returns which depended, in large measure, on Indian labor, productivity fell off sharply, yet the mining economy survived on a subsistence level throughout the colonial period.

The wealth of Buriticá had long been known to the Indians, and the Spaniards were impressed with the extensive evidence of abandoned mine workings.[10] The mines were spread over a mineralized zone of "lace gold" (*oro de encaje*) of considerable extent. The ore from weathered outcroppings of the veins was washed in wooden bowls (*bateas*). Where the gangue was not completely disintegrated and was rich enough in free gold it was first broken up by pick and hammer. Existing Indian tunnels (*socavones*) were apparently used. Scarcity of water for washing the pulverized ore was one of the principal limiting factors in the development of the Buriticá properties, aqueducts as long as 14 kilometers being required to reach the ridge-top mine locations."

In 1582 the twelve vecinos and two hundred commoners (*españoles de ordinario*) of the villa of Santa Fé were reported to be working 300 Negro slaves and 1,500 encomienda Indians in the Buriticá mines." The Indian labor force was by this time being recruited mainly from other sections of the province. Later, with the abandonment of the encomienda system in the seventeenth century, Buriticá became an Indian reservation (*resguardo*).

Like Zaragoza and Remedios, Buriticá seems to have reached its production peak before 1630. With the founding of Medellín in 1675 many of the Spanish proprietors of Santa Fé left for the new city. Moreover, the mines of Santa Rosa de Osos were being opened up and most of the slave gangs were transferred there to the more easily worked alluviums.

Between 1730 and 1800 there was a series of attempts to reopen the Buriticá mines but all ended in failure. Raids by hostile Chocóes continued and the yield from the mines was hardly sufficient to pay the soldiers employed to protect the workmen against Indian attacks." A 1730 report describes the mines as "much abandoned, with the remaining miners in a miserable state."" A new company which reopened operations in 1775, employing 75 Negro slaves, seems soon to have ceased work."

Visitors to the province invariably expressed surprise at the primitiveness of the mining techniques employed. At Buriticá all of the wealth was taken by pickwork in open cuts until water completely stopped operations." Pumps to remove water from the shafts were unknown, as was the technique of blasting and amalgamation, and the use of water-powered stamp mills. Elsewhere in the New World the Spaniards borrowed knowledge of vein mining from the Germans and the Italians, but in Antioquia they were on their own. Both Governor Silvestre and Mon y Velarde had plans, never realized, for bringing European mining engineers and mineralogists to Buriticá. Both were convinced that great wealth remained, and that it would be more easily taken here than from the newly discovered Titiribí mines.

Spanish Mines and the Labor Supply 43

No later attempts to reopen Buriticá seem to have been made. Boussingault,[17] who visited the area in 1830 and left one of the few accounts of the geology ("porphyritic syenite, dominated by amphibolite"), said that the town was still occupied at that date by Indians, many of whom still worked in the mines. But today mining is a forgotten art in Buriticá and its past greatness is only dimly remembered. The modern population is dedicated to subsistence agriculture and to the making of Panamá hats.[18]

Searching for the fabled wealth of Zenú, a party of seventy Spaniards from the villa of Santa Fé de Antioquia descended the Río Porce in 1580 to establish the town of Zaragoza de las Palmas, on the right bank of the Río Nechí a few miles below Dos Bocas. Here, in the extensive flood plain where Porce and Nechí join after leaving the crystalline highland, another gold camp was opened. The first deposits worked were the dry bench gravels (*aventaderos*) but soon the superior quality of the stream-bed materials, workable only in the dry months, became apparent. Veins in the residual hills away from the river seem also to have attracted attention.

As reports of the new strike were carried down river, Spanish merchants and slaveowners from Tenerife and other points along the lower Magdalena were drawn to the new settlement. At least eight Negro slave gangs (*cuadrillas*) were brought by Spanish captains from Veragua on the Isthmus of Panamá.[19] By 1582 Zaragoza had a royal smelting house and an office of the royal treasury, where the gold from Buriticá and Cáceres was also deposited.

The preamble to Governor Rodas' mining ordinances of 1587[20] stated that the great discoveries at Zaragoza had made the regulations necessary. These ordinances were to become the basis of all New Granadan mining law. Individual claims of 60 yards (*varas*) square were allowed; those in the hills back from the river were to be 80 yards square. It was specifically stated that the ownership of more than one cuadrilla of blacks would not entitle a man to additional claims, each of which had to be staked out and worked within a given period of time. A special court for settling disputes, including those over water rights, was established. Water rights were to become as important as mining claims in later litigation.

Fray Simón placed the Indian population of the Zaragoza region at 2,000 families and reported that in assigning encomiendas to the soldiers imaginary names were used by the officials to fill in the lists and placate the men. Within a very few years no natives remained, the last being taken by the smallpox epidemic of 1588. Vásquez de Espinosa explained the disappearance of the Indians in the region as being voluntary ("since rather than be subject to the Spaniards they preferred death and bled themselves to death through their noses"). Moreover, the country was "naturally unhealthy in the extreme."[21] In his day Zaragoza had 300 Spanish and 3,000 to 4,000 Negro slaves in cuadrillas.

Zaragoza loomed so important in the economy of the province in the seventeenth century that several of the governors made their headquarters there rather than in the city of Santa Fé de Antioquia, perhaps for the easier supervision of their own mining interests. Contemporary documents even referred occasionally to the "Gobierno de Zaragoza."

The appointment of one governor to Antioquia, in 1629, was made with the express condition that he should carry out a diversion of the Río Nechí for 7 leagues so that its river-bed gravels could be worked. If this audacious plan was successful, the appointee had assured the Crown, the annual income from the royal fifth alone would reach 200,000 ducats. He was provided with a hundred Negro slaves for the task and was promised the title of viscount on its completion, but he died in 1634, apparently before the work had started.[22] The project continued to be discussed for some time thereafter but was never carried out.

Zaragoza was the port of entry for the Guamacó camp, founded in 1611 in the high country of the Serranía de San Lucas between the Nechí and the Magdalena. Until the middle of the eighteenth century Guamacó remained under the political jurisdiction of Antioquia. Fray Pedro Simón described it[23] as reached by a hard, six-day trip from Zaragoza, the trail being so bad that the Spaniards were forced to proceed on foot. Another road was opened in 1613 from Simití on the Magdalena and it eventually became the principal route.

The early importance of Zaragoza[24] was forgotten in the eighteen century and it continued as a poor river hamlet of free blacks and mulattoes. Neither did the new Cáceres, founded on the low plains of the Cauca 30 miles to the north, attain significant importance. Both were placed under the jurisdiction of a *capitán de guerra* who was also the collector for the royal treasury. Economically and culturally both towns turned more and more toward Mompox rather than to Medellín.

Heavily wooded, rain-drenched southeastern Antioquia was first entered from the Magdalena by Bogotanos rather than by the men of the Cauca. It had been reconnoitered as early as 1535 by members of the Jiménez de Quesada party on their way to the Chibcha country, but the first entrada was that conducted in 1550 by Francisco Núñez Pedroso,[25] who returned to found the villa of Mariquita, attracted as much by the gold-bearing gravels of the vicinity as by its silver lodes.

Mariquita was first of a series of settlements to the north which in the next forty years extended to the present-day site of Remedios. First of these was Victoria, founded in 1558 by vecinos of Mariquita, 30 miles to the north in the valley of the Río La Miel in the modern department of Caldas. Two years later a group of forty Victorians under Captain Francisco Ospina moved to a new site in the "Valle de Corpus Cristi" (Río San Carlos) to establish the first town of Nuestra Señora de los Remedios. From here the villa was shifted briefly to Buenavista and, after the exhaustion of the local Indians and gold, to another site "six leagues to the west" in a valley called San Blas, probably in the upper Río Nus drainage or the vicinity of Yolombó. Here it remained for twenty-six years and became, according to Fray Pedro Simón,

> ... a goodly city compared with others in these Indies. It had a good site and climate, plenty of water and land for maize and many natives to serve it... as well as vecinos who were most sociable and agreeable, a good church, an hermitage, hospital and *cofradías* and such other things as contribute to urbanity. They took fair amounts of gold with part of the Indians while the others were used to cultivate maize. With all this the inhabitants lived content and well supplied, for reports of gold brought merchants there with foodstuffs and clothing.[26]

Forty-three encomiendas, representing 9,000 natives "able to serve," were awarded within 10 leagues of this new site,[27] although there was conflict with the few vecinos of Victoria, who were making "unauthorized raids" to the north to augment their diminishing labor supply.[28] The great 1588 smallpox epidemic[29] took a terrible toll among the Indians until the few remaining were required for work in the fields, since "without the attraction of gold the merchants who had formerly brought them their supplies failed to come." The following year Remedios was moved once more to the Sabanas de San Bartolomé (Cancán?) and shortly thereafter 18 leagues further north to its present site, then known as "Quebradas." Thus the fifth and final move of the city of Nuestra Señora de los Remedios was made in 1594, to a commanding ridge site on the eastern margin of the crystalline Antioqueño highland, almost 70 air-line miles from the point where it had originally been established thirty-four years earlier.

So rich were the new Remedios mines, says Simón,[30] that "in two years it became the richest town of its size in the Indies." Numbers of Negroes were brought in from Cartagena, the twenty leading citizens each having cuadrillas of a hundred or more slaves. Calculated on the basis of the royal fifth, Remedios produced six million pesos of gold between 1594 and 1620 and, in addition, there was much illicit production. "It seemed," reported Fray Simón, "that the land had made testament and given up its wealth."

The exhaustion of the labor force, not the gold, caused the decline of seventeenth-century Remedios. Epidemics so decimated the slave population by 1626 that less than five hundred remained, with less than half that number of Indians.[31] No replacement seems to have been attempted. Costs of supplies remained high, being brought in either through the Río Nechí or Río Nare ports. Livestock were driven in from the valley of Aburrá. The Spaniards who were able returned to Bogotá with their profits to partake of the attractions of that growing center of leisure and culture. They had few ties with the settlements farther west in Antioquia, and few if any of the leading Antioqueño families trace their origins through Remedios.[32]

As the Buriticá, Zaragoza, and Remedios camps faded in importance, widely dispersed placers on the highland massif of central Antioquia came into production. In 1636 a resident of Antioquia asked title to the "Río de los Osos and the gold mines on its margins" in the Santa Rosa area.³³ Many small strikes were made thereafter on the uplands. Some were pockets of alluvial gravel, others gold-bearing veins in the decomposed country rock. The gold ore was generally hacked and broken loose from the rock, crushed, and washed in bateas in the conventional manner.

Medellín and Ríonegro prospered as supply bases for the countless small diggings of the tierra fría east and south of the Río Cauca. Establishment of the curacies of Santa Rosa de Osos and Santo Domingo in 1659³⁴ suggest that the occupation of these uplands was already well under way at that time. The scarred red earth around San Pedro, Santa Rosa, Belmira, and Don Matías to the west of the Río Porce and at Retiro, Guarne, San Roque, San Vicente, and Concepción in the east (*Oriente*) still show the evidence of two centuries of primitive mining operations. Today there is not a single stream on these highlands that does not bear evidence of old workings. Even the *cañon* of Medellín became an important source of gold as the older valley-terrace gravels were worked and reworked, especially between Bello and Barbosa. Above Medellín, between Ancón and Caldas, the river was diverted from its bed for some 800 yards by a deep bed-rock cut which is still a striking landmark. Only the Tertiary beds about Amagá and Fredonia failed to yield gold.

INDIAN LABOR AND MISCEGENATION

The Indian encomienda in Antioquia, as in other parts of the New World, was at first used to insure cheap labor for the mines under the guise of spiritual trusteeship. In so doing it destroyed the economy and undermined the religious and ceremonial structure of Indian society. Virtually the first public act after the founding of a new settlement in the sixteenth century was the assignment of encomiendas or estates of 50 to 500 heads of families, thereafter obliged to provide services, or later tribute in gold or produce, to their encomenderos. By 1590 the reservoir of docile, native labor in Antioquia had become so reduced that Negro slaves had become the main labor force. The title of encomendero became increasingly an honorary one without economic reward, for it was more and more the owners of the slave cuadrillas who were taking the treasure.

In 1614 the Real Audiencia sent the Oidor Francisco Herrera y Campuzano to report on the status of the Indians and encomiendas of Antioquia. His lengthy accounts, spread through many manuscript volumes in the Archivo Nacional at Bogotá, offer a wealth of unused evidence on the conditions of native labor. For the nineteen encomiendas of "Antioquia" (including the haciendas of Sopetrán, Aburrá, Buriticá, and Ebéjico) he listed only 409 male tributaries, but 85 caciques, captains, and others exempt from tribute, and 1,082 women and children.³⁶ At Cáceres there were eighteen additional encomiendas and 346 male tributaries, and at San Jerónimo del Monte, north of Cáceres in the Río San Jorge drainage, the eight encomiendas included 90 "useful males." The average encomendero, then, had less than 25 Indian laborers and some had already become encomenderos in name only.³⁶

It was really the Indians who taught the Spaniards how to mine. When the oidor decreed that the natives should no longer be forced to work in the mines, the inhabitants of Cáceres appealed, pointing out, with good reason, that without the Indians mining would cease, both because it was the Indians who taught the Negroes the work and because the Indians were the only ones who had the skill to construct the very high aqueducts.³⁷

When he visited Guamocó, in the mountains east of Zaragoza, Fray Pedro Simón³⁸ criticized the practice of awarding encomiendas of *indios de minas* to poor common soldiers who "so overwork the Indians to enrich themselves quickly that they are finished with them in two days, for the natives are not accustomed to the hard work of the mines."

The terrible death tolls which followed the impact of the first Spanish contacts seem to have run their course in a single generation here, as elsewhere in the New World. The survivors of the first fifty years of epidemics,³⁹ forced labor, and acute psychological readjustments were a select group, numbering probably between 5,000 and 10,000, who were to provide an important part of the rootstock of the evolving "raza antioqueña."

Colonial census reports recognized four castes, of which the "first class citizens," the whites, were sometimes further subdivided into nobles and commoners. The "second class" was composed of mestizos and was usually the most numerous. The "third class" comprised the mulattoes, and the "fourth class" both Negro slaves and Indians. The mestizos and mulattoes together outnumbered the whites, slaves, and Indians by wide margins in almost all colonial communities in the seventeenth and eighteenth centuries. Sometimes the ratio was as high as ten to one. At the end of the colonial period, for instance, the population (1797) of the entire jurisdiction of Santa Fé de Antioquia, which extended from Yarumal to Urrao and Anzá, contained only 6 per cent whites compared with 65 per cent "free persons of color," including both mulattoes and mestizos.[40] Comparable figures for Medellín (1778) showed 18 per cent whites, 27 per cent mestizos, 35 per cent mulattoes, and 20 per cent slaves in a population of 14,507.[41] The mulatto element was especially strong in the mining sections and throughout the tierra caliente where today Negroid features predominate.

In the early seventeenth century the Spanish Crown began to show concern that the remaining indigenes should be dealt with fairly and justly. Following the recommendations of the Oidor Herrera y Campuzano the remaining Indians were gradually placed on reservations, the land being assigned to them in common in the name of their caciques. But those who had been on encomiendas were still required to give personal services to their former masters. The first reservations were established at Buriticá, Sabanalarga, Sopetrán, and San Lorenzo de Aburrá. The last was moved to La Estrella after the founding of Medellín. Another reservation existed briefly at San Juan de Piede-la-Cuesta, near modern Ebéjico, until it was absorbed into Sopetrán and its land were sold for the profit of the Church. Others were established in the following century at Peñol, Sabaletas, and Pereira in the jurisdictions of Ríonegro and Marinilla, and that at Cañasgordas served as a sort of frontier post for Church and State in the long campaigns for the subjugation and conversion of the less tractable Chocó Indians.

There was constant pressure by free citizens against the boundaries of the better reservations. At Sopetrán Mon y Velarde found so many free men (*libres*) living on Indian lands that he could not order houses built around the plaza as at other places "because it would have been in violation of the law prohibiting Indians and libres from living together."⁴² There was no such pressure at Sabanalarga, however, where he observed that the lands cultivated by the Indians "are rocky and sterile slopes, so precipitous that they work them only with great risk of life."⁴³

At the end of the colonial period the eight reservations in Antioquia had approximately one hundred tributaries each, their combined populations approaching 5,000. This latter figure included many mestizos and mulattoes who were married to reservation Indians. One census of La Estrella at the end of the eighteenth century showed 87 mixed marriages there between libres of various castes and Indians.⁴⁴

The reservation system, while serving to keep the small surviving Indian nucleus in a sort of ecclesiastical and economic bondage, also fed the racial amalgam with numerous fugitives and with children born to these cross-caste marriages. The latter were in most instances considered free. Less than a century after the liquidation of the reservations in Antioquia, the miscegenation had become so complete that a visitor at Sopetrán or La Estrella could discern few traces of their Indian background.⁴⁵

Negro Slaves and Slavery

The pattern for Negro slavery had been set up for the Spaniards in Hispaniola, Veragua, and other early mining camps of the New World; at Cartagena a major slave market functioned.⁴⁶ Negroes accompanied Badillo in 1539 and participated in all the later entradas. Cieza de León, first chronicler of Antioquia, early observed of Buriticá that only when the Spaniards got more Negroes would they get more gold.⁴⁷

The mines of Buriticá, Zaragoza, and Remedios were worked mainly by Negro cuadrillas during the bonanza days at the end of the sixteenth century and so continued until about 1650. The wealth of a vecino was determined by the number and quality of his blacks. Simón attributed the successes of a mestizo soldier of Zaragoza to his ability to obtain credit in buying Negroes from the slave merchants of Cartagena.

Spanish Mines and the Labor Supply 51

In 1598 there was a major rebellion of the blacks at Zaragoza, suppressed only in the following year by royal troops.⁴⁸ This was the forerunner to the great Cartagena revolt which began in 1600. The early uprising at Zaragoza was followed by others, including the 1706 rebellion in Marinilla, Ríonegro, and Girardota.⁴⁹ Such rebellions left a residue of escaped blacks who were able to maintain their free status, sometimes furtively. A curious reminder of one such movement is the settlement of descendants of runaway slaves (*cimarrones*) at Uré, 30 kilometers northwest of Cáceres on the Antioquia-Bolívar border. As color and caste became increasingly disassociated it must have been more and more difficult to retrieve runaways in a thinly settled, mountainous land.

Even among these African laborers, often immune to the European diseases which swept through the Indian populations so disastrously, mortality was at first high. Fray Pedro Simón blamed diseases among the Negroes of Remedios for the decline of that camp from its early prosperity.⁵⁰ Syphilis and smallpox took a heavy toll.

Starvation, resulting from the short-sighted policies of their owners in the provision of foodstuffs, was another cause of the decline of the slave population. A visitador to Antioquia in 1663 reported that "as a result of four years of scarcity many slaves have died of hunger."⁵¹ The decline of the Indian population, which had grown the food required for the cuadrillas, must have been a contributing factor in the decrease in the number of Negro slaves.

Emancipation of individual slaves, especially women, was a common practice in Antioquia and, almost from their inception, the colonial courts were much concerned with litigation over individual slaves and their descendants. The "free Negro" became a recognized category in eighteenth-century censuses. The first mass emancipation occurred in 1781 when Lorenzo Agudelo, a slaveowner of Santa Fé de Antioquia, announced the freeing of his eight Negroes employed at a mine called Buenaventura. His action was considered a rebellious one by the colonial government and he was arrested and exiled to Puerto Bello, Panamá.⁵² The movement spread in later years and it was on the initiative of Antioquia at the Congress of Cúcuta (1821) that the policy of progressive liberation was adopted.

In 1759 Governor Chaves wrote to the viceroy that "there are so many mines in the province that it is scarcely possible to set down one's foot except upon gold, and yet... the number of Negroes who work in them will not reach 900."[53] The mineowners of Río Chico and Río Grande near Santa Rosa de Osos complained of the scarcity of Negro labor and that "the best part of their yield is consumed in their purchase." Governor Silvestre noted in 1776 that the mines, having few laborers and fewer tools, were obliged to employ Negroes who

TABLE 3
NEGRO SLAVES IN THE PROVINCE OF ANTIOQUIA, 1808[a]

Canton	Slaves	Per cent of Canton's population
Santa Fé de Antioquia	4,401	9
Medellín	2,849	9
Ríonegro	2,056	8
Marinilla	424	6
Zaragoza	315	15

[a] *Anuario Estadístico* (Medellín, 1888), pp. 110-115.

cost at least four hundred pesos or else to pay wages at the rate of one peso or more a day. Even Zaragoza had more free Negroes than slaves in the late eighteenth century. One 1767 report indicates that at that time there were 4,296 Negro slaves in Antioquia (compared with 3,504 in the Chocó and 9,313 in Popayán),[54] but this figure had more than doubled thirty years later. The first complete census, that of 1808, showed 10,045 slaves in the Province of Antioquia (table 3). The cuadrillas were things of the past. Now the slaves were widely distributed as family retainers and hands on the ranches and in small mine workings scattered through the hills.

The mulatto caste in many areas was numerically superior to both mestizos and whites. Negroid elements were especially numerous in the mining camps. Judging from earlier census reports, when color lines were more carefully defined, Negro blood must have constituted at least one-third of the evolving Antioqueño strain. Thus, the 1778 census of the villa of Medellín[55] listed 55 per cent of the 14,704 inhabitants as either mulatto or Negro slave. For Santa Fé de Antioquia

Spanish Mines and the Labor Supply 53

an 1805 census[56] recorded 4,242 out of a total population of 5,945 as either mulatto or slave, and the near-by *partido* of Obregón listed 865 mulattoes and 70 slaves out of a total population of only 1,069. These were extremes, but even in the cooler uplands the Negro element was significant. In 1777 Pontesuelo (Santa Rosa) had 117 whites, 13 mestizos, 274 mulattoes and free Negroes, and 174 slaves.[57] At Guarne the Negroes and mulattoes owned two-thirds of the property listed on the assessor's books.[58]

The mixture of Negro blood has always been less in the Oriente, the region which provided the greatest number of the colonists who occupied Caldas, Tolima, and the trans-Cauca Occidente after 1800. Moreover, the rate of increase of Negroid elements has been lower than that of the highland whites. Thus, the modern Antioqueño racial amalgam is undoubtedly less Negroid than one-hundred and fifty years ago, although there has been virtually no white immigration from outside to change the elements in the racial mixture.

Mazamorreros and Barequeros

Until the advent of the dredges and monitors of the twentieth century, mazamorreros extracted virtually all of the placer gold taken from the province. They still number many thousand, the majority of them women. Their traditional implement, the batea, is an elliptical, shallow wooden bowl with a handle 12 to 14 inches long. Rocking this hand-fashioned tool with two hands and with a section of guadua or half a coconut shell tied to the belt to receive the product of each panning operation, groups of mazamorreros may work all day waist deep in the streams.

Two types of alluvial workings are distinguished, those worked during the dry season (*minas de verano*) and those which can only be worked during the rainy months (*minas de invierno*). The former, which include the high-grade river-bed gravels of the Cauca, the Porce, and the Nechí, are generally the more productive. From December to late March Cáceres, Remedios, and Zaragoza are half deserted, and great encampments of mazamorreros line the river banks at such places as the Charcón del Nechí above Dos Bocas, where "such astonishing returns are taken that they may pass the rest of the year quietly resting at their homes."⁵⁹ Where the water is deep, and the current not too swift, divers (*zambullidores*) sometimes plunge with bateas in hand to the bottoms of the rivers to obtain high-grade gravels concentrated there.

Several ingenious methods have been developed for the hand exploitation of gravels not easily worked by the individual mazamorrero. Those engaged in this type of communal work, usually in groups of from three to six, are often known as *barequeros,* a term apparently derived from the Spanish *bahareque,* a type of lattice construction. One such device is the *sombre,* a baffle of palm leaves suspended over a stream and so adjusted at the bottom that the churning water cuts down through the sands and gravels of the river bed to expose the gold concentrations overlying the bedrock. These concentrations are then worked with long-handled shovels or by divers, the gravels being brought to the stream bank where they are panned out in bateas, usually by groups of robust Negresses. Earlier accounts tell of some stretches along the rivers of Antioquia which were filled with stakes driven to hold such palm-mat barriers.⁶⁰

Sometimes crude, earthen wing dams (*tapados*) are extended into a stream in semicircular form and the water behind them then either pumped or baled out to expose the rich stream-bed gravels. Where the current is adequate a simple check dam may be all that is required.

A more ambitious operation is the *cortado* or diversion of an entire stream from its original bed. Such a project was proposed by the Real Audiencia as early as 1629 on the lower Porce and later was accomplished on several major streams, including the Nus, the Grande, and the upper Medellín.⁶¹

The *minas de invierno* are chiefly in the highlands where the scarcity of water restricts washing operations in alluvium and vein alike. Small tanks were, and still are, commonly used to collect rain water or surplus stream flow for use in panning or sluicing. Especially around Santa Rosa de Osos has this shortage of water been a serious problem. Boussingault, who visited the mines of this region in 1830 to lay out a plan for conducting water to them, reported to his financial backers that the only method known locally was praying to the miraculous image of San Antonio.⁶²

Spanish Mines and the Labor Supply

Tonga or small-scale strip-mining operations, in which directed streams of water are used to excavate dry gravels, are also usually confined to the rainy months. The washings are passed through a sluice channel where the heavier gold settles out in a sand which is then washed by bateas. Larger rocks are first removed by hand. In this manner wide areas of highland Antioquia have been stripped of soil and vegetation.

Modern Developments

There was widespread realization that precious metals alone could not provide a lasting foundation for prosperity and progress in Antioquia. "Instead of representing the wealth of the Crown," wrote Padre Joaquín de Finestrad in 1783, "the mines seem to have been responsible for the notable backwardness of certain provinces. Antioquia, which is paved with gold, is the poorest and most miserable of all." Finestrad, who visited every corner of the province, reported that poor people asking for aid assembled in groups wherever he went "although they were occupied in searching for gold."[63]

During the reign of Carlos II (1759–1788) the Spanish government made concerted efforts to introduce new European mining techniques into the New World. In 1784 the Crown sent Juan José d'Elúyar and Angel Díaz, who were familiar with the mines of France and Germany, to New Granada, where they directed their efforts to restoring the silver mines of Mariquita.[64] Earlier, in 1763–1764, two technical advisers from Perú had been brought to Mariquita and Pamplona with disappointing results. In 1788 eight Germans were brought to work in the silver mines of Pamplona and Almaguer (near Popayán) at the request of the mine operators.[65] But not one of these technicians seems to have visited the gold mines of Antioquia. It was silver, not gold, to which the Crown looked for revenue.

In 1808 José Manuel Restrepo could still write of the mines of Antioquia:

... Those in operation today are poor and only make enough profit to keep their owners alive ... Our knowledge of scientific mining has not advanced one step in over two centuries; we cannot follow a vein or seam; we are unable to sink a shaft; and in the end we shall inevitably lose everything in the grave of our disappointed hopes.[66]

Vein mining began in Antioquia with the development of the Cornish or Antioqueño stamp mill by a group of European mining engineers who had been brought to the government's Marmato mines in 1825 and who later drifted into Antioquia. The Antioqueño mill is still standard equipment in the handful of hard-rock mines that remain operating in the department today. It consists of an overshot water wheel which turns a wood camshaft 12 to 15 inches in diameter. The light and primitive stamps are built in multiples of three to six to a battery. The chrome-iron stamp shoes, cast in Medellín and weighing four to five hundred pounds, are the only replacements needed except for a few bolts and nuts. It is thus ideally suited for small-scale operations in the Antioquia mountains reached only by rough mule trails. Commonly the free gold is removed by hand washing or by running the triturated rock over an "Antioqueño table" of fibrous *yolombó* wood, the surface of which is cut in a crosshatch pattern to form a trap for the free gold.

Between 1835 and 1845 the Santa Ana mine at Anorí became the leading mining enterprise in Antioquia and more or less set the pattern for similar developments in later years. It was here that the principal techniques, and especially the Antioqueño mill, were perfected. In 1838 the rich placers and quartz veins of the Riachón, a few miles southeast of Anorí, had resulted in the establishment of the new town of Amalfi. It enjoyed a rapid growth and in a few years had outstripped the old centers of Zaragoza and Remedios as the most populous place in the northeast. Other important nineteenth-century centers were Santa Rosa, Titiribí, Concepción, Zea, Guarne, San Pedro, and Santo Domingo.

The gold-silver mines of Titiribí (Zancudo, Otra Mina, Chorros), in quartz veins along the margins of a small andesitic laccolith north of the town, were the most productive group of mines in Antioquia during the last century. It was here that La Sociedad Zancudo, the province's first large mining syndicate, founded in 1851, introduced smelting, cyaniding, ball milling, and other techniques for the first time. Much of the ore yielded one part gold to twelve parts silver, assaying at an average of $10.00 (U.S.) a ton."[47] The mines were described and studied by several European engineers who came to

Colombia to supervise various phases of their development, but in later years they were managed entirely by nationals. Several of the foreigners remained in the province to contribute importantly to its later industrial development. When Grosse visited the Titiribí area in 1923 the mines were still in full operation, employing 1,000 persons, but soon thereafter they were closed down.[68] Today they are in ruins, but the story of their development is the pride of Antioquia. Miller and Singewald estimated that the mines of Titiribí had yielded $30,000,000 (U.S.) in gold and silver in the period of their operation.[69]

Modern dredging techniques introduced on the lower Nechí by foreign interests have made gold-mining in Antioquia big business in recent years. Antioquia today produces about two-thirds of all the gold mined in Colombia, close to three-quarters of this coming from foreign owned and managed companies. The first successful steam dredge was placed in operation on the Río Nechí below Zaragoza in 1909 and four years later California interests commenced working with the first of the Pato electric dredges.[70] Pato Consolidated Gold Dredging, Ltd., a Canadian corporation controlled by the International Mining Corporation of New York,[71] operates five large floating dredges at El Bagre, below Zaragoza on the lower Río Nechí. Presently developed gravel reserves, to depths of 80 feet, are considered sufficient to support operations for another 15 years under existing economic conditions. The company employs about 500 workers in the El Bagre operation, all Colombians except for a few foreign engineers and dredgemasters. Production in 1966 was 80,000 ounces of gold, only half of the peak output reached twelve years earlier. Values, which currently run about 14 cents (U.S.) per cubic yard, have been declining as operations have moved downstream, farther from the source areas of the gold in the Antioquia mountains. The metal content is highest at the bottom of the old channels so only the largest, most powerful dredges can be used. The California-made dredges each has a capacity of about one-half million cubic yards per month.

The formerly English-owned mine at Segovia, a few kilometers north of Remedios, has been in recent years the most productive vein mine operating in Antioquia or in Colombia. The town of Segovia, a much larger and more flourishing settlement than its colonial neighbor, Remedios, has sprung up since 1860 to meet the needs of the mine. The company, Frontino Gold Mines, Ltd., became a wholly-owned subsidiary of the South American Gold and Platinum Company in 1956. Since the latter has been acquired by International Mining, it controls virtually all of Colombia's present gold production. Frontino Gold Mines, Ltd., was founded in 1864 to operate scattered veins at Frontino, in the Western Cordillera, and the "Bolivia" claims north of Remedios. The Frontino veins did not become major producers (they have been entirely closed down for many years because of damage from landslides), but the properties at Remedios (Segovia) developed well, especially the El Silencio mine, a deep-fissure vein (1,600 meters) which is today the source of about 70 per cent of the ore cyanided by the company. The name Frontino has been retained and has been the source of much confusion. At these mines the first steam engine in Antioquia was employed. A colony of some 25 foreign technicians and their families live in a model hill-top community at the mine. The company also operates a 16,000-acre ranch with a herd of 5,000 cattle to supply meat at reduced prices to the labor force. The 900-odd Colombian miners are predominantly highland Antioqueños, but there are also some workers from the Atlantic coast. Heavy equipment is brought in to the mine over a truck road from Zaragoza on the navigable Río Nechí or, more recently, on a new road from Medellín, but its early development was entirely dependent on mule transport. The gold is flown to the Casa de Moneda in Medellín from the nearby air strip at Otú which, like El Bagre, is now connected with Medellín by daily flights. Frontino's production in 1966 was 73,000 ounces. All gold is sold to the Colombian government at $35 (U.S.) an ounce, of which half is paid in Colombian pesos and half in United States currency, to be used to defray expenditures abroad and for remittance of any profits.

The other major, foreign-operated vein in Antioquia has been the Berlin mine near Yarumal, owned and developed by the Timmins-Ochalí Mining Company. Discovered in 1929, this lode was operated by Colombians using hand methods and Antioqueño stamp mills until it was purchased by North American interests in 1935. Since that time a modern, all-slime cyaniding plant has been installed, and the mine connected with Yarumal by a thirty-five mile road. The mine was closed down in 1946 owing to exhaustion of the ore bodies.

Several small hydraulic mining operations continue intermittently active in the auriferous gravels of the lower Cauca, Nechí, Porce and Nus drainages in Antioquia, but these and the folk miners with their wooden *bateas* together probably do not account for more than 15,000 ounces of gold a year. As recently as twenty years ago government leases in the Marmato mining district in Caldas were yielding some 12,000 ounces annually, and additional production came from a lone dredge at Supía, but these have all ceased operations, faced with the relentless pressure of rising costs while the price of gold has remained unchanged.

Vicente Restrepo estimated that the total gold production of Colombia and New Granada (including Panamá) up to 1886 had been $639,000,000 (U.S.), of which 39 per cent had come from Antioquia. Of Antioquia's production better than two-thirds must have come from placers. Production in the eighty years since Restrepo's estimate was made has approximately equaled that of the previous three and a half centuries, with Titiribí, Pato, and Frontino accounting for considerably more than half of the modern output.

V. COLONIAL AGRICULTURAL SETTLEMENT

THE GREEN and lovely mile-high valley of Aburrá, with its well-watered meadows and its equable climate, was visited by the first Robledo expedition of 1541, but it was not until the next century, when the mines of Buriticá and Zaragoza had declined and the supply of cheap labor had run low, that the big influx of settlers began in the valley which was to become the site of Medellín. From the beginning its economy was oriented as much toward stock raising and subsistence agriculture as toward mining.

In 1547 Gaspar de Rodas, later governor of the province, applied to the council of the villa of Santa Fé for a grant of three square leagues of land in the valley, northward from the old *pueblo* of the Aburráes near modern Envigado.[1] Four years later, when the Pedroso reconnaissance party visited the valley, it was apparently still occupied only by Indians.[2]

Royal grants of land were made in the ensuing years to several other wealthy residents of Santa Fé de Antioquia who established livestock haciendas to supply meat to the growing mining populations to the north and east. By sale, inheritance, and squatter occupance the valley was soon broken up into a comparatively large number of holdings. Vásquez de Espinosa (1628) called it:

> ...one of the most fertile and rich in pastureland in all the Indies,... it contains great numbers of cattle, sheep, horses, mares and mules and produces excellent vegetables and garden truck... They harvest here great quantities of corn, and four or five varieties of beans, some of them better and bigger than horse [Lima] beans (*pallares*). They grow an abundance of [sweet] potatoes; they get honeycombs in the trees, without care or effort; and on the land are wild and domestic swine and every variety of cattle.[3]

The first permanent settlement was made in 1616 on the site of modern Poblado, a few miles up the valley from modern Medellín. Established by order of the Oidor Herrera y Campuzano to bring together the encomienda Indians of the valley, it was named San

---

[1]For notes to chap. v, see pp. 198–199.

Lorenzo de Aburrá. Here a church was erected for its three hundred Indian householders and a handful of Spaniards and mestizos. The regulation against libres owning land within a reservation brought about the establishment of a second settlement in 1646 at the *sitio* of Aná, within the limits of the present city of Medellín, where another straw-roofed church was erected. In 1659 it was formally recognized as a parish church by the visiting bishop of Popayán. Among the inhabitants of the valley at this time were counted several of the wealthiest of the early settlers in the villa of Santa Fé, as well as a growing number of newly arrived Peninsular families who had come direct to the valley of Aburrá. They came from all parts of Spain, but especially from Asturias, Extremadura, and Jérez de la Frontera, forerunners of a wave of Spanish immigration to the valley in the latter part of the century.' Numerically, if not economically—for the land grants went to the nobility (*hidalgos*)—the mestizos, offspring here of soldiers and stragglers left by the several expeditions which had passed through the area, were probably already dominant. As has been said, "the wombs of the most arrogant and beautiful of the young Indian women were the crucibles in which the new race was molded."⁵ By 1630 other sitios in the valley besides Aburrá included Aná, Tasajera (Copacabana), Culatá (San Cristóbal), Itagüí, Santa Gertrudis, Hatoviejo (Bello), and Guayabal.'

In answer to an appeal by the inhabitants, who were still under the jurisdiction of Santa Fé de Antioquia, a royal cédula was issued in Madrid in 1666 authorizing the founding of another corporate city "in the most convenient place in the province" for the vagabond mestizo, mulatto, and Spanish population which numbered more than one thousand in the valley of Aburrá and on near-by mountain slopes. It was pointed out that these people, "so poor and without permanent homes," could not be properly punished for transgressions, much less taxed or encouraged to attend Mass, as long as they continued this "seminomadic life."⁷

Opposition from the council (*cabildo*) of Antioquia, jealous of the prerogatives and prestige of their capital, held up the founding of the new villa for nearly ten years, but on November 2, 1675, the Villa de Nuestra Señora de la Candelaria de Medellín was formally established on the authority of a second royal cédula issued the previous year. The new villa was named in honor of the Count of Medellín, in Extremadura, at the time president of the Supreme Council of the Indies, who signed the papers authorizing the foundation. Its jurisdiction at first included only the valley itself (*de cumbre a cumbre*), a narrow band about 8 kilometers wide and 70 kilometers long flanked on both sides by lands under the jurisdiction of the city of Antioquia.[8]

A census of the valley of Aburrá in 1674 showed some 3,000 inhabitants scattered from the modern town of Caldas to the *sabanas* of Barbosa. Of the 287 families, most were mestizo or mulatto. The settlement of Aná, the largest, contained eighty-five houses.[9]

Almost all the emigrants after 1650 came direct from Spain to Aburrá where they were joined by a considerable number of vecinos from Santa Fé de Antioquia. The latter movement reached such proportions that for ten years the settlement of residents of the former in Medellín was forbidden by law. There were only eighteen vecinos remaining in the old capital when the council met in special session in 1679 to consider possible remedies for the continued loss of population which had left the city without anyone willing to take over the duties of *alcalde*.[10]

The persistent but apocryphal legend that these sixteenth- and seventeenth-century immigrants were Spanish Jews fleeing the Peninsula to the refuge of these mountains has been effectively disposed of by the late Emilio Robledo of Medellín[11] who traced it to an obscure early volume on ecclesiastical history by Manuel del Campo y Rivas,[12] who had taught at Cartago before being appointed oidor to the Audiencias of Guatemala and México. Neither the early chroniclers nor the voluminous archival materials in Medellín and Bogotá hint at such origins. Nor is there any Inquisition record of Jews being found in Antioquia, although they were found in Tunja, Pamplona, and Bogotá.[13] Of the 767 sentences passed by the Cartagena tribunal in two centuries, sixty-eight were against Jews, but none of these were from Antioquia.

If the Semitic legend did originate in the del Campo y Rivas publication, it did not gain wide circulation until the middle of the last century when the revered Antioqueño poet, Gregorio Gutiérrez González, wrote his widely read *Felipe*, which hinted at the Semitic origin of the Antioqueño peoples. It was furthered by the Colombian Jewish author, Jorge Isaacs, whose *La Tierra de Córdoba* had also suggested the same origin for the Antioqueños. Isaacs, although a native of the Valle, had spent his later years in Medellín and was buried there at his own request, holding in his will that its "Jewish heritage" made it fitting.

It is, of course, admissible that the peoples who came to the New World from Spain in the sixteenth and seventeenth centuries included some newly converted Jews who were desirous of hiding their identity, but there is no evidence that they were more numerous here than elsewhere in Spanish America. Of the more common Antioqueño surnames only Santamaría and Correa are generally conceded to be of Jewish origin. The popular acceptance of the legend is clearly related to a feeling of inferiority which seems to exist among other Colombian groups, envious of the economic successes and the "Yankee materialism" of the Antioqueños.

The choice of the name "Antioquia" itself has been interpreted by some as favoring the Semitic story. It has been pointed out, however, that it might reasonably have been named in honor of St. Luke, possibly a native of Antioch in Syria (Antioquia de Siria).[14] Although December 4, 1541, has been officially adopted as the date of Robledo's founding of the city, the *relación* of Juan Bautista Sardela, who accompanied the expedition, gives November 25, which is the Fiesta de San Lucas.[15] The early chroniclers are silent about the choice of the name.

At the time of the formal establishment of the villa of Medellín five other settlements in Antioquia already carried the title of *ciudad*: Arma, Remedios, Cáceres, Zaragoza, and Santa Fé. All had seen better days and were gradually losing population as settlement extended into the cooler granitic uplands, where new mines were being opened. There were seventeen additional smaller pueblos (including Guamacó, Ayapel, and San Jerónimo del Monte, which later were placed under Cartagena), but the total population of the province hardly exceeded 25,000 inhabitants.

The Oriente, as Antioqueños refer to the old upland surfaces of the Antioqueño massif which lie to the east and south of the valley of Medellín, seems to have attracted settlement much more slowly. For one thing there were fewer Indian graves to be looted for gold. Moreover, with the more pleasant lands of middle elevations still open to settlement, where maize and beans yielded two crops a year and where a woolen *ruana* was never needed, there was little incentive other than the mines to move into the bleaker tierras frías.

At the beginning of the seventeenth century the meadowlands along the upper Río Negro had been deeded to the city of Antioquia as common lands (*ejidos*) by their first owner, Governor Gaspar de Rodas, and were being leased to stockmen from Arma, Anserma, and the upper valley of the Río Cauca as well as to residents of the capital. By 1663 Ríonegro is known to have had its own curate and in 1702 its one hundred vecinos were asking for their own *alcalde*.[16] The community's suit for separation from Santa Fé de Antioquia fills hundreds of pages of records in the archives of Medellín. Its claims were finally compromised in 1783 with the transfer of the title of the old city of Santiago de Arma (Arma Viejo) to the inhabitants of Ríonegro, who were also given title to the ejido lands.[17] Marinilla, a settlement only five miles to the east but originally within the jurisdiction of the old Province of Mariquita, had been made an ecclesiastical viceparish of Ríonegro in 1720. By viceregal decree in 1756 it was incorporated into the Province of Antioquia, to which it belonged geographically and economically, and in 1787 it was made an independent villa (map 5).

The best mines, mostly within the jurisdiction of Ríonegro rather than of Marinilla, lay along the west side of the valley toward Medellín. All were above 2,000 meters elevation, and thus well within the limits of the tierra fría as locally defined. The two leading centers of population at the close of the century were not Ríonegro or Marinilla, but the mining camps of San Vicente and Mosca (Guarne).

The wealth and gentility of the people of the Oriente elicited special comment from many early observers. Governor Silvestre noted that "the town of Ríonegro has a greater number of distinguished and wealthy inhabitants than the capital—and its climate is cool."[18] In 1788 its Church tithes, as reported by Mon y Velarde, were comparable to those of Medellín and Antioquia.[19]

A large proportion of the new settlers coming to Ríonegro and to Marinilla had come directly from Spain. Whereas during the seventeenth century the newcomers had gone almost exclusively to the valley of Aburrá, now it was the cooler lands of the Oriente which were attracting them. Of thirty-five Spanish families which arrived in Antioquia between 1750 and 1800, twenty settled in Ríonegro or Marinilla, and but nine in Medellín and five in Antioquia.[20] Other settlers came from the valley of Medellín, from Mariquita, and from the Province of Popayán.

The Oriente was early a crossroads of traffic into the province, both from Popayán and from the warehouses of Nare on the Río Magdalena, and a considerable merchant class developed alongside the nobility. Indians carried the bulk of the in-coming cargo as far as Peñol or Marinilla, where it was transferred to pack trains for Antioquia and Medellín. The route from Popayán passed through Ríonegro but not through Marinilla. As a result of commercial rivalries and historical differences Marinilla and Ríonegro have remained to this day intense rivals. The former is the great Conservative stronghold, the latter is Liberal. Governor Silvestre mentions the trials which the independent Marinillans were to the administration in 1776.

They maintain a very close society, especially those of quality, who are many, and the majority of one family. Caution is necessary to take cognizance of that which displeases them ... for some of them have been evading the tax on *aguardiente* ... with scandalous disdain for authority....[21]

The families, which he observed were mostly from Medellín, were not only wealthy, but hard working, although "spending too much of their time trading when they should be at the mines." In modern Antioquia it is still the Marinillans who have the greatest reputation for sagacity and shrewdness, although their curious customs and excessive politeness are proverbial. Duque, Gómez, Zuluaga, and Hoyos are names which today distinguish these proud gentry who are, by common consent, "much smarter than they look."

There was no observer of late colonial Antioquia who failed to associate the general poverty of the country with the high cost and scarcity of foodstuffs. Especially at the newly opened placers of the tierra fría, where transportation costs from the principal supply areas at Medellín and Ríonegro ran highest, did this condition exist. Mon y Velarde, who was concerned with establishing a better balanced economy, reported to the viceroy in 1788 that he had ordered everyone not employed full time in mining enterprises "to plant a stipulated quantity of maize (which is the common food) every year." Each district was ordered to choose a deputy to enforce this order and, further, to guard against any infringement of the rights of the planters by the mining population. He further advised that a commission be formed in Medellín to be concerned "with all matters affecting agriculture."

As larger harvests are obtained ... the increase in the numbers of hogs and chickens will follow as a natural course, thus contributing to the better maintenance of the miners and artisans and with reciprocal advantages for all. For if the farmer has no one to sell to he will be ruined and the miner or artisan with no one to buy from must either stop working or sell his services at excessive prices....[22]

One of the solutions to this dilemma which Mon y Velarde proposed was the establishment of several new agricultural colonies, a plan for which approval was granted by royal cédula in 1789. To each new town was given four square leagues of land to be distributed to the settlers by a land-title judge (*juez poblador*). Each family received a town lot and a rural finca, the size of the latter depending on the number in the family and their capacity for work. At San Carlos approximately 2 fanegas (3.2 acres) of land were awarded for each member of the family, so that an average-sized family of nine might receive 18 fanegas. Of the four new settlements only San Carlos was in the Oriente, on the road to the Magdalena. The other three, in the jurisdiction of Santa Rosa de Osos, were Yarumal (San Luís de Gongora), Carolina, and Don Matías (San Antonio del Infante). In later years the lands granted to these settlers became the subject of long-drawn-out litigation, for they had been expropriated from holders of vast royal grants.

Yarumal, which became the most prosperous of the new settlements, was in 1786 "a deserted and forgotten mountainside." Three years later there were 520 persons, "noble and honorable although poor," and including a number of malcontents, seeking titles in the area.

Miners in the valley of San Andrés enjoyed a sharp decrease in the price of maize as a direct result of the foundation. Coöperative road-building efforts cut transport time between the new town and the mines by half.[23]

The other settlements at Don Matías and Carolina were in older mining territory and their *colonos* were chiefly mazamorreros who were thus brought into organized communities for the first time and granted title to their own plot of land. This practice, it was hoped, would encourage both food production and attendance at Sunday Mass.

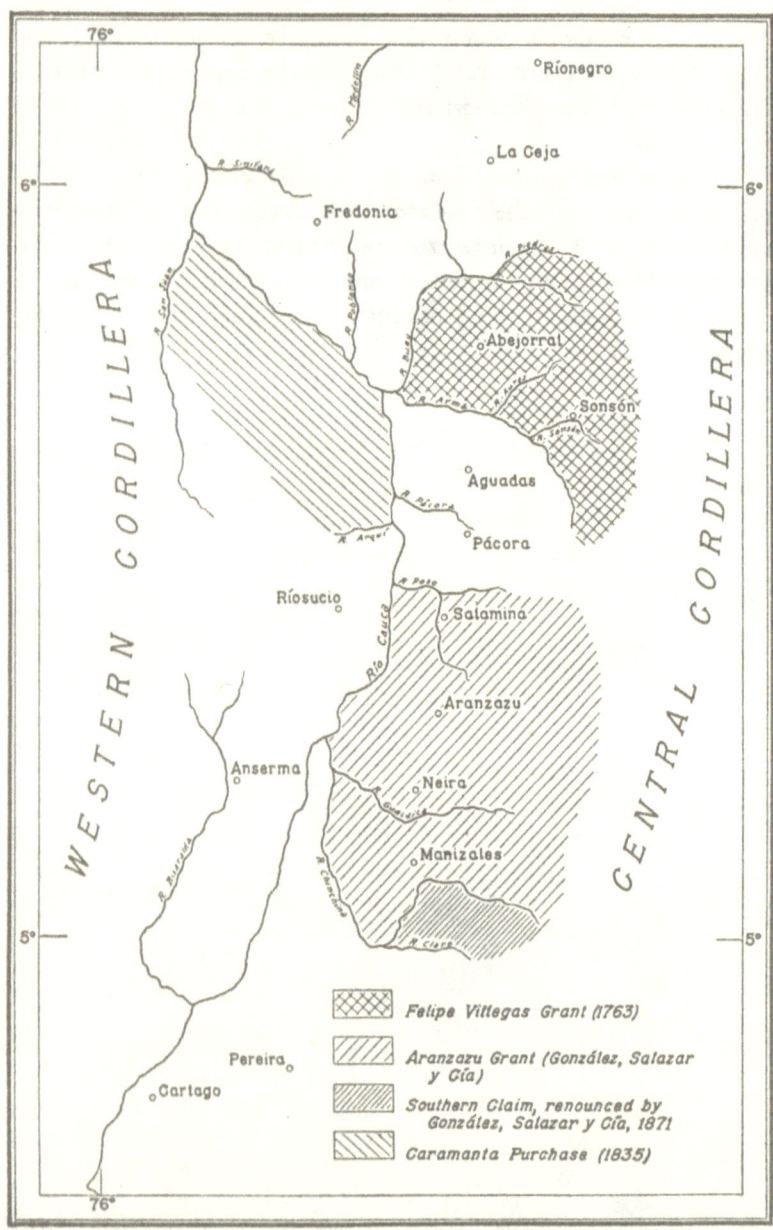

Map. 6. Nineteenth-Century Land Grants on the Southern Frontier.

VI. MODERN ANTIOQUEÑO COLONIZATION

SOUTH OF THE valleys of the Río Negro, beyond La Ceja, lay forested slopes, uninhabited, except for the few humble shacks of Arma Viejo, a way station for muleteers on the road to Marmato and Popayán. Apparently the first major Crown land grant in this southernmost part of the Province of Antioquia was that made in 1763 by the Audiencia of Bogotá to Don Felipe Villegas (map 6),[1] who had come to Ríonegro from Burgos in Spain twenty-eight years earlier.[2] Although he is reputed to have become fairly wealthy working the auriferous gravels of the Río Buey with Negro cuadrillas, Villegas' principal purpose seems to have been the construction of a new and shorter toll road which would connect Medellín and Mariquita. In his proposal, which was forwarded to the viceroy in 1776, he requested further grants along the eastern part of the route for the construction of inns (*tambos*), as well as titles to all gold mines found in connection with the work.[3]

A group of Antioqueño adventurers from the Oriente, briefly established, in 1787, at the bottom of the precipitous Quebrada de Arma, near its junction with the Río Aures, seem to have been the first organized group of settlers to venture into these lands.[4] Originally seeking gold, these people soon turned their attentions toward the higher, healthier, and more level "Valles Altos de Sonsón," near the site of the present town and above the falls of the Río Sonsón and its confluence with the Río Arma.

A memorial to the governor of the province,[5] dated August 27, 1789, in which the settlers set forth their grievances, suggests the forces behind the migration:

... We, the undersigned vecinos of the Ciudad de Ríonegro and the Valle de San Josef de Marinilla, come before you in all humility ... and declare: We have been led to make this move by our extreme poverty in material goods and by the scarcity of lands, either to till as our own or on which to build homes for ourselves and our families. These conditions have been caused by the rapid increase of our people. Thus we have come, penniless, to these mountains of Sonsón, where there is good soil, ample pasture for

---

[1] For notes to chap. vi, see pp. 199–203.

our stock, salines and rich gold mines, to make our homes and erect a new town. This will bring benefits both to ourselves and to the Royal Treasury... as a result of the discovery of said salines and alluvial gold deposits and of the opening of communication between the new settlement [*plantío*] and Mariquita, which is near said Valle de Sonsón....

Litigation over land titles occupied the new settlers for a good part of these first years. They petitioned as *pobres vasallos* for a validated title to that portion of the "uninhabited and unused" Villegas tract lying between the Río Aures and the Quebrada de Arma in the declivitous southeast third of the original Crown grant. The following year a revised petition to the governor⁶ proposed purchase of these lands, "full of abandoned cattle, undeveloped salines and alluvial mines," in order "to avoid the lawsuits experienced by the other new settlements at San Antonio del Infante and San Luís Gongoro, which cost their vecinos no little." The cost was to be distributed among the settlers in exchange for lands assigned to them by the land judge.⁷ Meanwhile the sympathetic Crown was challenging the Villegas title on the grounds that the lands had not been cleared and improved as required by the royal cédula of August 2, 1780.

Few settlers arrived during these early years, although there were lands available for distribution. One of the initial acts of the juez poblador had been to order trees felled for the town plaza, but the first houses were scattered through the forests on individual clearings. It was not until 1797 that the first thatched houses were constructed on the plaza, and the town lots were distributed to the eligibles three years later. At that time there was still no priest, and the nearest Mass, at Arma Viejo, was two and a half days for a peon on foot. "Having a curate would greatly increase the population...." read one petition to the governor.⁸

Of the 2,143 persons listed in the first census of the district in 1808, nearly half were women, sufficient testimony that this was a pioneer farm-family community and no mining frontier. In spite of the prevailing youth of the settlers, 22 per cent of the 292 families with children had eight or more of them.⁹

Although the territory of the district (*partido*) reached from the tierra caliente of the Arma to the tierra fría, virtually all of the early clearings seem to have been in these healthier, higher, and less precipitous lands. The site chosen for the town plaza (elev., 2,545 m.) was about a mile above the wide alluvial valley of the upper Río Sonsón. Excepting Santa Rosa de Osos, it was the highest Antioqueño settlement to that time.

A visitador in 1808 noted[10] that already the Sonsoneños were considering the empty lands across the cordillera for possible settlement, particularly the upper basin of the Río La Miel toward Mariquita. Early bumper yields from the newly cleared, humic forest soils of Sonsón had contributed to the relief of the general hunger caused by the drought of 1807.

Settlers were also moving into the forested slopes to the northwest, beyond the Quebrada de Aures. In 1808 the new partido of Abejorral ("bumblebee hive") had close to 1,500 inhabitants and was demanding a curate.[11] Like Sonsón, the first settlement had grown up around the camp of a mining cuadrilla in the Quebrada de las Yeguas, but soon was moved upslope to a healthier site. It stood within the Villegas grant on a high nose (elev., 2,186 m.) between the gorges of the Arma and the Buey. A son of Felipe Villegas formally ceded the area for the town in 1811 "from a portion of the vast lands that God has given me," but already there were many houses.[12]

In the earliest colonial days Arma had been one of the more flourishing settlements within the jurisdiction of Popayán, having been founded in 1542 under Belalcázar and settled by a few Spaniards from Cali and Popayán. In the early days it was famed for its gold, washed from the Río Cauca sands by Indians and Negro slaves. Lying on a low hill near the Río Cauca it was reputedly extremely unhealthy. When the Oidor Mon y Velarde visited Arma Viejo in 1788 he found seventy-seven families living in the district, many afflicted with a dermatosis (*carate*).[13] Both economically and culturally its dark-skinned population was more closely linked to the Marmato mines and Cartago than to Antioquia.

Although for nearly three hundred years the residents of Arma had ignored the forested mountain slopes above them, the arrival of the Antioqueños in these lands stirred them to activity. The formal foundation of the new town of Aguadas on a high ridge (elev., 2,214 m.)

overlooking the Quebrada de Arma was made in 1814 with the appointment of a juez poblador.¹⁴ Citizens of Arma Viejo settled both here and at Pácora, established sixteen years later, a few miles to the south.¹⁵

The political and economic unrest of the revolutionary period slowed but did not shut off this new Antioqueño immigrant stream. A memorial to the governor in 1817, signed by 145 heads of families, mostly from Sonsón, asked permission to found a town at Sabanalarga, above Salamina and a quebrada beyond Pácora.¹⁶ The previous year an exploratory party had found these lands "fertile, beautiful and of good temperature," with plenty of pasture and water. Although a cautious colonial governor had denied the request "as exceedingly prejudicial to Sonsón," a settlement began in the area soon after Independence.

The validity of titles to the extensive Crown grants of unsettled, forested areas vexed the courts and complicated problems of land tenure for many years. Of these latter none was so troublesome as the extensive Aranzazu grant, confirmed by the Supreme Court of the new republic in 1828.¹⁷ The grantee's original claim included all the lands east of the Río Cauca between the Quebrada de Arma and the Quebrada de Chinchiná. The Aranzazus eventually abandoned all of their claims between the Arma and the Quebrada de San Lorenzo, but to the south a long and bitter struggle between the squatters and González, Salazar y Cía. (successors to the Aranzazu title) was marked by incendiary fires, personal feuds, and, in 1851, by an assassination.¹⁸ The lands involved included all of the present Caldas municipios of Salamina, Neira, Aranzazu, Filadelfia, and Manizales, comprising an area of exceptionally rugged topography approximately 60 kilometers long by 40 kilometers wide (map 6).

The situation was clearly one of squatters against vested interests; in the end the former emerged with a compromise victory. Salamina had been established as a district in 1825 by a decree from Bogotá which, seemingly, regarded the lands as public domain (*baldíos*).¹⁹ By 1833, after the town had been moved to its present ridge-top site, the company of Gonzáles, Salazar y Cia. had won a decisive court victory against the colonists. Court dockets were jammed with suits originated by the company against both the Salamina squatters and the new settlements of Neira (1843) and Manizales (1848). The uncertainty of titles probably discouraged some immigration during this period, but it also stimulated a few of the more restless adventurers[20] to press on still further *arriba,* beyond the law. The settlers of Manizales capitulated in 1851 with an agreement whereby the company claims were recognized in return for a promise to sell to each vecino a town lot for half the evaluated price. González, Salazar y Cía. also agreed to provide lands for the plaza, church, streets, cemetery, school, and jail.

As custodian of all former Crown lands (now public baldíos), the government of the republic was deeply involved in disputes. In 1853 it negotiated an agreement with the company which finally brought an end to the unrest and uncertainties. The agreement stipulated:

(1) That the Government cede to the company all rights to the lands under dispute.

(2) That the company give free and absolute title, gratuitously, to 10 fanegas [16 acres] of land to each settler established within these lands who had built a house or made clearings or other improvements, providing it did not encroach on the rights of previous purchasers or concessionaires.

(3) That the company give to each town 12,000 fanegas [19,000 acres] of land, to be held for the disposition of the respective town councils.

(4) That the Treasury of the Republic become owner of one-quarter of the stock and other rights which were the property of González, Salazar y Cía.

(5) That for two years from date of the contract settlers who wished to purchase additional lands from the company should be granted an 8 per cent deduction from the purchase price for legal expenses and 6 per cent for public education.[21]

Manizales had commenced with a few scattered clearings in the forest of the broad amphitheater formed by the upper Río Chinchiná.[22] Leaving behind their new cornfields and herds of hogs,[23] the settlers returned to their homes in Neira, Salamina, Sonsón, and Abejorral for their families, reassembling at Neira in June, 1848, to form the Expedición de los Veinte with the announced objective of founding a new town to the south. The journey from Neira to the Chinchiná, although only 20 kilometers air-line distance, involved the crossing of two extremely deep canyons and the ascent of their high, abrupt interfluves. The trail was still not passable for pack animals.

After two false starts in the valley of the upper Chinchiná, the new town was finally erected on a commanding ridge top (elev., 2,153 m.) between the Chinchiná and Olivares on the new trail which linked Salamina and Sonsón with Cartago and the Valle. From this point, too, the new Camino del Ruiz branched off eastward across the cordillera to Mariquita and Bogotá. It was shorter and easier than the old route from Salamina over the Páramo de Herveo and was soon carrying virtually all of the traffic to and from the Río Magdalena.[24] As a result, Manizales soon became the principal trading emporium for all of southern Antioquia and much of northern Cauca, including the Chocó and the mines of Marmato. Moreover, its strategic position astride the main routes of communication was to give it a peculiarly important military role during the civil wars of the latter nineteenth century. It thus became not only a trade center, but a frontier garrison which controlled access to both southern Antioquia and northern Cauca. Here, more than elsewhere, gold mines or rumors of strikes seem to have attracted the new settlers flocking in from the north. For a time in the 'seventies is seemed that the future of Manizales lay in the auriferous veins which lay east of the town toward the headwaters of the Río Chinchiná, where the mantle of volcanic ash from Ruiz was thinnest. It was even suggested that miners be brought in from the fading Amalfi region of Antioquia.[25]

Despite the destructive earthquakes of the 'seventies and 'eighties and its cramped, ridge-top position which severely limited the physical expansion of the city, Manizales continued to grow. The cacao blight which wrecked the plantations of Antioquia and Sopetrán gave it the added role of entrepôt for a large cacao trade which carried this indispensable foodstuff of the Antioqueños on oxen from the Valle to Medellín. Schenck observed in 1880 that the powerful cacao middlemen of Manizales, who would stop at nothing to impede direct trade between the producers in Cauca and the consumers in Antioquia, had been able to block the reëstablishment of a telegraph line from Manizales to Cartago.[26]

The 12,000 fanegas of land given to the town were distributed in parcels of 10 fanegas (16 acres) each to 1,154 individuals, all being eligible who had been in residence at the time of the contract.[27] Those who lived across the river in the state of Cauca within the partido of Chinchiná (Villamaría) were also considered as "vecinos." Later, a commission of four, appointed by the Manizales town council, purchased the remaining company lands within the municipio for 22,500 pesos. But when the council decided that the cost was too high, the purchasers constituted a private company (Moreno, Walker y Cía.) which sold lots and stock to later settlers.

Modern Manizales (population 190,000 in 1964) is a startling city, perched precariously on the sky line, its huge, gray, unfinished cathedral visible for miles in all directions. Its future was assured when it was made the capital of the newly established department of Caldas in 1905 and, later, an aerial-cable and railway terminus. Today it is threatened by the rising commercial centers of Pereira and Armenia. for there is no site near the city suitable for a grade A airport.

Beyond the Río Chinchiná the densely forested volcanic-ash slopes east of the Rió Cauca were administratively a part of the Province of Quindío within the state of Cauca. Save for the pasture lands and cacao plantations of the tierra caliente near Cartago and along the Cauca and Río La Vieja, the entire province had remained an empty, forested frontier without attraction for the Cauca mulattoes.

Antioqueño settlers from the north had begun to move across this political boundary even before the founding of Manizales. The very border itself had long been under dispute, there being confusion as to which of the streams pouring down from Ruiz was the true Río Chinchiná. The name seems originally to have been applied to the next stream south, marked on modern maps as the Río Claro, and that separating Manizales from Villamaría was more properly the Río Manizales. But the settlers, not without guile, had soon altered the original terminology. The question was of importance in connection with the limits of the Aranzazu grant, which were finally settled in 1871 with González, Salazar y Cía. renouncing all claims to lands between the Río Chinchiná and Río Claro in return for other considerations, including title to 12,800 hectares of baldíos and 10,000 pesos cash.[28]

The earliest Antioqueño colony in this area had been the Fermín López settlement at Santa Rosa de Cabal in 1844. An original congressional grant of 12,000 fanegas of baldíos in that year was doubled in 1849 as a result of a petition from the settlers of the new parish.²⁰ Already, they reported, their clearings had spread beyond the limits of the original grant into baldíos which, as a result of the new importance their activities had given the region, would be subject to claim by rich persons "against whom we poor settlers cannot hope to compete for lack of resources." The sympathetic legislature, in granting the request, observed the advantages in trade with Buenaventura, Popayán, and Medellín that the prosperous new settlement was affording as a result of the new and shorter road from Manizales to Cartago which passed that way.

In 1852 the town, which lay on a gently sloping fan at 1,800 meters above the sea, was made seat of a district and the name changed from the earlier Cabal to Santa Rosa de Cabal after the saint's day on which the settlers had arrived from Salamina. Still later, Santa Rosa was given 24,000 fanegas more by the Constitutional Convention of Ríonegro in 1863, to make it the most richly endowed in government land grants of any nineteenth-century community in the republic.

The lands between Manizales and Santa Rosa were rapidly settled during the 'fifties and 'sixties. The Ríonegro convention had ceded sufficient baldíos to the state of Cauca to permit a grant of 5 hectares (12 acres) to each person in the *aldeas* of Villamaría, Santa Rosa de Cabal, San Francisco (Chinchiná), and Palestina who had not already received lands, as well as those who might arrive later. Veterans of the civil war, their creditors, and legitimate heirs, were to receive 10 hectares (24 acres) instead of 5 hectares. It was stipulated that grantees could not sell, transfer, or alienate these lands to individuals who possessed more than 30 hectares within the region, so that property would not "accumulate in a few hands." The right of proprietorship could be acquired by "cultivation," to be proved either by erecting a house or by making a clearing.

From such eminently sensible legislation emerged the small-holding society of Antioqueño agriculturists on these new lands of Cabal. The new towns continued to be built close to the 2,000-meter contour, which meant the healthier lands. They were situated well back from the Río Cauca except for Segovia (Marsella) which lay on the high nose (elev. 1,910 m.) of a ridge overlooking the river. The clearing of the lower slopes, especially below 1,500 meters, awaited the advent of coffee and commercial stock raising after 1880.

In this entire hill zone of the Province of Quindío only one successful settlement had a non-Antioqueño origin, and it, too, was soon engulfed by the immigrant wave from the north. This was Pereira, founded in 1863 as Cartago Viejo on the original, sixteenth-century site of Robledo's settlement on the banks of the Río Consota.[20] The new founders, a group of Cartago citizens, reported the same dense stand of guadua which the first chroniclers had described three hundred years earlier. Some of the old stone masonry of the original settlement, rediscovered by the Fermín López party, was used for the foundations of the buildings of the new town.

The Pereira district began receiving large numbers of Antioqueño immigrants after 1870.[21] Commercial ties with Santa Rosa and Manizales became as important as those with Cartago. At the time of Schenck's visit in 1880 Pereira had become the center of an important cacao-growing district, supplying the Antioquia market. These were lower, warmer lands than had previously been attracting Antioqueño settlement. The site of the plaza (elev., 1,476 m.), lying at the foot of the 2,100-meter high ridge, from which the vast, fertile plain of the Valle del Cauca spread out to the south, would hardly have been selected by men who had founded such sky-line settlements as Manizales, Palestina, Salamina, and Aguadas.

The hostile attitude of the residents of Cartago toward these aggressive, loquacious Antioqueño intruders undoubtedly deflected many of the latter to Pereira.[22] It was not until after 1900 that reprisals against the Antioqueño settlers ceased, their successful occupance of the rolling Quindío lands to the south having become a grudgingly accepted reality. Modern Pereira, with close commercial ties with Valle del Cauca, is one of the most prosperous and dynamic cities in Colombia. In 1967 it became the capital of the new department of Risaralda.

The rolling *altiplano* of the Quindío lies south of Pereira and east of the Río La Vieja, a 40-kilometer-square pocket of deep, volcanic-ash soils, nestling against the cordillera and shielded by the Cuchilla de Santa Bárbara from the floor of the Valle. Since the conquest it had remained a *terra incognita,* known only by the single trail which cut through the dense forests of its northern margins to link Cartago with Ibagué by way of the well-traveled Quindío Pass. At the foot of the cordillera stood the way station of Salento, established in 1843 as a government penal colony for convict laborers on the Quindío road. In 1866 it had become a *corregimiento,* with a government grant of 12,000 hectares of baldíos, but growth was slow until the first Antioqueño immigrants from the north began to arrive ten years later.

The unparalleled rush into these empty lands of the Quindío has been appropriately termed "the epic of Antioqueño colonization."[23] The long-evident colonizing fervor of these land-hungry mountain folk from the north seems here to have been intensified by at least four economic attractions: rubber, gold, high hog prices, and the area's advantages as a refuge from the civil wars which were desolating the republic.

Exaggerated reports by the first explorers of the abundance of Castilla rubber brought the first rush of adventurers. Samples of the latex had been sent from Salento in 1872 to a resident of Villamaría, Manuel Mejía Santamaría, recently returned from the Esmeraldas rubber district of Ecuador. Following a rapid inspection tour of the Quindío he proceeded to Manizales and Medellín, announcing that there was rubber "not only in abundance, but of superior quality." In a few months a contagious *fiebre de caucherismo* was sending a considerable number of latex prospectors southward.[24] Between 1877 and 1880 Pereira was the center of a fairly important rubber trade, but low European prices and the destructive methods of exploitation employed soon brought an end to this brief chapter in Quindío history. Fleeting hopes later held for the development of a cinchona, vanilla, and cochineal trade were never realized.[25]

But the rubber boom had led to something more remunerative, the fine-worked Quimbaya gold of the Quindío guacas (above, chapter iii). A blend of fact and fancy, the stories of the gold wealth of the Quindío spread like lightning to Antioquia. One of the most widespread was the legend of Pipintá,[26] a lost subterranean temple at the foot of the cordillera supposedly full of beautiful gold ornaments, including an enormous golden serpent. Its entrance, blocked by a great stone, had been found by a colonist hunting *iraca* palm leaves for sombrero making, but when he returned a second time he had lost his way. The story was received with enthusiasm in Antioquia and attracted many of the venturesome, most of them going to the Salento district where they were rewarded by a few traces of gold in the stream gravels. Several old inhabitants of the Quindío have said that it was the legend of Pipintá which first brought them into the region and, not daring to return to their homes without samples of gold, they remained in these lands. Others, of course, came seeking legitimate mines, of which a few of minor importance were found in the exposed parent rock of the steeper cordillera slopes.

The pattern of agricultural settlement here was not unlike that to the north, but as a result of the destruction in other areas brought on by the civil wars market conditions had improved. On the first clearings maize was grown for mazamorra; then, in increasing surpluses, to feed the herds of lean hogs purchased at the nearest Cauca towns. Fattened on maize and plantains, they were driven back to market three or four months later, occasionally in herds of two or three hundred, where they were profitably sold.

This system was followed by many [wrote one of the settlers], and it could almost be said at one time that Cauca and Antioquia consumed only hogs proceeding from the Quindío. Some of the great fortunes of those who live here today had their origin in that business, which was without doubt one of the most important factors in the colonization of the Quindío.[27]

Yet another cause for the immigration into the Quindío was the fury of the civil wars of 1885 and 1900, both of which were especially destructive in Antioquia and Cauca. The threat of expropriation and political retaliation sent many persons to the refuge of the Quindío.[28]

Improved traveling conditions between Antioquia and Cartago also contributed materially to the very rapid peopling of these lands. Filandia, first Antioqueño settlement in the Quindío, had been founded in 1878 on a commanding height on the Ibagué road. Elsewhere road building came after settlement, as had occurred with the earlier towns founded in the north. But the trip from Manizales to Cartago had been reduced from eight or ten days to one and a half days by 1890, an overnight stop normally being made at Santa Rosa de Cabal. At about the same time cheaper if not faster communication had been provided to Cali with the introduction of steamboat service on the upper Río Cauca from Cartago's new wharves at Puerto Sucre.

The founding of towns in the Quindío seems to have been more often a profit-making enterprise for a few large landowners than it had been to the north, where a sort of community socialism often ruled. Armenia (1889), Circasia (1889), Calarcá (1890), and Montenegro (1892) were all dominated by *guaquería* in their earliest years, and a general lack of interest in agriculture and land titles offered a few speculators opportunity for the development of large holdings. The modern municipio of Montenegro, for example, whose first residents were engaged in grave looting, is said to be largely controlled by a single family.⁸⁰ Circumvention of the laws limiting the size of baldío adjudications was accomplished by the use of dummy names.

Later, as settlement advanced, agriculture became increasingly important. The great coffee-planting mania at the beginning of this century made the Quindío the republic's most important coffee-growing section. It was especially Armenia and Calarcá and the more southerly settlements of Tebaida, Caicedonia (1905), and Sevilla (1903) which grew with coffee in these later years, the last two being beyond the limits of modern Caldas in the department of Valle del Cauca.

Sevilla stands on a high, gently tilted plain looking over the vast, level Valle floor, its back to the Quindío. It is the southernmost outpost of Antioqueño colonization of importance on the western slopes of the Central Cordillera. The explanation of this blunting of the southward finger of penetration here may be found to be related to the replacement of the Quindío ash by compact, sandy clay primary soils further south. Yet land clearing is still carried on, at a lessened pace, on this southern edge of the Quindío in the municipios of Sevilla, Caicedonia, Pijao, and Génova, with settlement gradually extending into the tierras frías of the upper Río Barragán and Río Bugalagrande.

The new highway across the cordillera has transformed the former quiet coffee plaza of Armenia into a busy rail and trucking center at the transport break between the Pacific Railroad from Buenaventura and the truck route to Ibagué and Bogotá. Armenia's population has increased fivefold in the past 25 years. It is one of the leading commercial cities of Colombia, a transport, coffee, and cattle center with somewhat of a frontier air and now a departmental capital.

Increasing numbers of settlers from Tolima, Cundinamarca, and the Santanders have been arriving in the Quindío in recent years as coffee workers, truck drivers, and tradesmen. With the advance into the tierra fría many people have also come in to take up baldío homesteads. Although the Quindío today is still 90 per cent Antioqueño, the new stratum of outsiders has, on occasion, been a source of local economic and social friction.

The Quindío colonists, too, fought a long and bitter contest with a powerful land company before their rights to possession through occupance were finally confirmed. The "Territory of Burila" extended in the form of a parallelogram from Bugalagrande (Valle) to the crest of the Central Cordillera behind Calarcá, covered the southern half of the Quindío and included all or part of the municipios of Calarcá, Armenia, Génova, Pijao, Sevilla, Caicedonia, and Zarzal. The claim was based on a royal cédula of 1641 which granted lands in the jurisdictions of Cali, Buga, and Toro within the old Province of Popayán to the brothers Juan Francisco and Juan Jacinto Palomino.[40] After passing through many hands the lands in question were sold in 1884 to a Manizales land company (La Sociedad Anónima de Burila) which planned to develop and exploit them for gold, salt, and charcoal, as well as to promote agricultural colonization.

Little attention was paid to the vaguely defined claims of the corporation until the beginning of the present century when it appealed to Bogotá for the ejection of the squatters in Calarcá from what was purported to be a part of the lands of Burila. A long and confused litigation, made more unintelligible by the contradictory policies of the various magistrates, governors, and ministers involved, only slightly slowed the pace of settlement. Although many land sales were made by the company to the more affluent settlers, the majority chose to continue as squatters, trusting to the efforts in their behalf of the influential and respected Antioqueño benefactor, Heraclio Uribe Uribe. The latter himself held a substantial claim within the jurisdiction of Zarzal, on which had been established the new and thriving town of San Luís" (later Sevilla), and thus stood in direct conflict with the Burila interests. Since 1926 the Empresa Burila seems not to have pressed its claims further, and in a 1939 test case the judge of the Circuit Court of Tuluá (Valle) declared its rights void as a result of its failure to contend further in the courts."

The narrow band of tierra caliente along the Río Cauca acted as an effective barrier against Antioqueño colonization westward until well into the nineteenth century. Lacking the placer gold of the granitic uplands, these lush tierra templada slopes, extending southward from Anzá, had remained for more than two hundred years an unpeopled wilderness save for the colonial mining communities of the Anserma-Marmato area. Neither a rich volcanic soil nor a climate conducive to two crops of maize a year was sufficiently appealing to the gold-hungry Antioqueños of the colonial period.

Mon y Velarde observed in his 1788 report" that forty landless families from Envigado had recently moved across the low divide at the head of the valley of Medellín to Amagá (elev., 1,392 m.) with the intention of founding a town. After 1800 the newly discovered Titiribí mines, near Amagá, were worked in a casual manner. By 1807 there were ninety-four families settled in the vicinity of Titiribí and others were arriving." The famine of 1808 is reported to have sent another wave of settlers into the district."

Another base for the movement into the trans-Cauca lands was Fredonia, on the upper slopes of the volcanic cone of Cerro Bravo. Until 1829 the region which included Fredonia (then Guarcitos) had been a part of the district of Santa Bárbara, but in the following year a new parish was founded at the site of the present town (elev., 1,859 m.). Its settlers were principally from Envigado, Itagüí, Medellín, and Amagá."

The census of 1828 listed the populations for the districts in question: Amagá, 4,300; Titiribí, 2,593; Santa Bárbara, 1,045. No settlement had yet been made on the other side of the Río Cauca, although

Modern Antioqueño Colonization 83

these lands were nominally under the jurisdiction of Titiribí and, after 1830, of Fredonia.

In 1830 the first groups of settlers from Titiribí crossed the Cauca and made their initial clearings on the forested slopes of the mountains of Comía.[47] Here, too, the Indian graves provided an important attraction. The provincial legislature of Antioquia passed the following historic resolution on October 2, 1834:

> Considering, first: that the establishment of new parishes on good lands contributes directly to the public welfare, giving value to the land which it did not have before and at the same time facilitating the support of a growing number of families who have no lands or occupations to secure the necessities of life, and second: that, in the mountains of Comía in the canton of Santa Fé de Antioquia, which are public property, there have been established hard-working colonists in considerable numbers, sufficient to form a parish and support a curate, and third: that said region offers many advantages for a new town; it is resolved that the *personería provincial* shall solicit the establishment of the parish of Comía and the adjudication of 12,000 fanegas of *tierras baldías* and other advantages which the law of May 5 last concedes to new settlements.
>
> (Signed) MARIANO OSPINA
> *President of the Legislature*[48]

The requested grant of baldíos was made the following year by the National Congress,[49] the first of many similar grants later made in Caldas and Tolima on petitions from Antioqueño colonists (below, chapter vii). Later grants were to be made directly to the settlers, in loosely organized communal societies, without the intervention of the provincial governments.

Auction of a part of the new lands at a minimum price of one peso a fanega (1.6 acres) was authorized by the provincial legislature the following year and, in 1838, first steps were taken for the gratuitous distribution of the remaining lands to eligible settlers. A citizen's committee (*junta repartidora*) appointed to assign the property showed the impartiality and concern for public welfare typical of nineteenth-century Antioquia civic leaders. Other lands were rented, the proceeds going to the support of the schools.[50]

The parish of Concordia, established in 1848 to include all of the lands lying between the Río Cauca and the Western Cordillera, bounded on the north by the Quebrada de Comía and on the south by the Río San Juan, apparently covered the approximate area of the original Comía grant. The census of 1864 showed a population of 4,692, larger than Titiribí and almost equal to Amagá.

In sharp contrast to the earlier settlements on the flanks of the Central Cordillera, where the great majority of settlers had come from the tierra fría around Ríonegro and Sonsón, the colonists who came into the Occidente were predominantly from the temperate valleys of Medellín and Amagá. Virtually none came from the tierra caliente along the Río Cauca, either north or south. A tabulation of the birthplaces of 434 heads of families, applicants for the drawings conducted in 1849 for remaining common lands owned by the province in the district of Andes in the valley of the Río San Juan, shows the following distribution: Medellín and vicinity, 99; Amagá, 75; Retiro, 73; Envigado, 59; Ríonegro, 27; Fredonia, 30; Santa Bárbara, 13; Guarne, 8; Anorí, 7; Sabaletas, 6; Abejorral, La Ceja, Heliconia, 5 each; Marinilla, Santa Rosa de Osos, 4 each; Girardota, Don Matías, Campamento, Anzá, San Pedro, Yarumal, 2 each; Angostura, Santo Domingo, Pácora, Amalfi, Carolina, Ebéjico, Antioquia, Urrao, San Jerónimo, Aguadas, Titiribí, Cartago, Buga, Roldanillo, 1 each.[51]

The few surviving Indians in the area were not forgotten in the distribution of the lands. The list of families eligible for the drawing referred to above included 18 Chamí Indians in addition to 434 Antioqueños. In 1852, when lands for the town of Andes were being allotted, 100 fanegas were reserved for the natives.[52] The Chamí were recent arrivals in Antioquia, having migrated a few years earlier from a pueblo on the Río Andagueda within the Chocó drainage.[53] Their settlement on the upper Río San Juan (Antioquia), named Golota, lasted until 1852. In addition to the Chamí there were a few other poor remnants of the Caramanta tribe near the headwaters of the Río San Juan, some of whom still come to the plaza at Andes and Jardín.

South of the Río San Juan lay the Caramanta country. The main section of these unoccupied lands, as far south as the Quebrada Arquí, had been granted in 1835 to three wealthy Antioqueños, Juan Uribe, Gabriel Echeverri, and Juan Santamaría, who obtained their titles by purchase of the bonds of the financially pressed young republic (map

6). The new owners immediately concerned themselves with the construction of a road from Santa Bárbara by way of the Paso de Caramanta (La Pintada) and across their new grant to Marmato and Supía. Free plots of land were offered to settlers agreeing to work five days a year on the road.[54] The earliest settlements were on the precipitous upper slopes of the Quebrada Arquí at Nueva Caramanta (elev., 2,121 m.). A few miles away the Marmato-Supía mining district offered a market for maize and meat. By 1835, when there were more than three hundred colonists, the owners ceded lands for the town and donated funds for a chapel. Four years later the same Gabriel Echeverri, now governor of the Province of Antioquia, signed a bill creating Caramanta an independent district within the canton of Medellín.[55]

Colonists came from Sonsón, Abejorral, Pácora, Fredonia, and Medellín. By 1865 Valparaíso, Támesis, Andes, Bolívar, Jericó, and Jardín had all been founded. Settlers at Jardín in that year included a priest from the Medellín cathedral and the former rector of the University of Antioquia, both refugees from the revolutionary government of General Mosquera.[56] In addition to political refugees, there were others who came in search of gold mines and Indian graves.

Schenck[57] observed in 1880 that "in a whole day's ride south from the crossing of the Cauca at Caramanta only a few isolated houses in the forests are to be seen." The new town at Támesis, founded by Sonsoneños, was known for its hard-working agriculturists, but Valparaíso he thought peopled by "worthless vagabonds" whose only activity was washing gold from the Río Cauca during the dry season. Elsewhere in the Occidente stock raising was important. From Valparaíso to the new Caramanta the road was through virgin forests where today the slopes are in coffee and introduced pasture.

The Anserma region, southward from the Caramanta country, had long been known to the Spaniards before the arrival of the first Antioqueño settlers. The city of Anserma, founded in 1539 a few miles west of its present ridge-top site, served as the early gateway to the gold fields of the Chocó and the Marmato district, as well as being the northern frontier outpost of the Popayán government. Fray Jerónimo de Escobar,[58] in 1582, had called it "the richest pueblo in all this province of Popayán," although the more than 40,000 Indians (adult males) who had lived in the area at the time of the Spaniards' arrival had been "so decimated through the secret wisdom of God that there are not eight hundred left." Activity centered around the *real de minas* of Quiebraloma, 7 leagues to the north on the shoulders of the Vega de Supía, where gold-bearing sulfide ores were taken by Indian labor from shafts as much as 150 feet deep.[59]

The Marmato mines were never self-sufficient, depending on Cartago, Mariquita, and occasionally Antioquia for many supplies. Thus Boussingault later wrote of his experiences there in 1825-1826 as a consultant for English mining interests.

Notwithstanding the Negro working population it was necessary to bring workers from Antioquia. They arrived supplied with food for two weeks and then returned to their homes, later to return again. To keep them longer I had to be able to guarantee their subsistence and for this purpose ... we planted a large area to plantains on the banks of the Río Cauca ... together with maize, yuca and beans. Traders from Antioquia soon brought wheat flour, cacao and coffee....[60]

The beginning of Antioqueño settlement in these lands dates from the refounding, in 1870, of the old colonial city of Anserma, a loyalist stronghold desolated by the revolution. At about the same time Antioqueño colonists began to swell the population of Quiebraloma (Ríosucio).[61] Thereafter a steady stream of settlers poured across the Río Cauca from Sonsón, Salamina, and Manizales, mingling with a considerable Indian element which had survived here in organized communities. Quinchía (1886) and Mocatán (1890) were on or near the sites of earlier Indian settlements. Pueblorrico (1884) was on the trade route to the Chocó. Apía and Santuario were first settled by guaqueros who found Indian graves here as rich as those of the Quindío, although less numerous. Only the tierra caliente of the valley of Risaralda, a northern arm of the Valle del Cauca projecting into the mountains below Anserma, was shunned by the settlers.

In the present century settlement has pushed steadily southward along the Western Cordillera. Balboa, established as a municipio in 1907, and the southernmost of the west Caldas settlements, has been followed by a dozen later establishments within the department of

Valle del Cauca. Among these are the Antioqueño municipios of Versalles, Trujillo, Darién, Restrepo and El Cairo, and the corregimientos of El Aguila, La María, Betania and El Porvenir. All are on the ridges or slopes of the same cordillera so long disdained by the people of the valley floor. Several, like Versalles and Restrepo, are across the crest line within the Pacific drainage, bounded on the west by the virgin rain forest of the rain-drenched lower Calima and San Juan basins.[62]

The opening of the road to Trujillo (founded in 1924) and the construction of the bridge over the Río Frío speeded the settlement of the upper Calima country and beyond as far south as La Cumbre, Dagua, and the Pacific Railroad. Further south, toward Popayán, settlers continue to arrive from Caldas and southwestern Antioquia to clear and claim the forests of this last great coffee reserve of Colombia.[63] Rejecting the fertile alluvial valley lands and the meadows along the upper stream courses owned by a few stockmen, they keep to the steep, forested slopes of the tierra templada. The colonists who are clearing the Valle del Cauca mountain baldíos have been estimated to be more than 80 per cent Antioqueño and Caldense, 10 per cent Nariñense, 5 per cent Vallecaucaño, and 5 per cent from other areas.[64]

Beginning about 1850, other groups of Antioqueño colonists had moved eastward across the Central Cordillera into the forested slopes of Tolima. The earlier migrations followed the main communication routes, among which the Aguacatal short cut (La Elvira) between Manizales and Mariquita soon became the most traveled. Along it, on the Tolima side, an early string of settlements appeared, including Fresno (1856), Soledad (1860), and Santo Domingo (1866), the latter two known today as Herveo and Casabianca. All were of Antioqueño origin and within a few years had received their 12,000-hectare (29,640-acre) baldío grants from the government.

Two other early settlements, Líbano (1860) and Murillo, were situated on the old colonial Camino del Ruiz between Manizales and Lérida, and Manzanares (1866) and Marulanda lay on the Camino del Herveo from Salamina.

Further north, near the Antioquia-Tolima boundary, families from Sonsón and Aguadas founded the new town of Pensilvania[65] on the

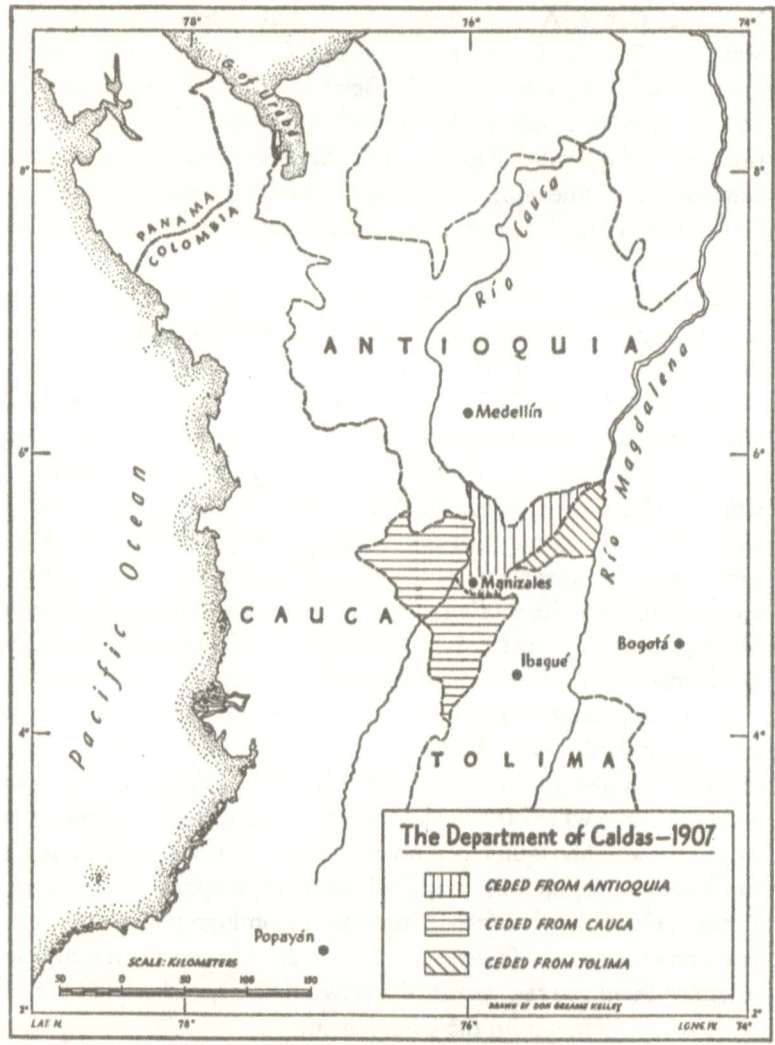

Map 7. The Department of Caldas, 1907.
(In 1966 the National Congress created two new departments, Quindío and Risaralda, from southern and western Caldas.)

old Villegas road between Sonsón and Mariquita. Permission for the establishment had first been asked of the governor of Tolima and refused, whereupon Governor Berrío of Antioquia authorized the new town in 1866 as a *fracción* of Sonsón, the land having been deeded by a resident of that place. Later claims by Tolima were denied in an arbitration award in 1870 which gave all of the area north of the Río Guarinó to Antioquia. In 1905, with Marulanda and Manzanares, it became a part of the new department of Caldas (map 7).

The early pattern of agricultural occupance in Tolima was similar to that within the Cauca basin. Only three or four harvests of maize were expected from a clearing, after which it was rested in native grass for ten or more years before being planted again. Even the pasture was of inferior quality and on the steeper slopes grazing usually led to early gullying. The destructive nature of this shifting, corn-hog agriculture was apparently recognized by the settlers. In 1906, a local editor wrote:

> The cultivation of maize has had the unfortunate consequence of destroying the centuries-old forests in such a thorough manner that many of the Antioqueño families which have emigrated to Tolima in search of new lands to clear are now at the banks of the Magdalena...⁶⁶

Low hog prices and poor roads, which made it at times impossible to get the fattened porkers to market, were common complaints. Only coffee growing, which was beginning to increase, seemed to offer the hope of a permanent, stable agriculture on the more rugged lands.

Most of the Tolima slopes of the cordillera were baldíos and the central government dispensed them liberally to groups of settlers who petitioned for the founding of new towns. An 8,000-hectare grant in Anzoátegui municipio (to the corregimiento of Caldas) in 1914 seems to have been the last grant of this kind made by the Congress.

There was a long litigation over the grants given to the settlers of Santo Domingo (Herveo) and Villahermosa. These lands had been previously adjudicated to private individuals, but in 1876, with two of the four owners deceased and the other two out of the country, the government redesignated them as baldíos. In 1890, when the two survivors returned to demand indemnification at the preoccupation value of the lands, there were 4,000 colonists within Santo Domingo alone.⁶⁷

Where the lands were privately held, as at Pensilvania, the titles were obtained either through purchase or gift. In 1916 colonists from an earlier Antioqueño settlement at Anaime, in a deep canyon west of Ibagué, founded the new settlement of Cajamarca a few miles to the north where Ibagué Viejo once stood, organizing a joint-stock company to purchase the land.[68] A traveler who passed through Cajamarca in 1918 described it as a zone of intense activity, with clearings extending "side by side for great distances" where six years earlier the slopes had been unpeopled and forested. Its location on the route of the Ibagué-Armenia highway, then under construction, has accounted for much of its late prosperity.

The heartland of Tolima, the vast, arid *llanos* of the middle Magdalena Valley, held no attraction for the Antioqueños, who here as elsewhere preferred the mountain slopes. Only at the departmental capital of Ibagué (elev., 1,284 m.), important trade center at the base of the cordillera, has there been a mixing of plainsmen and mountain folk.

Among the most southerly Antioqueño colonies in Tolima today is the new municipio of Roncesvalles, created in 1944 some 140 kilometers south of the capital. The town stands on a high spur (elev., 2,600 m.) at the approach to the Depresión de Buenavista, lowest pass across the Central Cordillera south of Antioquia.[69] Near-by Santa Elena, settled forty years ago, maintains closer commercial ties with Pijao and Armenia than with Ibagué. Here, as elsewhere in the tierra fría of Tolima, potatoes have become a major cash crop in recent years. There are other smaller Antioqueño settlements as far south as the coffee lands of the Río Saldana in the municipio of Ríoblanco (population 11,460 in 1964).[70]

Lower rainfall, poorer soils, and recent political *violencia* explain the lessened pace of Antioqueño settlement south of Ibagué. Coffee, at least, has not become the dominant crop here that it is to the north, for the movement has been especially up slope, into the tierra fría. In late years it has included considerable numbers of poor, land-hungry peasants from the uplands of Boyacá and Cundinamarca.

The main current of Antioqueño colonization in the nineteenth century was overwhelmingly toward the south and southwest, although there were other extensive, empty, temperate lands toward the east, north, and west which might equally have been taken up. The healthful Ríonegro uplands sent forth the earliest and largest number of colonists, and in the mountains of Sonsón were some of the closest available lands. Moreover, they were covered with a productive, volcanic ash, whereas in other directions lay the thin, primary soils of the granitic cordilleras or the malarial tierra caliente of the Magdalena, Atrato, and lower Cauca regions. In addition there were the supporting attractions of the mines and Indian graves and, briefly, the rubber of the Quindío. Bogotá, Cartago, Cali, and Popayán became closer, not further away, as settlement pressed southward. Thus, there was opportunity for the development of trade and commerce which, as it increased, in turn stimulated toll-road construction. Finally, there was the simple momentum of the movement, which, once headed southward, tended to surge ahead in the same direction.

Sealed off by colonial Spain to all but contraband trade, the conquistadores' route from Antioquia to the Gulf of Urabá had been overgrown and forgotten. The unsubdued Chocó Indians and, earlier, fears of English buccaneers had discouraged travel into the Western Cordillera by all but punitive expeditions. Even the validity of Antioquia's claims to an outlet to the Caribbean was long in dispute with the state of Cauca, which continued to monopolize the Chocó trade. The nineteenth century had heard much talk but seen little action in the occupation of the western flanks of the Western Cordillera. Early emphasis was on the construction of an improved road between Urrao and Quibdó which might capture some of the trade of that place for Antioquia, but after 1870 a campaign was opened for the construction of the Camino del Occidente through Dabeiba and Pavarandocito to the Gulf of Urabá." An earlier proposal to finance the settlement of "farmers and artisans from other parts of the Republic" who wished to settle in the region had come to naught, although the Antioquia cacao blight had sent a group of ruined campesinos to the Urrao district after 1852.

Two grants, totaling 300,000 hectares of baldíos, were made to the province in 1872 and 1886 to develop colonization and immigration on the lands between Frontino and the Río Atrato, but little of the land was adjudicated to settlers. Some went to the English contractor building the road to Pavarandocito, then the scene of considerable lumbering activity in native cedar. The lumber was rafted down the Río Sucio and Río Atrato for shipment to the United States.⁷² The contractors for the remarkable 940-foot cable-suspension bridge across the Río Cauca near the city of Antioquia received 10,000 hectares more. At least two companies were formed to foster the colonization of the region, but there were no takers for the contract, advertized by the 1894 Assembly, for development of a settlement of 5,000 persons within the ten years. The Secretary of Hacienda reported in 1898:

> The truth is that efforts toward the development of this rich region of the department have to date been quite ineffective and the colonization of the Occidente remains today an unanswered problem.... Antioqueño emigration to Cauca and Tolima is admittedly considerable but the encouragement of colonization in this highly fertile region ... should eliminate this daily drain on the population of the department which results from the aggressive, colonizing spirit of the Antioqueños and our failure to take advantage of our own immense baldíos.⁷³

The slow development of the "Occidente," especially beyond the crest of the Western Cordillera, contrasted sharply with the explosive expansion of the Antioqueño frontier that was occurring elsewhere.⁷⁴ The area was rainier than the Antioqueños had been accustomed to, so that fire could only be used to clear land with difficulty; and the soils seemed generally inferior. Dabeiba and Frontino, moreover, had the reputation of being the most staunchly "Liberal" municipios in Antioquia, and Conservatives from the interior highlands may well have considered this in deciding on which direction to go in search of new lands. But the most important deterrent to colonization appears to have been the unsettled nature of land titles. The Indian *resguardos* of Buriticá, Cañasgordas, Giraldo, Frontino, and Dabeiba had been broken up, at least in part, between 1832 and 1840, but in a manner that left titles cloudy and the lack of confidence general. Substantial numbers of Catío Indians remained in the area. In 1886 Juan Enrique White termed the situation "complete anarchy." He thought that there were not ten clear titles in the entire Dabeiba district. Twenty-five years later the complaint still existed that insecurity of land titles was a principal limiting factor to settlement.

The recent increase of interest in the empty lands of the tierras calientes is summed up in the unparalleled land rush into the Antioqueño Urabá in the past decade. The completion of the Carretera al Mar to Turbo in 1954, and the subsequent decision of the United Fruit Company to provide controlled credit to banana growers in the area, opened the way for a massive wave of settlers. The vast area of the municipios of Turbo and Arboletes had a population of 15,000 persons in 1951; today it has close to 100,000, an amalgam of immigrants from the Sinú, the *Sabanas* of Bolívar, the Chocó, and highland Antioquia. There were 15,000 hectares in bananas along the Carretera al Mar in 1966, mostly in holdings of from 50 to 200 hectares owned by people from Medellín. Turbo, almost overnight, has surpassed Santa Marta as a banana export port. A large plantation of African oil palms, a joint Dutch-Colombian venture, and a smaller plantation of Hevea rubber at Villa Arteaga planted during World War II under the sponsorship of the United States Department of Agriculture, give diversity to the economic base, along with coconuts and a rapidly expanding livestock industry. In the hill lands back from the Urabá coastal plain Sinuano colonists have felled the forest to plant rice, plantains, and maize on forest clearings (*rozas*) that are soon converted into pastures of introduced African pasture grasses. In little more than a decade the face of the land has been completely changed. Rapid population growth has brought in its wake staggering problems of health, education, and welfare. Earlier these were community matters, but the government is now looked to for direction and aid.

TABLE 4
RATE OF POPULATION GROWTH, 13-YEAR INTERCENSAL PERIODS
1938–1951 AND 1951–1964

	1938–1951	1951–1964
Urabá (Turbo)	31.9%	172.6%
Bajo Cauca (Caucasia)	21.0	335.9
Puerto Berrío	0.8	127.6
Medellín	73.3	95.9
Department of Antioquia	31.7	56.5

SOURCE: Ernesto Gühl, "Anotaciones Sobre Población, Poblamiento, Posición y Estructura Demográfica en Colombia," *Revista Academia Colombiana de Ciencias Exactas, Físicas y Naturales*, 12:377–386 (Bogotá, 1966).

To the northeast and east, where the cooler highlands of the Antioqueño massif drop off toward the Bajo Cauca and the Magdalena lowlands, the earlier settlement pattern reflected the region's historical orientation toward mining. The few "white Antioqueños" from the interior were either merchants or mine administrators who considered themselves temporarily exiled to Cáceres, Zaragoza, or Remedios while they made their fortunes. Such places were above all frontiers of economic opportunity for tradesmen. But malaria was a constant concern.

The forest-cloaked southwestern part of Antioquia, over which fly a steady procession of planes on the Bogotá-Medellín run, is still one of the least known and least peopled areas of the department. Clearings have been made along the Magdalena River and inland along the route of the railroad from Puerto Berrío, including the valley of the Nus. Here, as well as across the Magdalena River in Santander, the former forests have been converted to *potreros* that support a prosperous and expanding livestock industry based on zebu-*criollo* crosses. Large holdings are the rule in these low-lying *tierras calientes*. Puerto Berrío (pop. 15,800 in 1964), the commercial center of the Magdalena Antioqueña, was still without a road link with the rest of the department in 1967. Meanwhile the town was being served by river, rail, pipeline, and air, a new railroad bridge linking it with the opposite shore. Petroleum fields at Casabe (opposite Berrancabermeja) and Perales (opposite Puerto Boyacá) and the cement plant at Nare provide an industrial base to the area that is lacking in other parts of rural Antioquia, giving employment to some 1,100 persons along the Antioquia side of the Magdalena.

Another center of activity in the Antioquia tierra caliente has been the Bajo Cauca, a region long isolated from the rest of the department, which now lies astride the new and heavily used Troncal del Occidente, the highway linking Medellín with Cartagena. Between the 1951 and 1964 censuses the municipio of Caucasia (pop. 24,000 in 1964) registered one of the sharpest population increases of any place in Colombia. Its river-front *cabecera* (pop. 7,000), the commercial center of the Bajo Cauca, is the principal stopover point on the highway to the coast. In 1966 it had three banks and a *Caja Agraria,* two theaters, two fish-icing plants, and a modern hotel.

In recent years Antioqueño capitalists have invested heavily in land and livestock on the Sabanas and in the Sinú, but these hot lowlands with their long dry season have little appeal to the highlander without financial reserves. Montería (pop. 70,500 in 1964) is the principal Antioqueño outpost in the north, but merchants and bankers are dominant, not rural colonists.[75] In the cloud-shrouded upper basins of the Sinú and San Jorge rivers is one of the last major blocks of forested baldíos remaining in northern Colombia. The few hundred forest-dwelling Chocó Indians who occupy this vast tract are under increasing pressure from Antioqueño colonists,[76] but this is still a land for the future. Much of the more rugged headwaters area of both streams lies within the Antioquia municipio of Ituango.

The earlier history of government efforts at directed colonization schemes is generally a dismal one.[77] Since 1960 the national government through its Instituto de Reforma Agraria (INCORA) has assumed responsibility for virtually all colonization and agrarian development schemes. It provides supervised credit, land titles to baldíos, penetration roads, and technical aid. In Antioquia INCORA had three projects in 1966: (1) at Barbosa, below Medellín, where 460 sharecropper truck-farmers are being provided with title to land; (2) the Cáceres-Cacerí project in the Bajo Cauca, where a 55-kilometer penetration road has opened up the principal remaining block of baldíos in the Bajo Cauca; and (3) the Arboletes project in Urabá, involving construction of a 130-kilometer road between the coastal towns of Arboletes and Turbo, with land titles and agricultural credit to *colonos espontáneos*. The benefactors of the last two projects have been chiefly Costeños rather than Antioqueños.

VII. PUBLIC LAND POLICIES

THE NATURE and history of legislation affecting the disposition of the public domain is inevitably a critical factor in the development of a new country. In colonial New Granada, as elsewhere in Spanish America, all titles to lands were derived solely from the Spanish Crown, being issued under a wide variety of conditions, of which nobility and services to the King were the most common. With the end of Spanish rule many of the Crown grants were confirmed by republican courts. One of the stipulations in the transfer of sovereignty from the royal Audiencia to the new government had been the recognition of the validity of existing land titles.

As policies and politics gradually were formulated under the republic, five distinctive types of adjudications of unoccupied, unclaimed baldíos came to be recognized:

1) To homesteaders.
2) To purchasers of government bonds.
3) To new towns.
4) To private contractors for services rendered.
5) To institutions or provincial governments as income property.

The rights of cultivators to public lands which they have cleared or in other ways improved has been a basic concept of Colombian law since the first days of the republic. Laws affecting baldíos generally limited the size of the area adjudicable to homesteaders. In 1834 it was 60 fanegas (95 acres) to each family, a figure which was later reduced as good lands became increasingly scarce. Under recent baldío legislation a "small cultivator" may gain title to twice as much land as he has cleared, with a 50-hectare maximum. Other classes of adjudications authorize grants up to 800 hectares for livestock fincas, whereas on lands more than 50 kilometers from the seat of a municipio the limit is 1,500 hectares.

The controversial *Ley 200* of 1936 ("the Law of Alfonso López"), which defined "possession" as requiring active economic exploitation of one-half the area of all rural properties more than 300 hectares in size, paradoxically stimulated the felling of the forest reserves on the larger fincas to the point where the watersheds were seriously threatened. Cut-out-and-get-out "poachers," under the protection of the law, were able to sell the wood and charcoal and then abandon the newly stripped land.[1] This law, later modified, granted possession to squatters in five years if they believed, in good faith, that they occupied "baldíos" as defined by the law. "Baldíos" included "all private property not exploited by its owner."

Traditionally, Colombian campesinos have shown little concern for the confirmation of their land titles unless challenged by *latifundistas*, an apathy stemming from the law's recognition of possession and usufruct as tantamount to unwritten title.

Despite the evident concern of a frequently benevolent government for the development of a small landholder class, considerable amounts of public land have been distributed by sale or auction. The numerous civil wars of the nineteenth century, by keeping the treasury of the new republic in a permanently embarrassed condition, only encouraged disposition of baldío bonds at generously low prices.

Of the sales made in Antioquia, the 102,717 hectares granted in the Caramanta country in 1835 is the largest on record.[2] Others, ranging from 250 to 25,000 hectares, were concentrated especially in northern Antioquia and toward the Río Magdalena, as in the municipios of Yolombó, Yarumal, Cáceres, and Ituango. In Caldas, Tolima, and Valle they were fewer. The two 10,000-hectare blocks awarded in the mountains behind Ansermanueva (1873–1880) were among the largest. These two blocks were apparently obtained in anticipation of the arrival of the first Antioqueño colonists into the Valle section of the Western Cordillera. In 1908 the law set the top limit for such purchases at 5,000 hectares.

Very few of the larger blocks of land granted in this manner have remained intact. They have been disposed of by gift and sale to heirs and new settlers, usually at reasonable prices. The introduction of coffee, a crop well adapted to small-scale family enterprise, has contributed importantly to the shaping of this society of freeholders in the volcanic lands of southwest Antioquia, Caldas, and Tolima. Elsewhere, where livestock and mining are of greater importance, larger holdings have persisted.

---

[1]For notes to chap. vii, see p. 203.

TABLE 5
Grants of Baldío Lands for New Towns Made by the Republic of Colombia in Antioquia, Caldas, and Tolima

Year	Area	Settlement
1835	12,000 fanegas	Comía (Concordia), Antioquia
1838	9,000 fanegas	Riachón (Amalfi ?), Antioquia
1840	8,000 fanegas	Turbo, Antioquia
1840	9,000 fanegas	Aguadas (Ituango), Antioquia
1844	12,000 fanegas	Santa Rosa de Cabal, Caldas
1847	12,000 fanegas	Neira, Caldas[a]
1849	12,000 fanegas	Santa Rosa de Cabal, Caldas
1849	12,000 fanegas	Victoria, Caldas
1849 (?)	12,000 fanegas	Murindó, Antioquia
1853	24,000 fanegas	Chaldía (?)
1858	12,000 fanegas	Fresno, Tolima
1863	24,000 hectares	Santa Rosa de Cabal, Caldas
1863	16,000 hectares	Villamaría, Caldas
1863	12,000 hectares	San Francisco (Chinchiná), Caldas
1863	12,000 hectares	Palestina, Caldas
1866	15,360 hectares	Nuevo Salento, Caldas
1866	12,000 hectares	Manzanares, Caldas
1866	16,000 hectares	Líbano, Tolima
1871	12,000 hectares	Pereira, Caldas
1871	12,000 hectares	Santo Domingo (Casabianca), Caldas
1871	9,000 hectares	Nare, Antioquia
1873	12,000 hectares	Murillo, Tolima
1873	10,000 hectares	Soledad (Herveo), Tolima
1876	12,000 hectares	Marulanda, Caldas
1879	20,000 hectares	Ibague Viejo (Anaime ?), Tolima
1907	?	Calarcá, Caldas[b]
1912	10,000 hectares	Santa Isabel, Tolima
1914	8,000 hectares	Caldas, correg. of Briceño (Anzoátegui), Tolima

[a] The grant to Neira was contingent on the lands being declared baldíos. By the contract ratified between the government and González, Salazar y Cía. in 1853 the company agreed to set aside 12,000 fanegas of land for the *cabildo* of each town within the Aranzazu grant, thus including besides Neira, Manizales, Aranzazu, Salamina, and Filadelfia.

[b] Rules for the distribution of the public lands of Calarcá were published in the *Diario Oficial*, January 14, 1908, but no specific grant seems to have been recorded. Title to the lands in question was under dispute. As early as 1888 a group of settlers there had petitioned for 14,000 hectares of baldíos, but the request had been tabled pending an investigation.

At least twenty-six different grants of baldíos, averaging some 12,000 hectares each, were made to newly established Antioqueño towns between 1835 and 1914 (see table 5), following a policy designed to stimulate the colonization of unoccupied lands.[2] These new colonies, especially in Caldas and Tolima, were closely knit, fraternal, agrarian associations in which coöperative clearing, seeding, and harvesting, and the sense of communal responsibility were highly developed.

Government stipulations which went with the grants varied in detail but followed a similar pattern. Preparation of the list of eligibles was the responsibility of the elected council, which commonly appointed a three-man board to carry out the adjudications. Plots allotted ranged from 60 to 150 fanegas[*] at the earlier settlements, depending on the size of the family and the nature of the lands. Later, as at Líbano and Manzanares, 32 hectares were reserved for each eligible, without regard to family responsibilities. If lands were left over they were held for later comers.

Restrictive covenants generally governed the sale of the lands, providing that they could not be sold until cleared or, alternatively, until four years had elapsed. Accumulation of large blocks of land by single individuals was carefully avoided by restrictions on sales to owners of more than a given number of hectares within the tract.

With each grant of rural property also went a town lot, usually 800 square meters, in the new town. These, too, were distributed by the *junta repartidora,* which set aside common land for the town, laid out the street plan, and reserved sites for the plaza, church, jail, and town offices. This sensible, flexible system of land distribution, a legacy from colonial times, apparently worked very successfully here, in striking contrast to the contemporary experiences on the Great Plains of the United States. Complaints against the *juntas* were few.

An entirely different type of communal adjudication was made in connection with the Indian reserves inherited from the colonial regime.[5] One of the first acts of the new government had been to relieve the Indians of their tribute obligations, at the same time awarding them legal title to the reservations. As a protection against abuses they were temporarily forbidden to dispose of their properties. In Antioquia, an 1848 ordinance finally authorized the Indians of the province individually to sell their lands as they wished and this was further confirmed by the Constitution of 1863. In a few cases, although apparently not in Antioquia, reservations were "extinguished" because there were no longer Indians to claim them.

Communication has been a major problem of Colombia for four hundred years. The impoverished state and national treasuries rarely being able to finance road construction, "privileges" were granted to private contractors for their construction or improvement. Blocks of public lands were offered as payment upon fulfillment of the contracts, which also usually authorized the contractors to collect tolls for a certain length of time. Among such grants which exceeded 10,000 hectares were those for the construction of the Río Cauca bridge at Antioquia and the Quindío, Nare, Dabeiba, Ruiz, Urrao, and Ayapel roads.[6] Contracts made after 1900 generally provided for grants of 1,000 hectares for each league (2.6 miles) of new road completed. The railroads were also to become important land-grant beneficiaries, beginning with the 100,000 hectares awarded by the republic to the projected Ferrocarril de Antioquia from Puerto Berrío toward Medellín (1874). Between 1905 and 1927 the Ferrocarril de Amagá, running southwest from Medellín toward the Cauca, was granted 19,618 hectares on the basis of 300 hectares for each kilometer constructed.

A unique plan for the establishment of an English agricultural colony in the Valdivia region, north of Santa Rosa de Osos, was presented to the Congress of 1836 by Mr. Tyrell Moore, influential English mining engineer who had adopted Antioquia as his home, and in 1836 he was ceded up to 100,000 fanegas in the Cantón of Santa Rosa de Osos under the following conditions:

1. That he populate the area with European farmers, artisans, and miners, the number and time limit to be set by the government.
2. If the contract was not fulfilled within the allotted time Moore would pay a fine of 4,000 pesos and lose an amount of land proportionate to the number of settlers lacking.
3. That new settlers be naturalized within a fixed period of time.
4. That settlers would be exempted for twenty years from payment of ecclesiastical tithes (*diezmos*), and for twelve years from military service, dating from naturalization.[7]

Although a new road ("El Padrero") was built through the virgin forests to bring cattle from the Ayapel plains, and some supplies were brought in up the Río Cauca in sampans as late as 1839, the undertaking died an unrecorded natural death.[8] Apparently no Englishmen ever reached the country's shores as a result of the project, although a few mining engineers who had come earlier remained in the province with Moore. Objection of the Church to the establishment of a Protestant colony within the Catholic stronghold of Antioquia was apparently in part responsible for the abandonment of the plan.

To sum up, the extreme parcelization of the lands of recent Antioqueño settlement must be interpreted chiefly in the light of the recency of their occupation. Only the old granitic massif of the Río Negro-Medellín-Santa Rosa heartland was effectively incorporated into the colonial structure and even here the strong emphasis on mining and the scattered nature of the deposits did not favor the development of the deeply rooted feudal traditions which sprang from the agricultural and livestock haciendas in other parts of New Granada. In Antioquia mining rights have always taken precedence over agricultural rights, so that in effect all lands not immediately under cultivation are open to exploitation by the holders of mineral claims.' And this exploitation, moreover, has always been largely in terms of free labor, for in colonial times the supply of Indians and Negro slaves was insufficient. The concept of wealth, then, was not tied either to subject peoples or to the soil as much as to hard work and initiative. On the new volcanic lands to the south and west the extremely broken nature of the country, together with the coffee planters' proud, free, and independent spirit of self-determination combined to produce this anomaly of a democratic society of small holders on a continent dominated by traditional Latin latifundism. Only in recently opened tierras calientes, in Urabá, the Bajo Cauca, and the Antioqueño Magdalena, has this traditional, thermally oriented settlement shown signs of significant modification.

VIII. POPULATION GROWTH

THE GROWTH of the Antioqueño community since 1778 has been computed from census returns in table 6, although the spilling over into other departments after 1850 has made the later figures increasingly arbitrary. Today there are more than four million Colombians who call themselves Antioqueños, including many "half-" and "quarter-Antioqueños" who still boast of being *paisas*.

Since 1828 the rate of increase has been steady, with an approximate doubling of the population every twenty-eight years. This rate, which showed the first hint of a tapering-off during the 1918–1938 intercensal period, stands well above that for the republic as a whole and is one of the highest for any Latin American group. The ascendancy of the people of Antioqueño stock over the rest of their countrymen is numerical as well as economic. In 1835 they represented 10 per cent of the population of the new republic of Colombia; today Antioqueños, both within and without the department, constitute one-fourth of Colombia's inhabitants (table 7).

This vigorous growth of the Antioqueño nucleus is the more remarkable because it has been unaided by any foreign immigration. Social and religious exclusiveness, coupled with a high degree of geographic isolation, has been an effective bar to settlement by outsiders. The few Europeans who have taken up residence in these mountains have been contract mining and professional men. Some have married Antioqueña women and perpetuated their names in the population (e.g., Bedout, Cock, DeGreiff, Eastman, Walker, White), but virtually none have gone into agriculture.[1]

Large families have long been traditional among Antioqueños and the fecundity of the maize-fed Antioqueña women (*maiceras*) is proudly boasted of to this day. Significantly, large families have been as characteristic of the upper classes as of the poor. Boussingault, one of the first to call attention to this phenomenon, suspected that an abnormally high rate of twinning might be involved, but later statistics have disproved this hypothesis. A social and religious environment peculiarly favorable to early marriage and large families offers

[1] For notes to chap. viii, see pp. 203–204.

a plausible explanation. Especially on the cooler uplands of Ríonegro and Santa Rosa de Osos health conditions were and are undoubtedly superior, and in the tierras templadas they were probably much better

TABLE 6
ANTIOQUEÑO POPULATION GROWTH IN COLOMBIA

Census year	Antioqueño population	Remarks
1778	46,500	Census figures for all years between 1778 and 1883
1787	56,000	are for the old Province of Antioquia, bounded on
1808	110,000	the south by the Río Chinchiná and including the
1828	120,000	Pensilvania district of modern Caldas.
1835	158,000	
1843	189,000	
1851	244,000	
1870	395,000	Includes estimated 30,000 new settlers in Gran Cauca and Tolima.
1883	525,000	Includes 60,000 in Gran Cauca and Tolima. Estimate by F. von Schenck.[a]
1905	923,000	Antioquia, 650,000; Caldas,[b] 185,000; Tolima,[c] 56,000; Gran Cauca,[d] 32,000.
1918	1,377,000	Antioquia, 823,000; Caldas, 428,000; Tolima,[c] 81,000; Valle, 45,000.
1938	2,220,000[e]	Antioquia, 1,188,000; Caldas, 780,000; Tolima,[c] 152,000; Valle,[f] 100,000.
1964	4,210,000[e]	Antioquia 2,360,000[g]; Caldas 1,425,000[h]; Valle 227,000 [i]; Tolima 200,000 [j]; Chocó 7,000.

[a] "Reisen in Antioquia und im Cauca im Jahre 1880 und 1881," *Petermanns Mitteilungen* (1883) p. 441.
[b] At the time of the 1905 Census the newly established department of Caldas did not include either the Pensilvania-Manzanares region or the Province of Quindío in Cauca.
[c] Municipios of Fresno, Herveo, Casabianca, Villahermosa, Líbano, Santa Isabel, Anzoátegui, Cajamarca, and an estimated one-half of the population of Ibagué.
[d] Filandia, Armenia, and Calarcá.
[e] These figures do not take into account the scattered groups living in Córdoba, Bolívar, Cauca or the departments of the Eastern Cordillera. In Bogotá there is a large Antioqueño colony which includes many of the country's business and professional leaders while others have taken part in the colonization of the coffee lands of the lower Sumapaz and Fusagusagá. The Antioqueño cattlemen living on the coast are more than compensated for by the in-migration from those departments to the Bajo Cauca. Estimates for the Valle are probably low because municipio boundaries there are especially unsuited for delimiting ethnic and cultural zones of occupance. On the other hand the Caldas and Tolima figures include unknown numbers of settlers from Boyacá, Santander, and Cundinamarca who have moved to the higher slopes of the Central Cordillera in recent years as wheat and potato farmers.
[f] Municipios of Caicedonia, Sevilla, Ulloa, Alcalá, Versalles, and Ansermanuevo only.
[g] The censused population of the department of Antioquia in 1964 was 2,477,000. The figure employed here excludes an arbitrary three-fourths of the population of the Bajo Cauca, Urabá, and Magdalena municipios, where most of the population are in-migrants from neighboring departments.
[h] Excludes municipio of La Dorada on the Magdalena river.
[i] Municipios of Darién, El Cairo, Restrepo, Trujillo, Versalles, and Ansermanuevo lying west of the Cauca river and Sevilla, Caicedonia, Ulloa, and Alcalá to the east of the river.
[j] As in [c](above), together with Roncesvalles and Rioblanco.

before the introduction of coffee growing. The newly cleared lands settled during the nineteenth century may well have remained temporarily free from intestinal parasitism and dysentery, the two great infant killers, until the infection of the soil and water caught up with occupation.

The classical example of the large Antioqueño family is that of the Envigado woman who was mother of thirty-four children by a single marriage. Her case history has been sketched by the reliable geographer-physician, Dr. Uribe Ángel.[7] Nubile at the age of eleven and a half, she had had two robust daughters by the time she was

TABLE 7
NUMERICAL ASCENDENCY OF ANTIOQUEÑO PEOPLES IN COLOMBIA, 1835-1964

	Census of	
	1835	1964
Antioqueño population	158,000	4,210,000
Population of Colombia	1,572,000[a]	17,484,000
Per cent Antioqueño	10.0	24.1

[a] Excluding Panamá and Veragua.

fourteen. "It is not rare in this district," Uribe Angel wrote, "to see men less than fifty years old surrounded at the dinner table by twenty or more children, all in flourishing health and well-behaved."

Another family of thirty-three living children by the same mother was observed at Titiribí by the Swiss naturalists, Führmann and Mayor.[8]

TABLE 8
AVERAGE CRUDE BIRTH RATES, 1915-1942[a] AND 1964[b]
(Number of live births per 1,000 population)

	1915-1942	1964
Department of Antioquia	38.7	43.0
Department of Caldas	39.2	39.1
Colombia	30.1	36.9

[a] *Colombia: Summary of Biostatistics*, prepared by U. S. Department of Commerce, Bureau of the Census (Washington, 1944).
[b] Computed from Census.

Jorge Rodríguez,[9] who more than anyone else has concerned himself with the growth and fecundity of his people, has estimated that the average married Antioqueña today has seven children during her reproductive period, a decrease of two from the last century. This decrease is attributed largely to the rise in the average age of girls at marriage from eighteen to twenty-two years. Birth control is practiced by a small but undoubtedly growing segment of the educated classes. In 1965, for the first time, it had become a matter of open discussion in the public press.

From unpublished vital statistics for certain Antioquia municipios in 1840 it has been possible to make a comparison of the "vegetative" or natural increase (surplus of births over deaths) with that of a century later for the tierras templadas of the valleys of Medellín and Amagá and the tierras frías of the Oriente (table 9). These figures

TABLE 9
NUMBER OF BIRTHS FOR EACH 100 DEATHS*

	1840	1941
Canton of Medellín.	315	219
Cantons of Ríonegro and Marinilla.	398	272

* Statistics for 1840 (actually August 1, 1839, to July 31, 1840) are from *Censo*, tomo 17 (Biblioteca y Archivo de Antioquia); for 1941 from *Anuario Estadístico*, Medellín, 1941.

not only indicate a still vigorous natural increase in the Antioqueño heartland but also suggest the existence in the last century of a higher survival (or birth?) rate in the Oriente's cool uplands as against the lower temperate zones of the valley of Medellín. The differential "pressure" of population on the Grade C clay soils of the highlands would have helped explain the role of the Oriente as a reservoir in the peopling of the slopes of Caldas and Tolima. Today this same region is sending increasing numbers of its youth into the textile mills of Medellín.

The vitality of the modern Antioqueño community, especially in the tierras templadas and tierras calientes, is severely taxed by such debilitating, endemic diseases as hookworm, dysentery, malaria, typhoid, syphilis, and gonorrhea, which find in the humid, isothermal lands of the lower Colombian Andes an ideal medium for propagation.

Incomparably the most widespread and destructive of these is hookworm (*anemia tropical, unciniarias*). The damp, putrescent, insect-ridden atmosphere of the shaded coffee fincas makes coffee and intestinal parasitism inseparably associated.[5] The greater part of the soils and ground waters of the warm and temperate zones to at least 2,300 meters elevation are infected, but most completely in the densely peopled coffee lands. Rotting pulp from coffee berries and the almost universal absence of latrines in rural areas contribute to infection. Where the larvae penetrate the blood stream through the feet and hands (especially the tender interdigital areas) ugly lesions known as *candelillas* or *mazamorras* are left which are frequently accompanied by swelling of the legs. In Envigado, Fredonia, and most of the coffee plazas of Antioquia (in Caldas, where coffee is recent, they are rarer) several of these pitifully deformed human beings may

TABLE 10
AVERAGE CRUDE DEATH RATES, 1915–1942[a] AND 1964[b]
(Number of deaths per 1,000 population)

	1915–1942	1964
Department of Antioquia.	16.8	10.7
Department of Caldas.	16.4	12.8
Colombia.	14.9	9.9

[a] *Colombia: Summary of Biostatistics*, prepared by U. S. Department of Commerce, Bureau of the Census (Washington, 1944).
[b] Computed from Census.

commonly be seen begging on the square, their lesions displayed to the passer-by. These tragedies on every side give bitter force to the frequently heard expression: "With every coffee bean is exported a drop of Colombian blood."

Intestinal parasitism and dysentery both exercise their greatest influence on infant mortality rates. The close correlation between coffee-growing and these disorders[6] is emphatically demonstrated by statistics. In 1942 infant mortality (i.e., deaths under one year of age per 1,000 live births) in the *muy cafetero* department of Caldas was 193.4; in 1965, 144.[7] This is one of the highest rates recorded in the world and much higher than any other region in Colombia. In neighboring Antioquia, *cafetero* only in its southwestern section, it was 146.7 in 1942 but had been reduced to a more reasonable 86.2 by 1965 (average for Colombia, 83). Childhood mortality (deaths under five years per 100 deaths of all ages) is likewise higher in Caldas than in any other department. The coffee municipios have much the worst records. The situation becomes even more alarming when it is realized that the Caldas campesino is probably better off economically and better educated than those of most other parts of the country.

Typhoid is another killer, frequently unrecognized in the past, which has found a favorable environment in the coffee lands. In 1965 Antioquia and Caldas together reported 3,700 cases, representing half of all of the typhoid cases in that year in Colombia. Aqueducts and sewers have been installed in late years in most of the larger towns, but few rural fincas have running water or toilets. The dank environment of the cafetales, too, offers ideal conditions for typhoid survival. Human excrement, clothes washing, and a general absence of a sense of sanitation contribute to the fouling of drinking water, probably the most common source of infection. In the larger cities, however, advances in sanitary engineering in recent years have made the public water supplies quite safe.

Malaria (*fríos y fiebres*) has been virtually eliminated as a public health problem in most of the Antioqueño country as a result of an effective eradication campaign with DDT by the *Servicio de Eradicacción de Malaria* (SEM). It is still endemic, however, in Urabá and the Bajo Cauca and Magdalena valleys. In the past it was present almost everywhere in Colombia below 1,500 meters, reaching its maximum virulence during and immediately following the clearing of the forests. Antioqueño homesteaders in Caldas and Tolima recognized this when they built their towns on high, well-ventilated ridge-top sites during the nineteenth century, almost always above 1,800 meters and the anopheles belt.[8] Twenty years ago it was even endemic in the lower swampy lands along the Río Medellín in the western suburbs of the city. It has now completely disappeared.

It is difficult to divorce the industrial-urban development of Medellín, Pereira, Manizales, and Armenia from the alarming increase in tuberculosis and venereal diseases which has aroused health authorities to active campaigns of suppression in recent years. In 1965 Antioquia and Caldas together reported 3,700 cases of tuberculosis and more than 25,000 cases of venereal disease. The latter represented 40 per cent of all such cases reported in Colombia. Its prevalence must be largely attributed to the extraordinarily widespread occurrence of prostitution among Antioqueños. Every town has its *barrio de tolerancia* under casual regulation by municipal authorities.[9] In 1946 the city of Medellín alone had 4,260 registered *mujeres de vida pública*, something like one out of every fifteen adult females.[10] In no other part of the country or probably of Latin America does prostitution play such a prominent role.

IX. THE AGRICULTURAL BASIS OF OCCUPANCE

ANTIOQUEÑO crops and cultivation techniques followed closely the pre-Conquest pattern. Whereas the highland Chibchas to the east and the Inca outliers to the south had made the potato their chief starch staple, in Antioquia the triumvirate of maize, beans, and sweet manioc (*yuca*) predominated. Supplemented by plantain and sugar cane, they still provide the basis for the common diet.

The shifting field system of the Indians had been well adapted to the steep slopes and thin soils, but it also fitted naturally into the semimigratory mining-camp environment of colonial Antioquia. Later it was adjusted to the frontier occupance pattern of Caldas and Tolima. Fire was always used for making clearings and after two or three crops of maize or yuca the plot was allowed to revert to brush and tree growth for ten or more years. Wherever land is cheap today the system still persists.

It has only been recently, with the introduction of coffee and planted pasture grasses, that an intensive, permanent agriculture has been developed beyond the confines of a few privileged alluvial valleys. This, in turn, has made possible the marked increase of the rural population in the last fifty years. Further, it has encouraged the parcelization of land into small holdings and the accompanying rise of a numerous and independent small landed class.

Under the colonial regime agricultural production was closely adjusted to the requirements of the province. Occasional drought years or locust invasions brought hardship and famine, but in good years there was no outlet for surpluses beyond the restricted local market. Not until the beginning of coffee cultivation in the latter part of the nineteenth century did the pack trains moving out of Ríonegro and Medellín toward the Río Magdalena begin to carry articles besides gold and silver bullion and an occasional shipment of hides, Panamá hats, and cinchona bark.

Even the measures initiated by the energetic Oidor Mon y Velarde in the 1780's to stimulate agricultural production had been conceived as but a means for reviving the mining industry. Yet such official concerns for agriculture within the province, coupled with the founding of the new agricultural settlements, may well have increased the available food supplies to the point of favoring larger families.

José Manuel Restrepo[1] wrote in 1808 that agriculture and industry offered Antioquia the only hope for a stable economy and a better life. In Chocó and Barbacoas, he said, there were richer mines for those who insisted on that business. So far, it had been the internal trade that had kept the colony going, with Antioquia, Medellín, and Ríonegro providing Santa Rosa, Yolombó, and Cancán with all that they consumed. For a beginning he recommended that the 500 mule loads of wheat and 2,200 mule loads of cacao beans annually brought into the province from outside might well be produced at home. And with the new Otahiti sugar cane there were even prospects for developing an export trade in *panela*.

Prophetically he observed the advantages which might be derived from the growing of indigo, cotton, and coffee, the latter "a drink popular in Europe which has enriched the Antilles and which prospers so happily in the Valley of Medellín." Conditions, he thought, seemed ideal for such a development in a land where two-thirds of the citizenry were landowners. Here the great haciendas were lacking, and if there were no very rich vecinos there were few who were desperately poor. For further expansion of agricultural production he urged the founding of new towns in the direction of the Río Magdalena "on the fertile lands of Nare, Guatapé, Samaná and the Río Nus ... to which the Valley of Medellín and other large settlements could send colonists."

Antioquia was too involved in the settlement of its southern frontier and in the new gold strikes to the north to take part in the boom-and-bust hysterias in exportation of agricultural products which swept other parts of the republic during the nineteenth century. Not until 1869, when the departmental assembly exempted cacao, indigo, and mulberry plantations from the payment of local taxes, did the government at Medellín indicate concern for the development of an export agriculture. An 1877 resolution went further, providing monetary

[1]For notes to chap. ix, see pp. 204–207.

awards of 50 pesos for each flock of two hundred or more sheep; 100 pesos for anyone producing fifty or more quintals of cotton; 500 pesos for the first person producing at least one thousand liters annually of good wine; and, finally, 4 pesos for each one hundred coffee trees planted (maximum award, 100 pesos). These offers were reaffirmed in 1881 and extended to include tax exemptions for plantations of cotton, indigo, cacao, coffee, mulberry, vanilla, grapes and their products, and those of mining, sericulture, sheep raising, and palm and laurel wax extraction. Appropriations were also made for the introduction of new seeds and new livestock for breeding purposes.

Since the introduction of coffeegrowing the Antioqueño occupance pattern has shifted still further from its earlier mining orientation toward small-scale agriculture. The tradition of an independent yeoman class, from which title to a few hectares of land has become the ambition of every campesino, has fitted the new crop extraordinarily well. Most of the small growers have continued to provide for their own subsistence on part of their fincas, sometimes disposing of small surpluses of plantains, maize, or garden fruits at the nearest market. The common adage that "maíz comprado no engorda" (purchased maize does not fatten) merely emphasizes the integrated role of the independent farm.[3]

MAIZE

When compared to that of many other parts of tropical America the maize[3] of Antioquia is strikingly lacking in varietal diversity. Monotonous whites and yellows replace the bright and variegated colors of the Indian corn of Guatemala and Perú. This may point to the relatively late introduction of maize into this part of Colombia, notwithstanding the strategic position of Antioquia at the stem end of South America on what should have been an important route of passage for culture elements, including domesticated plants, between the two continents. Yet maize was the basic staple everywhere in pre-Colombian Antioquia as it is today. The modern Antioqueño likes to be called a *maicero* (maize eater) and the most characteristic of the Antioquia regional dishes have been derived from Indian methods of preparing maize.[4] Among these the unsalted cornbread balls (*arepas*), whole hominy (*mazamorra*)[5] and its watery liquid (*claro*) are overwhelmingly the most important. The maize kernels are decorticated in the traditional Indian manner by pounding with a heavy pestle in the hollowed-out end of a log (*pilón*) which stands upright in front of every home.

Chicha, the corn beer of the Chibchas, has always been much less important in Antioquia than in other parts of highland Colombia. In 1808 Restrepo⁶ wrote that the people lacked a common fermented drink and that chicha was made nowhere in the province. Yet at the time of the Conquest it was consumed in large quantities by the Arma Indians and the tribes to the south, and jugs of it have occasionally been found in guacas.⁷ There is no evidence that fermentation here was induced by mastication as it was on the *altiplano* of Bogotá.

Although maize cultivation extends from the banks of the Magdalena and Cauca virtually to the upper limits of human settlement in Antioquia and Caldas, it is most widespread in the lower, warmer zone where two crops a year may be taken. The most common variety here is a white, flour-capped, slightly dented flint corn of considerable uniformity with ears five or six inches long. The kernels are flattened and elongated, a characteristic feature of all maize from lower elevations, and are easily decorticated by pounding for the preparation of mazamorra or the coarse meal (*arroz de maíz*) from which arepas are made. These hot-country varieties are variously known as *diente de caballo, fino, maíz negro,* and *cuba* by Antioqueño cultivators. According to Edgar Anderson, they are very similar to the common white corn of the west coast which in México, however, is much longer eared, becoming progressively shorter in the southern areas. A common feature is a deep purplish coloring of the cob which is sometimes transmitted to the base of the kernels, accounting for the term *maíz negro.* Toward the Magdalena this same color gene reappears frequently in degenerate Caribbean flints.

Another entirely distinct hot-country maize is the rarely encountered *piru* or *pirulera,* a small-eared, small-kerneled white corn quite similar to the ancient popcorn of western Mexico (*maíz reventador*). In Antioquia and Caldas it only occasionally finds its way into the markets, but is reported more common among the Chamí Indians of the Western Cordillera.

The transition from tierra caliente to tierra fría in the maizes is through a slow gradation, with the commonest type of the middle lands (e.g., the valley of Medellín) being a transitional white variety (*blanquillo*), somewhat fuller grained than that of the tierra caliente. Generally speaking, maize seems less cultivated in the tierra templada than either above or below, perhaps in part owing to the competition of coffee for the best lands.

The maizes of the Antioquia tierra fría have a strong tendency toward longer, narrower ears and larger, more round kernels (i.e., more globous than acuminate) when compared with those of lower elevations. In this second characteristic they follow the pattern of the kidney beans which are also strikingly larger and fuller than those grown within the tierra caliente. The most common maize grown around Ríonegro today is a yellow, large-kerneled dent corn (*maíz criollo*) which is much prized for the making of mazamorra. In the markets of Medellín and Manizales it is referred to as *maíz de la montaña*. This is also the zone of the giant Antioquia flour corn known by the Quechua name of *capio* and which Anderson suggests provides a link between the similar flour corns of Perú and Bolivia and the *salpor* of Guatemala and the *cacahuazintle* of the Mexican plateau. All of these varieties have large, white, hexagonal kernels evenly spaced on the cob and tend to cover the tip. Around Ríonegro the cobs average eight to nine inches in length and have considerably enlarged butts. A black variety is also known. *Capio* is much less commonly grown in Antioquia than in many other parts of Colombia (e.g., the Bogotá cordillera), for it is never used in making the indispensable *arepa* and *mazamorra* which together account for perhaps 90 per cent of the maize consumed in the department. It is eaten green (*choclo*) and its flour (*maizena*) is used for making *buñuelos*.

On philological evidence it was once suggested that Colombia might have been an early center of maize selection and improvement.[9] Certainly the wide range of environmental conditions in these northernmost Andes must have been congenial to early man's efforts to assure and regularize his food supply by domestication of the more promising economic annuals. But if Sauer[10] is right in insisting that plant reproduction from settings or rootstocks involves a quite different set of agricultural attitudes from those implicit in seed reproduction, then Colombia quite clearly belongs within the root-crop complex rather than with the grains. Recent work, in fact, by Reichel-Dolmatoff and others has demonstrated that maize must have arrived rather late in the Colombian area, being introduced from Meso-America about 700 B.C. The few varieties and the monotonous white or yellow colors of Antioquia maizes may be interpreted as lending support to this view.

KIDNEY BEANS

The common kidney bean (*Phaseolus vulgaris*) is an extremely important food in the diet of the present-day Antioqueño. Considering its remarkable diversity of form and color, it may be inferred that it was a highly favored food of the Indians of the area and possibly of considerable antiquity. In its vertical range it is a faithful companion of maize, extending from the tierra caliente to the upper limits of settlement around 2,800 meters.

Local usage divides the beans into two categories, the early bush beans (*cuarentanos*), so named from the belief that they mature in forty days (the average is sixty to ninety days), and the climbing beans (*bejucos*) requiring upwards of six months to mature a crop. Both have an exceptionally vigorous vegetative growth. The bush beans are typical of the tierra caliente and the lower tierra templada whereas the climbers are largely confined to the tierra fría. Although they grow well on the higher slopes above Medellín, many of the latter will not flower under the higher temperatures of the valley floor.

In the markets the cuarentanos can be distinguished by their small size and the flattened, elliptical shape of the seeds. The most common, a blood-red variety known as *sangre de toro*, is also one of the smallest. Red is the predominant color in most of the cuarentanos, modified by mottling, striping, and stippling. The common black bean of México, although not absent, is of very secondary importance.

The later-maturing climbing beans have much larger, fuller-bodied seeds which are very frequently blunted into oblong parallelograms by crowding within the pod. This latter characteristic is especially pronounced in the highly prized *liborino*, a handsome, fleshy, bright

Agricultural Basis of Occupance 115

yellow bean mottled with red which is common around Ríonegro, and in the *cargamantas,* a variegrated group of fat beans (*frisoles gruesos*), found at even higher elevations than the liborino.

The scarlet runner (*Phaseolus coccineous*) is found as a semiwild, rank-growing vine of the upper part of the temperate zone around Fredonia and Santa Bárbara. It is used both for stock and for human consumption. At least three distinct varieties are known, a yellow, a violet, and a violet mottled with black. The local names for the species are *petaco* or *frisol de vida.*

The curious scarcity of Lima beans (*P. lunatus*) in the markets and fields is surprising, for they are common both northward in Central America and southward toward Popayán. Of the forty bean varieties I collected in Antioquia and Caldas during the summer of 1946 only one, called *carcha* or *huevo de pinche,* was a Lima.

ROOT CROPS

Maize and beans have been supplemented by an assemblage of at least five species of plants cultivated for their starchy roots, including sweet yuca (*Manihot utilissima*), arracacha (*Arracacia xanthorrhiza*), mafafa (*Xanthosoma* spp.), sweet potatoes (*Ipomoea batata*), and the small native Andean potato (*Solanum andigenum*). This impressive array of edible rootstocks, which in the higher elevations of southern and eastern Colombia is augmented by the *oca* (*Oxalis tuberosa*), the *añu* (*Tropaelum tuberosum*), and the *ulluco* (*Ullucus tuberosus*), clearly associates these northernmost Andes with the root-crop complex of highland South America. The early Spanish chroniclers in Antioquia and Caldas were all impressed by the variety and importance of roots in the Indian diet.

Of the five tubers known in Antioquia the sweet yuca (manioc) has always been much the most important. In Antioquia it is found in great varietal range, its cultivation reaching to at least 1,800 meters, or almost as high as the upper limits of coffee. It is still one of the principal foodstuffs sold in the markets of Antioquia and Caldas and in some parts of the tierra caliente it is the principal starch, not excepting maize. A common ingredient of soups, it is also baked (*pan de yuca*).

The two other root crops of the tierra caliente, the mafafa and sweet potato, are little grown today, although they may have been of greater importance in earlier times. An explanation for this presumed decline might be found in the better keeping qualities of the yuca which meant so much in the provisioning of the early mining camps. The latter also gives higher yields and is more resistant to drought. The mafafa, an elephant-eared aroid with a tuberlike rhizome closely allied to the Asiatic taro, is still occasionally planted inconspicuously in gardens below 1,500 meters, usually in moist places. A variety known as *chunga,* distinguished by its glaucous stalk, lacks the acridity of the common mafafa.

The common white potato of Europe and the United States has been shown by Russian investigators to be unrepresented in Colombia, probably because it cannot adjust itself to the short day of the tropics. In its place are found the red, blue, and mottled varieties of the tiny Andean potatoes which formed the food basis for the Chibcha civilizations. In Antioquia the potato was of minor importance in colonial times, for thermophilous varieties which could be grown below 2,000 meters seem to have been lacking, but in the last century its cultivation has become increasingly important as the tierra fría has turned from mining to agriculture. Peñol, San Vicente, and Ríonegro have become important potato-growing municipios in Antioquia. In Caldas a campaign to encourage the crop increased production five times between 1937 and 1942 in the higher parts of Manizales, Villamaría, Santa Rosa, and Marulanda. Some of the crop is now being marketed in Bogotá.

Of greater importance is the much-prized rootstock of the arracacha, with its celery-like top and long, finger-like, edible tubers, usually of clear white but occasionally yellow or red colored. Its taste has been described as a combination of chestnut, parsnip, potato, celery, and asparagus. Its greater tolerance for high temperatures may well have given it a competitive advantage over the potato in Antioquia, where settlement has been almost entirely confined to lands below the 2,500-meter contour. In some Antioquia markets the arracacha is still the most important tuber displayed. Of all the root crops it is generally considered the most characteristically Colombian, and Bukasov[11] be-

Agricultural Basis of Occupance 117

lieved it to be one of the oldest as well. It is little known to Europeans, its range being restricted to the Andes between the *yungas* of Perú and Chiriquí (Panamá).

Garden Miscellany

The cucurbits seem to have been much less important in Antioquia than in many other parts of Latin America. Most common today are the two giant squashes, the white-seeded *ahuyama* (*Cucurbita moschata*) and the black-seeded *vitoria* (*C. ficifolia*). The former is a warty, yellow-meated squash which grows at lower elevations and is usually eaten candied or boiled with kidney beans. The brown-seeded type reported by Bukasov as common along the Río Magdalena is not encountered in interior Antioquia. The vitoria, known from Peruvian graves dating back to the third millenium b.c., is a stringy, white-fleshed squash with figlike leaves used as a vegetable in soups and sometimes as a sweetmeat. It is characteristic of the tierra fría, and in Rionegro gardens produces mature fruit weighing more than a hundred pounds.

A third species, the yellow-meated *C. maxima*, although commonly considered to have been limited to the Inca territory in its pre-Colombian distribution, is also found in Medellín markets. It is grown at least as high as 2,200 meters, and like the vitoria reaches great size. None of these rank as vegetables of first importance in the diet, being considered primarily a food of the poorer classes, like the chayote (*Sechium edule*) and the cucumber-like *pepino hueco* (*Cyclanthera pedata*).

Garden peppers (*Capsicum* spp.) are not especially common, nor do they have the varietal diversity of the capsicums of Mexico.

The *achiote* (*Bixa orellana*), a tree whose red seeds provided the Indians with coloring matter for both dyestuffs and cosmetics, has continued to be cultivated. It is used today in all Antioqueño households for the coloring of boiled rice dishes, cheese, and soups.

Crescentia gourds (*totumas*) and Lagenaria (*calabaceras*) are both abundant and still are widely used by the country people for containers. At least one variety of the latter (*tarralí*) was formerly used by the natives as a container for burnt lime, made from snail shells, with which they chewed the leaf of the coca (*Erythroxylon* spp.). The coca grew wild, especially in the tierra caliente of the Río Arma.[12] Antioquia seems to have been near the northernmost limits of coca chewing in aboriginal America. Both the plant and the custom have long since disappeared from the culture traits of the region. Seemingly its cultivation has been abandoned since the arrival of the European.

Among the legion of native fruits still commonly grown are the red-seeded watermelons, cherry tomatoes, avocados, pineapples, cherimoyas, *guanábanas,* and *ciruelas* (*Spondia* spp.). Others are the bright, orange-fruited *lulo* (*Solanum galeatum*), the tree tomato (*Cyphomandra betacea*), and the *curubo* (*Passiflora* spp.). The mamey (*Mammea americana*), *níspero* (*Achras zapota*), and mamoncillo (*Melicocca bijuga*) are considered to have been introduced from other parts of tropical America during the colonial period.

Sugar Cane

Everywhere below 1,800 meters sugar cane is today an important crop in Antioquia and Caldas. Although figures are not available, its acreage must approximate that of maize or coffee. That its cultivation is essentially a small-scale business is indicated by the very large number of small mills (*trapiches*).[13] Principal areas of cultivation are in the valleys of Medellín (Barbosa, Girardota, Copacabana) and Amagá, but from Yolombó, Campamento, and Frontino also comes a considerable quantity of Medellín's supply. In Caldas it is especially important in the Risaralda Valley and south of Manizales, including the Quindío. Everywhere panela is the principal product, an unrefined brown cake sugar made by boiling the cane juice in great copper cauldrons over a fire of bagasse or wood until it has crystallized. It is molded into half-grapefruit shapes which are sold in pairs in the markets. The little white sugar consumed is all imported from modern refineries in the Valle del Cauca.

In the tierra caliente the cane may be harvested in eight to nine months, the ratoons being cut as many as eight times before replanting, but toward the upper limits of cultivation the plant may take as long as twenty-one months to mature.[14] Nowhere is irrigation employed, and contour cultivation is confined to a few experimental fincas. Yields commonly average 1.1 tons of cane per hectare.

The white-stemmed Otahiti cane, introduced to Antioquia in 1804, was first invaded by leaf-mosaic in 1933. When Chardón visited the Amagá region in 1937 he reported the devastation there worse than the worst years in Puerto Rico, with production down as much as 50 per cent on most of the plantations.[15] Some mosaic-resistant East Indian canes were being planted at that time and have since largely replaced the older varieties.

TABLE 11

AVERAGE DAILY FOOD CONSUMPTION OF ANTIOQUEÑO WORKERS
(In grams)

Food	Agricultural workers (Caldas)[a]	Railroad workers (FC de A)[b]	Miners (Charcón del Nechí)[c]
Meat	180	320	340
Maize	575	500	565
Beans	143	100	115
Panela	500	250[d]	345
Yuca or plantain	500	400[e]	[f]
Lard or butter	15	15	40

[a] Emilio Robledo, *Geografía Médica ... de Caldas*, p. 302.
[b] Juan B. Londoño, "Climas de Antioquia," *Anales de la Academia de Medicina de Medellín* (1933-1934), p. 1063 f.
[c] *El Colombiano* (Medellín), November 30, 1946.
[d] In 1894 the Ferrocarril de Antioquia panela ration was one pound (454 grams).
[e] May be replaced by 115 grams of rice.
[f] 225 grams of rice.

Among the Antioqueños panela is used not as a sweetening but as an attractive and exceedingly cheap human fuel carbohydrate (*el dulce de la fuerza*), probably the cheapest source of caloric energy easily available to modern man. Its importance in the diet is shown in the average worker's daily rations in table 11. Another measure of the standard Antioqueño diet (as well as family size) is provided by the cost-of-living index of the municipio of Medellín,[16] computed for a family of ten persons of the urban middle class on the following weekly basis: maize, 46 pounds; beans, 5¼ pounds; rice, 3 pounds; potatoes, 8¾ pounds; panela, 20 pounds; meat, 21 pounds; chocolate, 2 pounds; and 50 eggs.

Much of this caramel-like panela is taken dissolved in water as a beverage (*agua panela*). It is also eaten as candy, with mazamorra, milk, or rice. *Aguardiente,* the common man's traditional intoxicant, is distilled from its molasses, and cane-field refuse is an important fodder for mules and horses.

PLANTAINS

The record of the introduction of the plantain or cooking banana (*Musa paradisiaca*) is missing, but it seems to have obtained complete acceptance by Indian and white alike almost from the first days of European settlement. It was a warm-climate crop which yielded bounteously with a minimum of care, and, furthermore, the great green bunches could be easily handled on pack animals. They also kept well. Documents of the seventeenth and eighteenth centuries indicate that even on Indian lands the plantain was the cheapest and most abundant food available, especially below 1,500 meters. The varieties distinguished were *hartón, dominico,* and *guinéo,* still the most important in Antioquia and Caldas. Giant plantains are an important element in the shade forests of the modern Antioqueño coffee plantations (*cafetales*) and provide the major starch food for the coffee workers. The sweet or commercial banana of United States markets has only recently become generally available, trucked in from Urabá.

CACAO

Chocolate, not coffee, is the traditional drink of the Antioqueño campesino. Commonly thickened with corn meal, flavored with peppers, vanilla or panela and drunk from large bowls, it provides an important source of nourishment for the workers on the modern coffee fincas. Cacao cultivation seems to have been practiced only on a very limited scale in colonial times, principally around the old capital where irrigation was easy and temperatures sufficiently high. Imports of cacao beans constituted approximately one-fourth of all goods by weight brought into the province in the latter part of the eighteenth century, coming mainly from Timaná (upper Huila) and Buga (Valle). Yet Mon y Velarde had observed that the cacao seemed to do better at Antioquia than at either of these places. Although he attempted to encourage its cultivation, imports continued on a large scale. In 1808 José Manuel Restrepo wrote that 2,200 mule loads of cacao were imported yearly "although we are just starting to grow it near Antioquia and it does very well."[17]

Large-scale plantings were made around Antioquia and Sopetrán after 1830, only to be devastated by a fungous disease which brought ruin to the growers. The *mancha* (*escoba de bruja*) first appeared at the end of 1851 in the plantations east of the Río Cauca and north of Sopetrán.[18] The fruit was covered with virulent, velvet-like fungi which dried into an impalpable dust. It spread rapidly to all of the *cacaotales* along the Cauca, causing the loss of the 1852 crop. In the first years hopes were held for recovery since the foliage continued to do well, but eventually, when even the chocolate provided for the plantation workers had to be imported, its cultivation was abandoned. It was this calamity which gave rise to the big cacao trade with the Cartago area, later to be so important a factor in the growth of Manizales as a trade emporium.

Gradual revival of cacao growing has been spurred since 1928 by a government campaign urging replacement of the original high-quality but low-yield *criollo* stock by the disease-resistant Central American *pajarito* (*forastero*) and crosses between the two. Production has also spread into the rainy lowlands of the Atrato drainage (Turbo, Urrao) and the lower Cauca, where irrigation is not necessary. In Caldas the bulk of the cacao is grown in the municipio of Pueblorrico on the boundary of Chocó, much of it by Chamí Indians.[19]

INDIGO

The failure of the cacao industry of Santa Fé de Antioquia brought efforts to develop indigo as a substitute. In 1869 the Secretary of Hacienda reported that there were six indigo establishments operating at Antioquia, Sopetrán, and Liborino, with five others planned. With Antioquia *añil* bringing 2 pesos a pound in France, profits could be calculated at close to 50 per cent annually on the capital investment; but the industry was soon ruined by the competition of aniline dyes.

VANILLA

Another brief stir was caused by efforts to develop vanilla plantings in the same area. By 1882 there were 18,000 vines near Antioquia and shade trees had already been planted for 50,000 more.[20] Samples sent to Paris and Bordeaux brought low prices and the efforts were soon abandoned.

Anise Seed

The Antioqueño taste for anise has a Spanish origin, but ever since the introduction of sugar cane it seems to have been used for flavoring *aguardiente* (or, colloquially, "José Anís"), just as cumin seed has been popular for flavoring food. All aguardiente produced in Antioquia is still strongly anise-flavored and apparently has been ever since the institution of the royal monopoly nearly one hundred and seventy-five years ago. Mon y Velarde attempted to stimulate the production of anise in one year by offering 12 pesos of gold to the leading producer. He noted in his final report that "in spite of the characteristic skepticism" a few arrobas were already being produced, principally around Sopetrán.[21] This minor specialty crop, still grown to meet local requirements, is sold entirely to the state-operated distillery in Medellín.[22] Its cultivation has become highly localized in the tiny mountainside municipio of Giraldo on the dry flanks of the Western Cordillera on the Antioquia-Cañasgordas road.

Rice

Among the Old World grains only rice has made much headway among the Antioqueños, ranking now with sugar cane and plantain as the major introduced foods in the local diet. It is seldom that the visitor, even at the most isolated finca, is not offered boiled rice with his meals. Its consumption has greatly increased in recent years as standards of living have risen, especially in the cities, for rice carries the same connotation of a white, upper-class food that wheat does in many other areas.

Given the extremely broken nature of the topography of Antioquia and Caldas, it is not surprising that most of the rice consumed in these departments is brought in from outside areas, especially from the Caribbean coast, the Valle del Cauca, and the plains of Tolima. Despite the new producing areas in Urabá and the Bajo Cauca, Antioquia produced only 35,000 tons of rice in 1965, about 6 per cent of the nation's output.[23] Rice imports into Antioquia and Caldas today probably exceed all other nonprocessed foodstuffs combined, if beef-on-the-hoof is excluded.

Rice growing seems to have been introduced into Antioquia about the middle of the eighteenth century by Jesuit priests. By 1788 it had already become concentrated around San Jerónimo on the elevated, impermeable terraces where the Río Aurrá debouches into the low plains of Sopetrán. Mon y Velarde reported that here was produced all of the rice consumed by the province. San Jerónimo is still the only important rice-growing municipio of interior Antioquia. Irrigation here is indispensable, the fields being flooded as often as every four days during protracted dry seasons, but the gentle slope of the land does not permit water to stand for more than a few hours. Two harvests a year are occasionally taken, but the principal crop is that sown in January and cut in June. In recent years the plow and reaper have been used with some success on the more level fields which, unlike most Antioquia farm lands, are commonly leased out to tenants on a share-crop basis.

Recently the rainy lowlands of the lower Cauca and Urabá have surpassed San Jerónimo as rice-growing areas, but from these outlying sections much of the harvest is exported either to down-river Magdalena ports or to Cartagena. High precipitation and the single pronounced dry season has generally made irrigation unnecessary. An extraordinary cultural adaptation is found on the steep, rocky slopes below Valdivia (elev., 1,200 m.) where large cornfields are interplanted with rice (*arroz de la montaña*). For those who associate upland dry rice cultivation with the isolated, usually primitive areas of southeast Asia it comes as a surprise to find it being grown on the Antioqueño pioneer fringe, half a world away from its original home. But Fray Pedro Simón's allusion in 1580 to rice in the Magdalena Valley, where it was growing with maize, proves it to have been an old practice.

At Mariquita ... rice (*arroz*) yields abundantly and without the labor required to grow it in the Kingdoms of Murcia and Valencia in Spain, for it is seeded in the same manner as wheat and without any other attention or irrigation until harvested.[34]

Tobacco

The large numbers of pipes which have been found in the Indian graves of Antioquia and Caldas are evidence that tobacco was widely used in the area before the Conquest. During the colonial period it was grown to some extent in local Indian communities, but it early became one of the principal imports brought in over the Nare road.[25] Governor Silvestre observed in 1776 that although the leaf grew well in the province, the inhabitants were generally ignorant of curing techniques.

Antioquia did not participate in the great Ambalema tobacco boom which followed the lifting of the government monopoly in the 1850's, but production to meet part of the local need has always been maintained on the warmer lands along the Río Cauca. The plant here is a perennial, and statistics published are for "producing trees," which at maturity are the height of a man or higher. In 1942 there were 4.9 million tobacco trees registered in the department of Antioquia in 1,067 separate plantations, a decrease of two-thirds from twenty years earlier.[26] By 1965 there had been a further substantial decline in production and only 300 hectares were reported under the crop. Tobacco consumption, however, has continued to increase. The big home plant of the Companía Colombiana de Tobaco is in Medellín.

Cotton

A woody, perennial cotton seems to have been extraordinarily widespread and important among the aborigines of Antioquia. Both their extensive *algodonales* and the great quantities of woven cotton cloth repeatedly brought comment from the early chroniclers. Clay spindle whorls by the thousands have been recovered from the Quindío. At first the Spaniards purchased their clothes from the Indians or ordered them made by their encomienda natives, but as the Indian skills, and probably the cotton fields, disappeared, clothes from Socorro, Quito, and Castile (*ropas de Castilla*) came to constitute the most important single class of imports. If the cultivation of foodstuffs seemed unattractive to a mining community it is understandable that the cultivation of cotton might have been completely abandoned. Observing the fine stockings and hats woven in the province, one official urged that the women of Antioquia engage themselves in this business of cloth making (*fabricación de lienzos*) so that imports might be reduced.[17] He proposed, but apparently did not effect, the bringing of two families of weavers with looms and spinning wheels to teach Antioquia's women the necessary techniques.

From time to time waves of enthusiasm have swept Antioquia for the development of commercial cotton cultivation to supply the textile mills of Medellín, but results have always been disappointing. In 1880 the press of Manizales thought a textile industry offered the one hope of interrupting the emigration toward the Quindío and asked that the local government take steps to distribute cottonseed, for which there were many requests. One editor wrote:

Our mission now is to plant cotton and increase our flocks, for as the sheep multiply and the cotton fields are extended the textile factories will increase, the poorer class will find productive occupation, prices will fall and emigration will cease.[28]

Later, in the present century, the developing, tariff-protected mills of the valley of Medellín distributed free seed to cultivators in the hope of developing a cheaper source of raw cotton within the department, but there has been little response. In 1908–1910 more than 1,400 pounds of cottonseed were distributed and planted in the municipio of Ebéjico on the southern margin of the arid zone near Santa Fé de Antioquia, but the crops were lost to weevils and caterpillars. Two other failures followed and the project was finally abandoned.[29]

Trees of cotton are to be seen today in the dooryards of most homes in the smaller settlements below 2,000 meters. As late as 1940 the small rain-shadow pocket on the far slope of the Western Cordillera above Dabeiba was supplying perhaps 2 per cent of the requirements of Medellín's expanding textile industry. Today cotton is no longer grown at Dabeiba. The mills are supplied with all of their raw material needs from new producing areas on the coast and in Tolima.

SERICULTURE

A brief attempt was also made in the last century to establish the silk industry in Antioquia. Silkworms had been introduced into the department by a French resident of Medellín, Manuel Vicente de la Roche. Samples of the first cloth made from them were presented to the governor in 1869, who ordered a gold medal be awarded their maker.

After some early disappointments a Sociedad Serícola de la Roche was established in 1888 under a 30,000-peso subsidy voted by the departmental assembly.[30] The grant called for establishment of a model farm near Santo Domingo for "the growing of mulberry trees, silkworm culture, cocoon reeling and silk weaving" as well as to carry on experiments with the native Colombian worm, *Attacus spondae*. But long bickering over financial aid led to abandonment of the project, although de la Roche, disillusioned and bitter, still held out hopes for it until his death in 1897.[31]

Cabuya

Cabuya (*fique*) is a name given in Colombia to both the fiber and the plants of the various species of the agave-like *Furcraea* which are cultivated throughout the upper tierra templada and the tierra fría.[32] Although it is seldom mentioned in the literature, cabuya plays a role of at least equal importance to cotton among the fibers for the campesino. From it are produced twines, ropes, hammocks, saddle girths, and halters and, most important, sacks for coffee, cacao, maize, and panela. The fiber is finer in texture than henequen and is lustrous and of excellent quality when well cleaned.

The most common method of preparing the fiber is by means of the *carrizo*. The leaves are split into narrow strips and are pulled between two sticks pressed together to scrape away the pulp. Its production is highly localized, in Antioquia the municipios of San Vicente and Guarne accounting for the largest part of the production. The demands of the coffee industry have given rise to the establishment of a large modern sack factory in Medellín that today purchases virtually all of the dried fiber produced in the department for the manufacture of the familiar coffee sacks, each with a green and red stripe woven lengthwise around it. Previous to the entry into the field of the Companía de Empaques, S.A., cabuya weaving had been a household industry, the principal looming centers being at Guarne, Rionegro, and La Estrella. Only the last, site of a former Indian reservation by that name, lay in the valley of Medellín.

STOCK RAISING

Everywhere European livestock formed an integral part of the Spanish colonial complex. Cattle, sheep, and hogs brought to Perú by way of Panamá shortly after 1530 provided the stock which accompanied the conquistadores in their movement northward toward Quito, Popayán, and Antioquia. Additional cattle, horses and asses, brought in through Buenaventura by Belalcázar, became the property of the Cauca Valley Spaniards. The evidence at hand indicates that this livestock was the foundation stock for all Antioquia herds.[33] There are no records of any cattle having been imported from the north, either by the Magdalena-Cauca river routes or over the soon-forgotton Urabá road of the first conquistadores.

Unmolested by predators, the stock multiplied rapidly. As early as 1569 the municipal council of the villa of Santa Fé de Antioquia had ordered all cattle (*ganado vacuno*) corralled each night because "... they do great damage to the *estancias* of this villa, eating the maize and beans and other crops which grow on them."[34] Thereafter loose cattle doing damage to private property might be killed without penalty. At the same time common pasture was assigned on the hill of Buriticá "for this villa and its livestock."

Elsewhere in the province the number of cattle also increased. Of a herd of five hundred being driven from Arma to the mines of Remedios in 1573, more than a hundred had strayed along the road in the valley of Aburrá.[35] In 1581 the son-in-law of their original owner, petitioning for a grant of 2 square leagues near Guarne "for an *estancia* on which to round up these cattle and establish plantings," observed that

... they have so multiplied in the last eight years in this area that they are now in great quantity and many persons, without conscience or fear of God, come to kill them with harquebuses or dogs or by other means as they are able, and as a consequence incurring on me great damage and injury.

The common pasture owned by the vecinos of Santa Fé in the valley of the Río Negro also developed as an early stock center. Grazing privileges were leased annually to outsiders at the rate of 4 pesos per hundred head and between 1644 and 1647 the tax collector's records show 900 steers (*novillos*), 1,696 cattle (*ganado vacuno*), and 480 hogs registered there.[36] Most of these had been brought from Arma, Buga, and Popayán for fattening prior to sale to the mining camps of Antioquia where there was a demand for beef and tallow, as well as for rawhide ropes and buckets. Others were to be sold as pack oxen, for during the rainy seasons the heavy clays of the uplands made roads impassable for mules and horses.

Although there seem to be no early descriptions of the Antioquia cattle which would indicate them as being in any way unusual, three centuries of isolation and selection have established a unique, well-fixed bovine race, variously known in Colombia as *blanco oreji-negro, Antioqueño,* or *criollo.* Its outstanding immunity to the tick (*garrapata*) and warble fly (*nuche*) have made it eminently adapted to Antioquia conditions. It is a frugal animal of small size with very white, fine, short hair except on the ears, which are black. The muzzle is also black and occasionally the tips of the horns and tail as well (pl. 5*b*).

As a thrifty, triple-purpose, milk, meat, and pack animal especially adapted to the steep slopes of the tierra templada, the blanco oreji-negro has been the faithful companion of the Antioqueño colonists both in the coffee zone and on the new clearings in the crystalline highlands toward the north and east. Viewed from the air their snow-white forms stand out sharply against the rich green of the grassy hills. They especially like to huddle together on the circular, earth-bare knolls in this region. Like the *arepa* and *carriel,* these cattle are everywhere reliable indicators of Antioqueño settlement, or were until very recently.[37] Increasingly these distinctive criollo cattle are being displaced at middle and lower elevations by zebu crosses, in higher zones by European dairy breeds. Their days appear to be numbered.[38]

The enormously expanded demand for fresh milk recently has given rise to a substantial dairy industry in Antioquia, centering on the cooler uplands around Don Matías and the *vegas* of the upper Río Negro near La Ceja. Plots of Imperial or Guatemala grass, set out in individual clumps that are periodically cut for fodder (*pasto de corte*), give a distinctive character to the landscape of these tierra fría dairy districts. A large modern pasteurizing plant in Medellín (Proleche) handles most of the output, collected from the farms by a growing fleet of tank trucks. Price controls on fluid milk, in the face of rising costs, have probably restricted the expansion of production to some extent in recent years.

The blanco oreji-negro, like the people of Caldas, have been said to be "more Antioqueño than the Antioqueños." Although they have spread into the coffee lands of Cundinamarca and the Popayán plateau, the center of their range remains the northern tierra templada of the Central Cordillera. Their distinctively white hair and black skin, which make them unique among Latin American cattle, have led to conjecture concerning their origin. Possibly the type traces back to the Roman white sacrificial cattle which were taken to Spain two thousand years ago. There they were largely mixed with native breeds, but in isolated mountain districts of the Peninsula some white cattle had survived at least until a recent date.[39] Introduced into northern South America, their subsequent isolation in the mountains of Antioquia has resulted in a natural selection toward frugality and parasite resistance, accompanied by a possible revival and stabilization of certain primitive characteristics, including the white hair, black muzzle, and black ears.

Darwin observed seventy years ago that "there is a strong tendency in wild or escaped cattle under widely different conditions of life to become white with colored ears."[40] As examples he cited the white, black-eared Park cattle of Great Britain, the common Hungarian oxen and herds reported on the Falkland Islands, the Mariana Islands, and in Wales. The English cattle, especially, have been the subject of much attention. The four or five existing Park herds and those earlier extinguished were all white with either black or brownish-red ears and black points.[41] Sometimes dark spots occurred about the neck and over the ankles; this last characteristic is fairly common among the native cattle of Antioquia. Although these wild white cattle of Great Britain have been suggested as descendants of the original wild *Bos primogenus* of the islands, a more reasonable thesis would seem to be that they have descended from cattle brought by the Romans from southern Europe and left to shift for themselves when the invaders were driven from England. Their occurrence in at least two isolated Spanish colonies and in England strongly favors a common Roman ancestry for both branches of the stock.

The first blooded foreign breeds were imported into Antioquia about 1880 and their numbers have continued to increase as milk consumption has skyrocketed in recent years. Holstein-Frisians and Ayrshires have been most successfully introduced, the latter representing close to three-fourths of the blooded cattle in the department of Antioquia. Hacienda Zulaibar (elev., 2,500 m.) near Angostura, established in 1910 by Tulio Ospina, has more than a thousand Ayrshires, most of them of pure blood. Other European strains have included Red-polled, Jerseys, Durham, and Brown Swiss. Arsenic baths and other cattle dips have made it possible for some European dairy types to be successfully introduced into the warmer lands.

More successful has been the crossing of blanco oreji-negros with other imported types. One of these, the criollo-Durham cross is widely distributed in Caldas where it is known as *azul y pintado* or *Caldense*.

Antioquia's livestock population has apparently declined somewhat in recent years (1,070,000 in 1965). The internal market for beef is being supplied increasingly from the savannas of Córdoba and Bolívar since the opening of the Cartagena-Medellín highway in the mid-1950's. *Costeño* cattle, with strong admixtures of zebu blood, today dominate the weekly Medellín cattle auction.

Importation of cattle dates from the early colonial mining period in Antioquia, but most of them were brought from the Valle del Cauca rather than from the north. The possibilities for Bolívar cattle were recognized by Governor Silvestre in 1776 when he proposed the opening of an overland road to Ayapel:

... it would also be useful for the traffic which would develop in driving cattle from the savannas of Ayapel and Tolú. There are very few stock in this country, but they will be necessary to cheapen the cost of meat to our settlers and mine workers and for foundation stock on our haciendas."

Imports seem to have been on a small scale, however, until the latter part of the nineteenth century when Valle surpluses began to be diverted to the new markets of Manizales, the Quindío, and the urban centers of the upper Cauca.

Prior to the opening of the Troncal del Occidente there were two principal ways of moving the cattle from the Caribbean plains to the interior. One was the overland trail ("La Trocha") from Montería through Cáceres, Valdivia, and Yarumal to Medellín. The other involved a shorter drive from the Sinú to the Magdalena river port of Magangué (Yatí), from where the cattle were moved on great three-decked barges either to Puerto Berrío for transshipment by rail to Medellín, or to La Dorada, from where they were driven over the cordillera passes to Manizales." A few cattle also moved to the interior markets by way of an overland trail to Turbo on the Gulf of Urabá and thence by water up the Río Atrato."

As many as 70,000 head of cattle per year moved by "La Trocha" to Medellín. It was a 45-day drive from Montería and weight losses en route averaged 30 per cent, to which had to be added a further 5 per cent allowance for deaths. On the fluvial route via Puerto Berrío losses ran 12 to 14 per cent but costs were higher.

Today the moving of cattle from the Caribbean lowlands to the Medellín market is a major industry involving several hundred trucks and truckers. Transport costs are 160 pesos ($10 U.S.) per head from Montería, 130 pesos ($8 U.S.) from the Bajo Cauca. From the Puerto Berrío district along the Magdalena river, the other major source area for the Medellín market, stock are moved by rail, but this will change with the completion of the truck road from the river port to the departmental capital.

Cattle from Córdoba, Bolívar, and the Bajo Cauca are normally thin (*flacos*) and must be fattened on artificial pasture for four to twelve months before they are ready for sale as fat cattle (average weight, 500 kg.) to slaughterers. The largest part of this stock is fattened on the Pará or India grass pastures of the tierras calientes either along the middle Cauca lowlands (La Pintada to Bolombolo) or on the lower Nus and Magdalena grasslands. Both of these areas have good transportation facilities.

The revolution in livestock transport brought by the truck coincided with the opening, in 1956, of the impressive municipally-owned livestock yards and auction grounds a few miles north of Medellín. The *Feria* of Medellín is said to be the largest and best appointed livestock auction yard in Latin America. In 1966 it handled 474,000 head of cattle with total sales of 778 million pesos ($50 million U.S.)— a figure almost identical with the total sales of Coltejer, the largest textile firm in Colombia, in the same year. Cattle from the northern savannas and the vegas of the Magdalena move through it not only to the nearby municipal slaughterhouse (capacity 55 head per hour) and to fattening pastures in Antioquia, but also to markets in Caldas, Valle, Santander and Cundinamarca. Medellín's Feria is the focal point for stockmen throughout western Colombia and activity there is intense, especially at mid-week. Facilities at the Feria grounds include five banks, twelve restaurants and numerous kiosks selling saddles, riatas, clothing, and other manufactured items for stockmen.[45]

Introduced Pasture Grasses

Introduced pasture grasses, most of them native African species brought to Colombia by way of Brazil, have permitted the development of a prosperous livestock industry in Antioquia. More important, they have provided a promising check to an accelerating erosion problem which has been threatening the region's agricultural economy.

A demand for finishing pastures for the increasing numbers of thin Bolívar cattle arriving over "La Trocha" led to the establishment of the first tierra caliente cattle-fattening haciendas in the 1870's. Stimulated by the successful plantings of Pará grass (*Panicum barbinode*) on Hacienda Túnez, almost all the virgin forests along the Antioqueño Cauca between the Río Arma and Bolombolo were turned into either Pará or India grass (*Panicum maximum*) between 1870 and 1900. Unlike the temperate slopes above, the land here was held in large parcels by wealthy absentee owners. Such a development would hardly have been possible without the barbed-wire fence which was introduced from the United States during this period, replacing the traditional, hand-excavated ditches (*chambas*) which previously had marked field and property boundaries. Both Pará and India grasses require rotational grazing. Continuous use throughout the year may be ruinous, especially on thinner soils, so that it was necessary to break the haciendas up into numerous smaller *potreros* of about 75 acres each. Túnez, with more than 3,000 cattle, has more than seventy of these individual pastures.

Pará grass, which is generally limited to the moist lowlands subject to inundation, has been more and more replaced in recent years by India grass (sometimes known as *pasto de Guinea*). India grass is adaptable to the thinner upland soils and does not suffer from periodic drought as does Pará. Both grasses are coarse and exceedingly rank growing so that it is sometimes difficult, even for men on horseback, to find cattle grazing in them. They have a similar nutritive value, their carrying capacity being generally rated at one head per cuadra (1.54 acre). There are extensive forested regions along the lower Cauca and Magdalena that are adaptable to these grasses, as indicated by their successful establishment in recent years around Cáceres, Puerto Berrío, and La Dorada. In this type of extensive, large-scale livestock ranching there is no room for the traditional small holdings of the Antioqueño colonos.

Although Pará and India grass have made available many thousands of acres of previously unproductive land in the tierra caliente, more importance must be attached to the recent explosive invasion of the African molasses grass (*Melinis minutiflora*) into the steep, worn slopes of the tierra templada. This soft, bluish-green grass which has come to be known in Antioquia as *pasto gordura* or *yaraguá*, is covered with fine hairs and has a characteristic, lemonlike odor which, after a rain, permeates the atmosphere. From the base of each hair is secreted a tiny drop of sweet, viscous fluid (unique among known Graminaceae) which makes it sticky to the touch and which is reputed to repel mosquitoes and cattle ticks. Animals first placed on this pasture are indifferent to it, but, once accustomed to the grass, favor it over others. Its carrying capacity is two-thirds that of Pará or India, but unlike the latter it can be used for dairy herds as well as for fattening beef. It is also thought to give a special sheen to the coats of cattle feeding on it.

The revolutionary importance of yaraguá to Antioquia, however, lies less in these qualities than in its exceptional soil-holding properties and its tolerance of the eroded, steep soils of low fertility which characterize the granitic Antioqueño massif and some of the abandoned coffee lands of the southwest. Its long trailing culms, which root at the joints, continue to grow on top of the old vegetation, sometimes forming a deep, loose mat of one or more feet in thickness through which new aerial roots from the nodes are continually extending to provide further anchorage with the ground.

This extraordinarily adaptable grass was introduced into Colombia in 1906 when a few of its seeds were inadvertently included in a shipment of seeds of the entirely distinct Brazilian jaragua grass (*Hyparrhenia rufa*) sent by the Colombian Minister to Brazil, General Rafael Uribe Uribe.[46] The Brazilian jaragua at first took hold only slowly and unimpressively and since two species of grass resulted from the seeds sent by the General, the public gave the name hold only slowly and unimpressively and since two species of grass resulted from the seeds sent by the General, the public gave the name "yaraguá" to the plant which prospered better, the Melinis. The confusion of names which has resulted from this circumstance is still far from resolved. Among the terms frequently applied to the Melinis in Antioquia have been "común," "gordura," "peludo," "melado," "Ospina," and "yeraguá de Colombia," but most common of all has been the erroneous "yaraguá." The same misunderstanding has spread to Puerto Rico and Venezuela, at least, where Melinis is also known as "yaraguá."[47]

Meanwhile the Brazilian jaragua, which General Uribe observed had already replaced molasses grass in most of Goyaz and was causing an agricultural revolution in Brazil,[48] became popularly known as "yaraguá Uribe" in Antioquia to distinguish it from its more aggressive counterpart.[49] It has been gradually extending its range, especially on the warmer, drier sites where other grasses do not do so well, such as the mountain slopes west of Santa Fé de Antioquia and Anzá.

The astonishing rapidity with which the Melinis yaraguá has taken over the temperate lands of Colombia may have few counterparts in agricultural history. It is in a sense comparable to the invasion of the

Mediterranean wild oat into California. At first carefully seeded after a preparation of an ash bed in new clearings, it has long since become a volunteer, invading abandoned cafetales, road cuts, railroad embankments, and even native pastures. Moreover, its range of tolerance extends well into the tierra fría and the tierra caliente, being limited approximately by the 17° and 24° C. isotherms. Only three years after its introduction into the Amalfi region (1912) a hacienda there had demands for more than 4,000 kilograms of seed, which came from all parts of the republic and from Ecuador, in response to some articles published in a Bogotá newspaper.[60] By 1926, just twenty years after the first seeds had been received in the country, it was already being called "the salvation of Antioquia." Today it may be found almost everywhere in the Antioqueño country, from the new road cuts near Zaragoza to the pinnacled top of Cerro Tusa, its seeds scattered by the agencies of wind, birds, and man with uncommon ease. As coffee passes from the Antioqueño economy in marginal areas it is yaraguá which is moving in behind it, checking further soil loss on the steep slopes and giving the land a new economic value as pasturage, especially for that short-legged rustler, the blanco oreji-negro.

The principal rival of yaraguá in the tierras templadas has been the native Colombian Micay grass (*Axonopus* spp.), an unnoticed component of the natural vegetation of the Río Micay region west of Popayán which was first planted on a hacienda near Cali in 1887.[11] It was a factor in the agricultural revival of Santa Rosa de Cabal at the beginning of this century, whence the first plants were sent to Medellín in 1910. Reproducing by root sets instead of seed, it has been much slower and more expensive to establish than yaraguá. It is especially valued as a pasture for milking herds, and is sometimes used to fatten cattle which have been raised on common yaraguá. Although it extends much further into the tierra fría than does Melinis, it does not tolerate the warmer temperatures of the lower temperate zone. Like the latter it does well on the sterile granitic uplands.

The tierra fría grasses are a much less promising assemblage than those being grown at the lower elevations of Antioquia. Among the introduced varieties which have some importance, especially in the dairy regions, are *elefante* (*Pennisetum purpureum*), *gramalote* (*Pas-*

palum dilatum), *imperial (P. fournerianum?) Guatemala (Tripsacum laxum*), and *Janeiro (Eryochloa polystachya*). Here, more than elsewhere, native grasses have provided useful pasturage, improved by the annual weeding to keep down the bracken which is here considered one of the routine tasks of the finca. This weeding is traditionally done with the Antioqueño *güinche,* a unique, sharp-edged instrument of local invention with which weeds are cut with a swinging stroke.

X. COFFEE

ALTHOUGH COFFEE was grown commercially on the French islands of the Caribbean as early as 1720, and was later well known in Venezuela and Costa Rica, its introduction into Colombia was curiously late. It was first grown on a commercial scale during the first years of the republic in the valleys of Cúcuta, having been introduced from the neighboring Venezuelan canton of San Cristóbal where it had been a cash crop for many years. From Norte de Santander its cultivation spread gradually southward along the slopes of the Bogotá cordillera, where several influential landowners took an active interest in its promotion. But even as late as 1890 one-half of the coffee exported from Colombia left the country through Cúcuta and Lake Maracaibo.[1]

From 1850 on coffee had been increasingly grown by a few people of means in Cundinamarca and it was here that most of the early experimental plantations were situated and the early advances made. An extensive pamphlet and periodical literature appeared in Bogotá during the latter half of the nineteenth century extolling coffee as a desirable export crop for Colombia and describing the methods of its cultivation.[2] The first of such *folletos* seems to have been that published in 1856 by the venerable Antioqueño historian, José Manuel Restrepo, who in his youth had pointed to the coffee tree as being well suited to his home province. In urging the extension of its cultivation he pointed out that coffee was the only exportable crop which could be grown on the slopes of Colombia's mountains:

> The Republic of Costa Rica is daily adding to its wealth and prosperity by the cultivation of this berry. There is no doubt but that this will also occur in New Granada. Most of our provinces lack export crops. In certain altitudinal zones of our cordilleras where the climate is temperate there is no fruit of value cultivated. Coffee will fill this void, for it yields excellent harvests and sells at good prices.[3]

It is curious that the first coffee planting of any size in Antioquia was made on the crystalline uplands, today recognized as marginal

---

[1] For notes to chap. x, see pp. 207–208.

coffee lands both as to soil and climate. In 1861 a plantation of 2,000 trees was made at El Tablazo, a few miles from Ríonegro, by José María Jaramillo.[4] It was the well-to-do landowners with surplus time and capital available, who were largely responsible for the spread of coffee cultivation in the years that followed. During the 'seventies Jaramillo played a major role in engendering enthusiasm for the new crop by taking an active part in promoting the new railroad outlet to the Magdalena, sending samples of Antioquia coffee to the European markets, and publishing and disseminating instructions for coffeegrowers.

The signing of the contract between the government and the Cuban engineer F. J. Cisneros in 1874 for the construction of the Medellín–Magdalena railroad gave coffee planting a tremendous boost in Antioquia. Jaramillo optimistically wrote to Cisneros that within three years there would be more than a million bearing coffee trees in the province to provide the new railroad with an eastbound cargo of 1,000 tons annually.[5] In his 1878 report, published in New York, Cisneros told prospective stockholders:

> Coffee is one of those things that are destined to change the aspect of Antioquia, for there is in it an abundance of lands unsurpassed for its cultivation; and above all those which the railroad crosses, irrigated [sic] by numerous waterfalls that can be converted into driving power for small mills at moderate prices to shell the bean and clean it.[6]

The report listed existing plantings of 328,000 coffee trees, or, at 1,000 trees to the hectare, 328 hectares of coffee. There were individual plantings of more than 10,000 trees at Yolombó, Yarumal, Copacabana, Medellín, Titiribí, and Concordia. Others, smaller, were at Ríonegro, Jericó, Fredonia, and in the valley of the Río Nus. By the time the railroad was built, he predicted, there would be 3,000 tons of coffee exported every six months. The promise of early completion of the new railroad seems to have attracted several early planters to the eastern slopes of the Antioqueño massif (e.g., Yolombó). Along the old Nare road, too, plantings began to appear in new clearings below San Carlos and it was here that Tulio Ospina, a young graduate of the University of California, first established a plantation.[7]

Coffee 139

Although the Antioquia provincial assembly's bounty appropriation in 1881 had been directed toward sheep and wine as well as coffee, all but one of the payments which were made in the first two years were for new coffee plantings. Santa Bárbara and Andes each had three of the new plantations and there was one each in Ebéjico, Concepción, and Aguadas.⁸ A larger, but unrecorded number of claims had been disallowed on technicalities, and the enthusiasm of others who had already set out seedbeds had been dampened by a drop in prices. But the subsidies had apparently been effective, for eighteen years later the prizes offered under the law of 1881 were cited as having been an important factor in setting off the Antioquia coffee boom.⁹

Coffee was also being planted on the steep slopes of the southern frontier around Manizales.¹⁰ Between 1865 and 1870 at least four small plantings had been made, but all were soon abandoned because of the lack of an adequate market or the consequences of the civil wars. In 1877, at the same time that the twin enthusiasms for coffee and the railroad were at their peak in the north, the first 10,000-tree cafetal was planted by Antonio Pinzón, native of Santander, on the steep slopes of the Quebrada Guacaica. The enthusiasm for coffee planting was caught by a Manizales editor, who wrote:

> It has made us envious to learn that the District of Sasaima (Cundinamarca) has now 1,108,000 coffee trees of which 580,000 are bearing. This should provide us with a worthy goal for the future. When shall we have the pleasure of being able to see even half that number of coffee trees in this district, each yielding its own abundant harvest, no less estimable than gold or diamonds?¹¹

The publication in Medellín of Mariano Ospina Rodríguez' *El Cultivo de Café* in 1880 gave coffeegrowing in the department a further stimulus. Although written for all Colombians, it had its widest circulation among Antioqueño colonists. A former governor of the province and president of the republic, Ospina, was a revered and respected public figure whose son was to follow him as chief executive of the country. During his eight and a half years of political exile in Guatemala he had studied the methods of coffeegrowing practiced in that country where some of the first large and efficient coffee fincas in Central America had been established. In his 1880 brochure, the most comprehensive study of coffeegrowing that had yet appeared in Colombia, he observed:

> Few crops adapt themselves so well to both large- and small-scale enterprise as coffee. If the first is profitable the second is more so, for without noticeable increase in the labor required by his maize and yuca each settler can convert a portion of his land into a cafetal.... All the effort required is the digging of holes and the setting out of the transplants at the time of seeding the maize and yuca. The weedings that these crops demand will suffice for the coffee. After three years... the land will have been converted into a producing cafetal... which will give an income which could never be hoped for from a similar acreage of maize or yuca....

Even newly cleared primary soils of the old uplands, he thought, would yield good crops where adequate organic matter was present, but he wisely observed that "the soil composed of humus and small stones, such as that in Amagá," should make the best coffee land of all. Here was the first recognition of the superior productivity of the young volcanic soils of the slopes of Cerro Bravo and beyond which were soon to become the forcing bed of the coffee boom which was to sweep the province. He recommended the altitudinal belt with an average temperature of 18° to 22° C. (64.4° to 72.6° F.), with the best quality to be expected from the higher plantings. On the question of shade he was noncommittal but skeptical, urging planters to experiment with its use before arriving at a decision. The shaded cafetales of Cundinamarca and Santander represented, he was sure, simply the transfer of a Venezuela culture pattern which had not yet been proved scientifically valid.

In 1882 Ospina began to put his recommendations to the test when, with Julián and Eduardo Vásquez, he established the first of several large-scale coffee haciendas, using scientific methods of cultivation and beneficiation, on the volcanic outwash slopes of Cerro Bravo, north of Fredonia. Here were installed the first pulping machines and mechanical threshers (*trilladoras*) in the department. As other wealthy *hacenderos* followed them to these fertile, stony soils the Fredonia region rapidly became the center of the Antioquia coffee industry. In 1888 coffee production in the municipio of Fredonia was 13,100 arrobas, no other municipio producing more than 2,000 arrobas (arroba = 25 pounds). In contrast to other Antioqueño districts coffee here has remained an estate crop, produced by modern technology and mass-production techniques. Workers on the Fredonia haciendas, who have constituted an unusually large proportion of the colonists who have settled the new lands to the south and west, have been responsible for the dissemination of coffee knowledge.

Improved river transportation and a rise in prices had combined to encourage the expansion of acreage in Cundinamarca after 1860, but in Antioquia, where access to the Río Magdalena waterway was more difficult, the sharp rise in production was not felt until after 1890 when construction of the Ferrocarril de Antioquia was well under way. Even as late as 1913 Norte de Santander and Cundinamarca were the two leading coffee-producing departments of Colombia, but after this date the shift in the center of cultivation from the Eastern to the Central Cordillera came with almost dramatic suddenness. The development of an organized buyers' market further favored the expansion of production, especially after 1920.

Coffee, by its nature, is not well adapted to a frontier economy. As a tree crop it lends a certain stability to agriculture which may be inimical to the new settler, who is never quite sure that he has gone far enough or staked out the best piece of land remaining unclaimed. Moreover, it yields its first berries only in the third or fourth year after planting, and not until the fifth year does it reach full production. Its cultivation implies a capital reserve and a permanence of occupation not commonly found among the men who cleared the virgin forests. Its adoption as a major cash crop by Antioqueño homesteaders usually followed by a decade or more the initial clearings, after the rich humus soils had given up their early bumper harvests of maize, beans, or tobacco. Even in the Quindío basin, where settlement has been relatively recent and where today, more than anywhere else in Colombia, coffee is king, most of the cafetales were set out on land previously in pasture. Although the crop fitted admirably into the established homestead settlement pattern, it was never a part of the frontier complex.

The climatic and soil requirements of the coffee plant are combined to an unusual degree in the mountains of Colombia. The tierras templadas, between 1,000 and 2,000 meters, offer optimum temperature requirements for coffee and virtually everywhere at these elevations rainfall is adequate to support normal growth. It is on the flanks of the three great cordilleras, their well-drained slopes so steep as to be entirely unsuited to mechanized agriculture, that the cafetales are found. No other crop of sufficient value to withstand the high transportation costs to export markets has been able to compete for these lands. Moreover, the simplicity of processing coffee for shipment has

TABLE 12
PERCENTAGE OF TOTAL COLOMBIA COFFEE PRODUCED IN VARIOUS DEPARTMENTS, 1913–1914 AND 1956–1959[a]

Department	1913–1914	1956–1959
Caldas	18.7	30.5
Antioquia	17.3	16.5
Valle	4.7	13.0
Tolima	5.6	16.2
Cundinamarca	18.7	8.0
Norte de Santander	18.7	3.1
All others	16.3	12.7

[a] Kathryn H. Wylie, *The Agriculture of Colombia*, United States Dept. Agriculture, Foreign Agriculture Bull. No. 1 (Washington, 1942), p. 40; *Boletín de Estadística*, F.N.C.

made it a crop particularly attractive to the hard-working peasants who have settled this part of the cordillera.

It is clearly the extensive volcanic soils in the middle Cauca trough and on the flanks of the Central Cordillera which have tipped the balance of coffee production so strongly from the Eastern Cordillera toward the Antioqueño departments in the last thirty years. Here the requirements of the coffee tree, a well-drained, unleached soil, rich in organic content and available plant nutrients, were especially well met both on the Tertiary lavas of the Cerro Bravo-Mellizos complex and on the more recent tuffaceous ash mantle which has been superimposed upon the slopes of the Central Cordillera as far north as Sonsón (map 2). The deep, loess-like Quindío ash soils of Caldas and northwest Tolima, particularly the rolling hills of the Quindío basin, where erosion is at a minimum, are considered the most productive coffee lands of Colombia.

Coffee

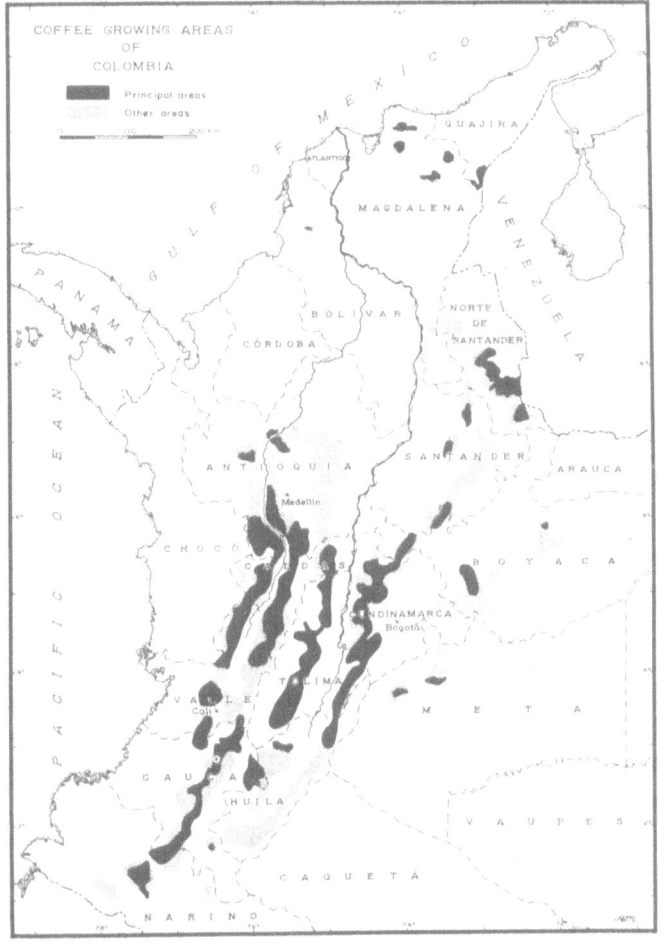

Map 8. Coffee Growing Areas of Colombia.
(Source: Federación Nacional de Cafeteros)

The overwhelming dominance of the Antioqueño departments in Colombian coffee production today, and the shift of the center of the industry westward from the Eastern Cordillera, is clearly indicated in table 12. If half of the Tolima production is considered to originate in the Antioqueño municipios of the northwest, then better than 70 per cent of Colombian coffee production is today of Antioqueño origin. In addition, a considerable part of the trans-Magdalena production of Tolima and Cundinamarca, especially from the larger plantations, is

TABLE 13
NUMBER OF COFFEE PLANTATIONS OF MORE THAN 60 HECTARES, 1932

Department	More than 100 hectares	60–100 hectares	Total
Cundinamarca	91	68	157
Santander	63	51	114
Tolima	60	62	122
Antioquia	41	65	106
Norte de Santander	38	38	76
Magdalena	15	7	22
Caldas	5	23	28
Valle	4	3	7

in the hands of transplanted Antioqueños. The valley of the Río Cunday in Tolima, near the Cundinamarca border, is reported, for instance, to be settled predominantly by people with Antioqueño surnames.

In 1932 the National Federation of Coffee Growers conducted a coffee census of Colombia which has since been repeated only for Tolima and Cundinamarca (1940).[11] It provided striking evidence of the parcelization of the land in the Antioqueño coffeegrowing regions (see table 13). In *minifundista* Caldas, which produces one-third of Colombia's coffee, there were only 28 cafetales of more than 60 hectares. Only in Fredonia (Antioquia) and Líbano (Tolima), among the Antioqueño municipios, are large coffee haciendas numerous. In comparison with those of Brazil, where plantations containing several million trees are not uncommon, even the largest Colombia plantation looks small.[12]

Colombia's favored position in the world coffee market has undergone substantial erosion in recent years as low-cost African producers have invaded the world market. Colombian production currently (1966) accounts for 12 to 14 per cent of world output, down from more than 20 per cent two decades earlier. World green coffee production averaged 46 million sacks per year in the 1961–1965 period, distributed approximately as follows.[14]

Area	Percentage
Brazil	35.4
Colombia	13.2
Central America-Mexico	13.3
Other Western Hemisphere	5.9
Africa	28.4
Asia and Oceania	3.8

Oversupply has brought continuing weakness in world prices and the growing realization in Colombia that the country has become excessively dependent on a single crop (coffee produces nearly 70 per cent of the country's export earnings; the 900,000 hectares in coffee exceeds the area planted to maize). Since 1963 Colombia has been a party to the International Coffee Agreement which is designed to stabilize world prices through the employment of export quotas. Present Colombian coffee policy is to reduce the amount of land under coffee but, especially on the more rugged volcanic slopes of the Antioqueño country, there are few alternative forms of land use available.

Until the completion of the railroad linking Antioquia with Cali and Buenaventura in 1942 virtually all Antioquia-grown coffee was exported by the Magdalena river route and the Atlantic ports of Cartagena and Barranquilla (map 9). Today the movement is almost completely reversed and almost all Antioquia coffee (and 85 per cent of all Colombian production) moves either by rail or truck to the maritime terminals at Buenaventura. The new complex of 60 coffee-storage silos recently constructed in Medellín seems likely to divert some of this traffic back to the Caribbean ports via the Troncal del Occidente, but there are no prospects for revival of the

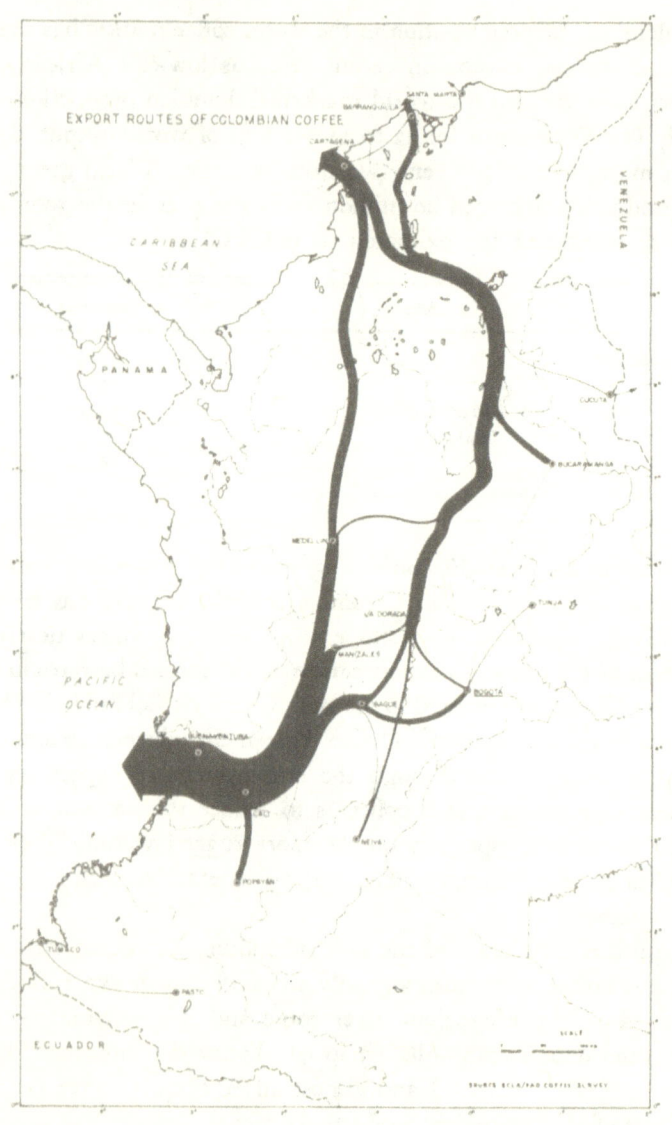

Map. 9. Export Routes of Colombian Coffee. (Source: ECLA/FAO Coffee Survey)

slow and costly Magdalena river coffee trade.

From the beginning Caldas-grown coffee moved chiefly to the port at Buenaventura, first using river transport on the upper Cauca between La Virginia and Cali and later the Ferrocarril del Pacífico which, by 1928, had penetrated inland to Manizales and Armenia. Earlier, in 1922, another competitive factor had been introduced by the opening of the Manizales-Mariquita aerial cable which until recently diverted a small proportion of the coffee from northern Caldas to the Magdalena river route.

Despite the revolution in transportation which has swept Colombia in the last twenty-five years, the mule is still the basic vehicle of transport. The topography of most of the coffee zone virtually forbids the construction of feeder truck roads, so that probably 80 per cent of the crop must move by muleback for at least part of the journey to the local markets. This dependence on pack transport seems certain to continue for as long as coffee is grown on these precipitous slopes. In 1945 costs of moving coffee from interior markets to the coast ranged from 1 to 2 cents (U.S.) a pound, the figure for most of Antioquia and Caldas being slightly higher than for other producing regions.

On small coffee fincas, where the family members are able to handle the work and where most of the food requirements may be grown within the cafetal, the only equipment necessary is a cheap, hand-operated pulping machine (*depulpadora*) to remove the outside skin and pulp from the ripe berries. After pulping, the beans are fermented, washed, and dried on little transportable trays or on cement patios, the resulting product being parchment coffee (*pergamino*). Some of the first coffee exported to England went as parchment.

Large trilladoras, in which the parchment hull is mechanically removed and the olive-green beans are polished, graded, and sacked, first appeared in Cundinamarca and then on the large haciendas of Fredonia. Soon contract trilladoras operated by steam or electricity were established in the larger market centers. Antioqueño towns with more than three operating public trilladoras in 1945 included: Medellín 13, Armenia 7, Líbano 6, Pereira 5, Manizales 4, and Santa Rosa de Cabal 4. Others were situated in smaller towns such as Andes, Bolombolo, Bolívar, Concordia, Sonsón, and Belalcázar.

To combat monopolistic tendencies, to improve credit and marketing facilities, to promote sales, and to establish research centers, a semi-official organization, the Federación Nacional de Cafeteros, was founded in 1927, financed by a tax on each sack of coffee exported from Colombia. Soundly and intelligently administered for the common benefit of all Colombian coffeegrowers, it has had a salutary effect on the industry, and has remained happily aloof from internal politics. Among the services of the Federation has been the standardization according to producing regions of Colombian coffee types, formerly in chaos on the foreign market. It is interesting that these arbitrary geographical areas are not related to elevation, soils, or methods of beneficiation but simply follow administrative lines. Thus "Medellín" coffee, which has brought a slight premium over the other grades in the foreign markets, may include coffee from anywhere in the departmeht of Antioquia, whether from the red schist soils of Cañasgordas, the crystalline uplands of Campamento or Caracolí, or the rich volcanic regions of Fredonia and Andes. "Manizales," "Armenia," and "Sevilla" coffee have all sold at prices only fractions of a cent below "Medellíns" and, on brief occasions, above it. The maintenance of this price differential in favor of the Antioqueño coffees involves a curiously empirical set of standards, in part fixed by tradition. It has been commonly said, however, that Antioqueño-grown coffees have brought premium prices because they have been more carefully picked and processed and also because they are, on the average, grown at slightly higher elevations than the coffees of other regions.

The widespread use of shade on Colombia plantations gives the country the superficial appearance of a natural woodland. The earliest Antioquia plantations were apparently shaded by trees intentionally left from the virgin forest, as is still occasionally done in areas of marginal productivity such as the valley of the Río Nus. Complete clearing, burning, and replanting of selected and properly spaced shade trees soon become general, even though Doctor Ospina, on the basis of his Guatemala experience, had left the question open. His son Tulio had returned from Costa Rica urging the abandonment of all shade trees.[15]

The merits of shade in coffee culture have been discussed for many decades in Colombia, as in other coffee countries, but few Antioqueños today would consider setting out a plantation without it. The evidence, much of it empirical, suggests that any superiority of shade-grown coffee must be attributed to something other than any better quality inherent in the flavor and aroma of the bean.[16] The principal influence of shade is on the vegetative growth habit and life span of the plant, one of its most important consequences being a prolongation of the ripening period. As a result, the bushes have to be gone over many times and each ripe, red berry picked individually by hand. In Brazil, on the other hand, where coffee is grown without shade and the market quality is inferior, the berries ripen sufficiently close together to permit the harvesting to be completed at a single picking. In stripping the clusters of berries from the plant with a single pull of the hand some dried berries and some green berries are inevitably included. It is these latter especially which are believed to contain the acids which give the harsh bitterness to coffee and distinguish the Santos types from the suaves of Central America and Colombia.

In wet, cloudy years shaded cafetales are at a disadvantage, and at the upper limits of coffee cultivation the lower temperatures make shade less important. In most years and within most of the coffee belt, however, plantations grown without shade go excessively to woody growth, the fruit is smaller, and the flowers are likely to drop during hot days. Moreover, although the unshaded coffee yields very abundantly in its first harvests, it is much shorter lived than the shade-grown variety and its entangled, woody growth soon makes picking excessively difficult. The nitrogenous litter from leguminous shade trees has generally been considered an important factor in maintaining high yields. In Antioquia and Caldas the larger trees serve as soil anchors on the steeper coffee slopes, which would wash and gully within a very few years under clean cultivation were it not for the stabilizing effect of the root systems and the organic litter derived from the shade trees. Finally, there is the recently recognized function of trees and tree crops in minimizing leaching and consequent deterioration of soils under conditions of tropical rainfall, a consideration which has long-range implications of paramount importance.[17] In establishing his cafetal under shade the Antioqueño settler may have been even wiser than he knew.

During its first three or four years, or until a plantation is in bearing, provisional shade is everywhere provided by plantains (*dominicos*). Maize and yuca are also frequently grown as intercalary crops, providing an important food reserve for the small grower and a margin against the contingencies of the coffee market. Occasionally, as at higher elevations in the Quindío and around Salamina, plantains provide the only shade in mature plantations. Everywhere some of them are allowed to remain to supply victuals to the owners' or workers' families even after their shade function has been taken over by the larger trees. They require no care, reproducing themselves naturally from suckers wherever the shade is not too dense. Oranges, grapefruit, avocados, and mangoes are also commonly encountered in mature cafetales, providing fresh fruit for the workers and their families. Other economic plants occasionally encountered include *chachafruto* (*Erythrina edulis*), *cañafístula* (*Cassia moschata*), and cinchona; even the sweet, white pulp of the giant beans of the *guamo machete* are loved by children and sometimes sold in markets.

Among the permanent shade trees every section has its favorite. For Antioqueños the many species of native *guamos* (*Inga* spp.) are overwhelmingly the most important. They are rapid-growing, leguminous trees with broad, leathery leaves and a spreading crown. Of them, that most commonly used in the past has been the *guamo bejuco* (*I. spuria*), distinguishable by its long, twisted, hairy, cylindrical pods, striated longitudinally. Subject to a blight in recent years, it has been increasingly supplemented by the larger, better spreading *guamo machete* (*I. spectabilis*), already common in the Quindío where it is sometimes known as *Santafereño*.

In earlier Antioquia plantations a much-favored shade tree was the handsome *pisquín* (*Albizzia* spp.) which was especially desirable for its high, umbrella-like crown which permitted a soft sunlight to filter through to the ground. Short-lived and shallow-rooted, it was easily toppled by heavy winds with consequent damage to the coffee trees beneath and was finally abandoned. Many of the cafetales of Fredonia and Venecia are strewn with giant logs of fallen shade trees in partial decay.

Although shade may improve the vigor and longevity of the coffee plant, it brings with it evils, especially where it is excessively dense. Fear of the leaf blight *Stilbum flavidum* (*gotero*) has in recent years led some planters to dispense with all shade except bananas, but this in turn has led to serious die-back at lower elevations where *gotero* is the most serious. More important but less understood is the threat to human health of the damp, putrescent environment within the deceptively beautiful cafetales.

The problem of shade has been complicated by the exhaustion of the easily available supplies of fuel wood and lumber in many regions, such as the Quindío, where the only utilizable reserves are the shade trees within the coffee fincas. Wood thinned from them provides an important source of supplementary income which, during periods of depressed coffee prices, may be valued even above the coffee. Local legislation has been necessary to restrict the cutting of shade trees in cafetales, which woodcutters have frequently invaded in preference to the long trips into the forested upcountry of the cordilleras.

In Antioquia the common method of pruning is to top the coffee tree at a height of 1½ meters after the first harvest. This cutting must be made, the campesino is likely to tell you, during the period of the crescent moon. It leaves a single-trunked tree which can easily be picked without the aid of a ladder and has been favorably compared to the Costa Rica (multiple-trunk) and Guatemala (double-trunk) systems which have been under experiment at the Chinchiná experiment station. Free growth, without any pruning, was the original system employed in Santander. It is still practiced in some cafetales on the east flank of the central range (Manzanares, Fresno) and in the Nus region of Antioquia, but always on marginal plantations.

Use of seedbeds for propagating plants for new cafetales has long been practiced by most Antioqueño coffeegrowers. It was strongly urged in Ospina's brochure of 1880. However, many campesinos still make their plantings from chance volunteers which spring up in the cafetal and do not make any seed selection whatsoever. According to Chardón, this seedbed preparation by the "Antioquia System," which he described, after a visit to Fredonia in 1928, has since been adopted in Puerto Rico.[13] Where he observed Antioqueño colonists of small means clearing new lands in the Valle del Cauca, however, he was surprised to find that they did not employ the seedbed method which he had seen first practiced in Fredonia.

Harvest congestion is minimized in Colombian cafetales because of the prolongation of the picking period over two periods of several weeks each, normally falling during the time of heaviest rains. As a result, almost no migratory labor is employed, the few large haciendas maintaining resident families on the basis of one to each five thousand trees, these families may contract to work either for wages or on shares. In the latter case a family head is assigned a given part of the cafetal for which he is responsible, and if outside assistance is required it is obtained and paid for by this subcontractor. Picking is especially the occupation of the young girls (*chapoleras*) and their group singing as they work their way through the ripening coffee is one of the traditional features of the season.

As with many other tree crops there is a tendency for good years to follow bad, probably owing to the strain placed on the plant during seasons of exceptional yield, induced by either the weather or overpruning. In 1944 thousands of trees died off in the Quindío following a year of bumper crops. The 400,000-tree cafetal of Luís Arango at Tebaida alone lost 50,000 trees from this cause.

Coffee planters have favored the steeper slopes for their plantings both because of their better drainage and because they fall predominantly within the tierra templada. It is not unusual to find slopes of 40 to 45 degrees under cultivation in northern Caldas and southwestern Antioquia, and there are frequent reports of injuries and deaths to campesinos falling from their clearings (*rozas*). Clean cultivation, as is practiced with maize, is especially disastrous on such slopes. The rate of soil wastage in coffeegrowing is only moderate, for the broad leaves of the coffee plants and shade trees both cushion the force of torrential rains, and the more elaborate root systems help anchor the soil.[19] In some areas, as around Fredonia and Venecia, large lava boulders provide a sort of natural terracing which may prolong the life of the plantations. Yet on few of the steeper slopes are worn-out cafetales ever replanted. More frequently, declining production in the later years leads to premature abandonment to yeraguá gordura pasture for a few blanco oreji-negro cattle. Such steep-sloped municipios as Sonsón, Salamina, and Aguadas have long been major centers of emigration, their worn-out lands being abandoned[20] for the new and better soils toward the Quindío and Tolima. Yet, given the steepness of these slopes, it seems astonishing at first to find the country in as good shape as it is. The explanation lies in the recency of occupance together with the conservative nature of tree-crop cultivation. Colombia has some badly eroded lands—Hugh Bennett of the United States Soil Conservation Service has said that 50 per cent of its arable lands have either been ruined or badly damaged by erosion[21]—but they are the older areas of occupance, especially on the thin primary soils of the uplands of the Eastern Cordillera[22] and the gold-bearing region of the Antioquia massif. A growing recognition of the seriousness of the erosion problem has not yet brought any widespread adoption of methods for reorganization of the cultivation system. Indeed, it appears probable that the cultivation of coffee without protective shade trees may increase. In the last few years a new variety known as Caturra, introduced from Brazil, has been experimentally planted without shade on a substantial number of fincas. It comes into early and flush production, with yields sometimes three or four times that of standard types, but the life of the coffee tree is short. The area in Caturra seems likely to increase sharply for, despite inferior quality and aggravated erosion hazards, returns on invested capital appear to be higher than from shade-grown varieties.

A five-year plan for the development and economic diversification of coffee-rich rural Caldas (1963-1967), supported by external loans, aimed to increase the rate of economic growth while reducing coffee's role in the department's gross product from 61 to 49 per cent, but alternative uses of the steep volcanic slopes that are the most marginal cafetales has proven difficult to find. In Antioquia, too, an *"Operación Café,"* initiated in 1964, aims at increasing coffee yields and quality but not total production ("más cafe en menos tierra") which, at 1.3 million sacks, makes the department the leading producer in Colombia. It is significant, however, that present levels of coffee production in Colombia have been maintained in the face of highly discriminatory special taxes and a dollar conversion rate which, in 1966, represented the equivalent of a charge of 51 per cent on the original value of the crop.

XI. TRANSPORTATION

RESPECT FOR the poisoned arrows of the unreduced Chocó Indians and the region's reputation as a fever-ridden swampland contributed to the abandonment of the first route of the conquistadores into Antioquia from the Caribbean by way of the Gulf of Urabá. The overriding factor, however, was the restrictive trade policy of colonial Spain which made Cartagena the only legal port of call and which entirely excluded trade with flags of other nations. Only contraband traffic followed this short cut to the sea after 1540, for, although the Caribbean coast here was only half as far from Antioquia as at Cartagena, navigation of the Río Atrato and its tributaries and the entry of foreign ships into the Gulf of Urabá were prohibited under penalty of death. Nevertheless the contraband trade was at times considerable. Antonio Arévalo described it in 1761:

> From the mouth of the Río Guacuba [Río León] to the city of Antioquia is sixteen leagues, eight of these by boat and eight by good trail. But use of this route is for the illicit introduction of goods bought from foreign ships which frequent the gulf for this purpose. These are very numerous because of the speed and ease of transport, which is much cheaper than the regular overland road, which takes three months.[1]

Another account in 1793 also mentions the Río León route to Antioquia as still "well-known to smugglers."[2] Other contraband for the upper Cauca region ascended the Río Atrato to Lloró (above Quibdó) and thence a one-day canoe journey up the Río Andagueda to Bagadó where cargo was reloaded for land transport to Cartago and Cali.

Commercial relations between Antioquia and the mines of the upper Chocó seem to have been slight until after 1779, when a new route was opened linking Urrao with the warehouses at Arquía (adjacent to the pueblo of Bebará) on a navigable branch of the Río Atrato.[3] Traveling time on this route for a loaded Indian carrier was ten days from Santa Fé de Antioquia. This trade, however, was of a very limited nature and the upper Choco, long politically attached to the province of Cauca, continued to be supplied through Cartago until the recent opening of the Bolombolo-Quibdó automobile road.

---

[1] For notes to chap. xi, see pp. 208–210.

Puerto Espíritu Santo is a place name almost forgotten in Antioquia, yet during most of the colonial period it was the principal port of entry for merchandise and travelers proceeding to Santa Fé de Antioquia from Cartagena and Mompox.⁴ The lower Río Cauca was easily navigated as far as Cáceres, and with more difficulty dugouts and rafts could be poled upstream thirty miles to Espíritu Santo, from which point it was ten days overland to Santa Fé. It was a fifteen- to sixteen-day journey for *canoas* ascending from the Río Magdalena, but going downstream required only two and a half days. Numerous early accounts describe the dangers of navigating the deeply entrenched Cauca gorge above Cáceres, where losses of cargo in the rapids and whirlpools were numerous. Traffic ceased during the summer months when the river was low.⁵

In 1788 Mon y Velarde wrote that Espíritu Santo was still the port of entry for all commerce with Santa Fé de Antioquia, but that there were no buildings standing.⁶ Less than twenty years later the route had been abandoned, although canalization of the Cauca was beginning to be discussed. The abandonment of Espíritu Santo, in an inaccessible, broken, and only recently settled part of Antioquia, followed the decline in importance of Santa Fé⁷ and the opening of the new Palagua and Juntas roads from the Río Magdalena to Ríonegro and Medellín.⁸

The old Nare road had been the most important Indian trade route linking the Magdalena with the interior of Antioquia even before the coming of the white man. During most of the colonial period it was the chief link between Bogotá and Medellín. From Bogotá the route descended to the river port of Honda, from where dugouts or rafts were taken down the Río Magdalena for two and a half days to the tiny settlement at the mouth of the Río Nare. From Nare the road went overland in a northwesterly direction, following the valley of the Río Nus to Yolombó and thence to the Río Porce. An important branch continued northward from Yolombó to the gold camps of Zaragoza and Remedios, and another connected westward with Santa Rosa de Osos and Antioquia.

The privilege of maintaining the warehouses at Puerto Espíritu Santo and Nare was much sought after and was the subject of much eighteenth-century litigation. The concessionaires were in a strategic

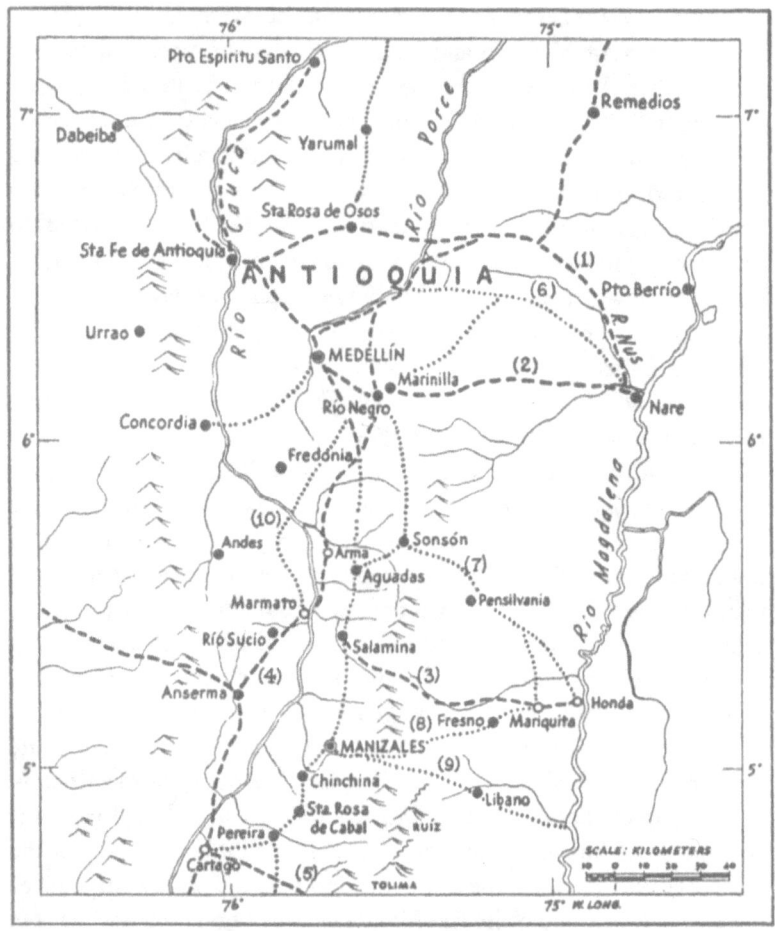

Map. 10. Major Pack Trails (*Caminos de Herradura*). Broken line represents Colonial trails; dotted line represents nineteenth-century trails.

(1) Nare
(2) Juntas-Palagua
(3) Herveo
(4) Popayán
(5) Quindío
(6) Nus
(7) Villegas
(8) La Elvira
(9) Ruiz
(10) Caramanta

position, for river craft were seldom available to permit outbound travelers to continue their trip either to Honda or Mompox. Likewise cargoes and passengers destined for Antioquia were subject to even longer delays because the lack of pasture made it impossible for pack trains to be held at the ports for more than one day. Although a warehouse charge of 2 *reales* a mule load (*carga*) was authorized on all goods passing through Nare, the buildings were mere straw structures, leaky and worm-eaten.[9]

So long and arduous was the overland trip from Nare that it was generally necessary to take twice as many mules as there were loads to be carried. Not infrequently in winter entire mule trains were lost in the quagmires of the deeply worn trail and, occasionally, a mule was killed by pumas (*tigres*). Governor Silvestre's relation of his experience on the Camino del Nare in 1775 was typical:

> When I entered by said road to serve this government, having brought down 50 mules to carry me with my servants and baggage, I spent seventeen days getting to Yolombó and was detained there for fifteen days more while they went after some mules loaded with clothing and supplies which we had been forced to leave in the forests. Twice additional mules had to be sent to our aid, the owners having lost 17 of them....[10]

Delays at river crossings were especially numerous and irritating. The crossing of the Nus, accomplished by an unsteady rope bridge, usually consumed an entire day. The average time required for a trip from Nare to Medellín was twelve to fourteen days, which in good weather might be reduced to ten days. As a general rule two drivers (*arrieros*) could handle ten mules, each animal carrying 200 to 250 pounds.[11]

A new and more direct road to Ríonegro was ordered constructed in 1779. It ran from the new Palagua warehouses, seven miles upstream on the Magdalena from Nare, directly west through San Carlos and the flourishing commercial centers of Marinilla and Ríonegro to Medellín. It was not only shorter than the older road by way of Yolombó, but provided some pasturage in its higher sections and abundant palm nuts toward the river. Very few travelers passed over the old Nare road without contracting "the fever," yet witnesses in its first years claimed that the Palagua route was singularly free from pests or illnesses.

Within a few years after the opening of the road the principal warehouses had been moved inland to Junta del Nare, at the confluence of the Río Nare and the Río Samaná, five leagues upstream from the Magdalena and at the head of canoe navigation. These warehouses soon became the most important point of deposit for merchandise destined for the interior of Antioquia, and the Juntas road became the principal link of the province with the outside world.[12]

In the early nineteenth century a second new route cutting several leagues off of the old Camino del Nare came into use. This by-passed Yolombó to the south, following the high interfluve between the Río Nus and the Río Nare and passing through Santo Domingo. The warehouses for this road were at Remolino, one league below Juntas on the left bank of the Nare, near the site of the plant which today supplies Medellín with cement.

This development considerably increased the importance of the old river town of Nare (Islitas) which now became a collecting point for goods entering Antioquia over either of the roads.[13] Merchants from Mompox moved here in some numbers when that old colonial trading center on a shallow arm of the Magdalena found itself stranded following the introduction of the first steamboat in 1824. Freed slaves, especially from the Yolombó mines, added to the population in the 'forties and 'fifties so that since that time the population has been predominantly Negroid. Not until the end of the Thousand Days War in 1902 did Puerto Berrío, at the railhead, finally replace the Nare ports as Antioquia's front door.[14]

Another alternate route between Bogotá and Antioquia, occasionally used in early colonial times, was the long, tedious trip over the Herveo. It was a one month's journey in good weather and two months' in the rainy season, with numerous uncertain stream crossings. Between Mariquita and Ríonegro it was through unsettled, forested lands except on the páramo, where there was "pasture for 200 mules." On the eastern side of the cordillera the trail crossed the turbulent Río Guarinó more than thirty times. However, the tax on cacao and clothing levied on goods passing through Honda was thus avoided.[15] Although traffic between Bogotá and Antioquia ceased using this route after the opening of the Juntas road, it remained in use for many years as the main supply line to the mines of Marmato and Supía, until it was supplanted by the new roads built from Manizales to the eastward after 1850.

Throughout the colonial period Antioquia's commercial and ecclesiastical ties with the south were much closer than with other parts of New Granada. Yet the Popayán road was always in extremely bad repute. The pack-train trip to that city from Medellín required twenty-five days in good weather and more in bad, most of it through malarial lands. Restrepo[16] called it "perhaps the worst and most dilapidated" of all the routes entering the province, so that the mail and much of the traffic in clothes from Quito and cacao from Timaná passed by way of Honda and Nare.

From Medellín the route went by way of Ríonegro and Arma Viejo, crossing the Río Cauca at the Paso de Bufú and proceeding through Anserma, Cartago, and Cali. The trip as far as Cartago was considered half way (eleven to twelve days). It was across extremely broken terrain which necessitated the crossing and recrossing of a large number of streams and during rainy seasons and, frequently, they were not fordable.

In 1808 one witness[17] testified that with loaded mules it was impossible to make the round trip to Popayán in less than two months and that on one of his trips he had been gone four months owing to bad weather. To return in two months it was necessary to change mules at Cartago "since there are no animals with sufficient strength to carry a load the entire distance to Popayán." He recalled that on one occasion he had been detained eleven days at one river crossing and for shorter periods at other streams in which mules were drowned.

Antioquia has always been renowned for the poor quality of its roads. The hearsay report of Alexander von Humboldt, who ascended the Magdalena to Honda and, later, crossed from Bogotá to Popayán by way of the Quindío road without entering Antioquia, was to be elaborated on by many later travelers:

> The whole of the Province of Antioquia is surrounded by mountains so difficult to pass that they who dislike entrusting themselves to the skill of a carrier and who are not strong enough to travel on foot from Santa Fé de Antioquia to Boca de Nare or Río Samaná, must relinquish all thoughts

of leaving the country. I was once acquainted with an inhabitant of this province so immensely bulky that he had not met with more than two mulattoes capable of carrying him; and it would have been impossible for him to return home if these carriers had died while he was on the Magdalena, at Mompox or Honda...."[12]

Even today, when railroads, trucks, and aircraft have penetrated the outer barrier of forests and mountains, the pack mule and pack ox remain indispensable to the mountain-bound Antioqueño economy. Loaded pack trains still tread the paved streets of Medellín every morning, and in Manizales prices of maize, yuca, and plantains rise abruptly in rainy weeks when the city is isolated from the surrounding fincas which supply its public market.

Wheeled vehicles remained a novelty in many parts of Antioquia until late years and many Antioqueños campesinos have flown from cow-pasture airports to Medellín to see their first automobiles. Two-wheeled, high-set jaunting carts were used in the valleys of Aburrá and Río Negro, where the topography was favorable, but elsewhere dependence was wholly upon pack trains. President Berrío's project to extend a wagon road to the Río Magdalena by way of Yolombó had been abandoned with a change of administration in 1876 and the substitution of the ill-starred railroad from Puerto Berrío to Medellín. Today, ninety years later, there is still no road for wheeled vehicles, except the railroad, to the Río Magdalena. Motor roads did not begin to be built until World War I, the first one having been built from Cisneros to Santiago over the *cuesta* of La Quiebra to link the two completed sections of the Ferrocarril de Antioquia.

Construction and maintenance of pack trails (*caminos de herradura*) during the colonial period had been most frequently the responsibility of Indians who gave their labor in lieu of taxes. In the nineteenth century it was more often accomplished through privileged companies which were given the right to collect tolls as well as title to public lands. The contracts stipulated the tolls which might be collected, the bridges, pastures, warehouses to be maintained, and the engineering specifications of the road. This system, in essence a heritage from Crown privileges, provided the means for meeting the growing demands for more and better roads during a century of political instability and empty treasuries, when the financing of major public works of any kind was notoriously difficult.

The Sonsón-Mariquita road, urged by Villegas forty years earlier, finally was completed by forced patriot labor during the revolution. As Antioqueño settlement penetrated into the volcanic uplands of Ruiz and Tolima, other transcordillera routes were constructed to the south. The difficult Herveo route which had carried traffic from Honda via Salamina to the Marmato mines, was replaced by two new roads terminating at Manizales, the Camino del Ruiz from Ambalema and La Elvira from Honda, both operated by privileged companies for many years. Two new parallel, north-south routes followed the Antioqueño settlement frontier on either side of the Río Cauca, replacing the old camino real to Popayán. The more traveled of the two went by way of Abejorral, Sonsón, Aguadas, Salamina, and Manizales to the Quindío and Cartago; the other from Santa Bárbara through Caramanta to Ríosucio and Anserma. Several bridges were also constructed across the turbulent Río Cauca by privileged companies, especially after 1850, including those at Marmato (La Caña), La Pintada, Jericó (La Iglesia), Antioquia (Puente del Occidente), and Ituango (Pescadero).

The Quindío road, classical route across the Central Cordillera for travelers going from Bogotá to the Valle, Popayán, and Pacific ports, was not important for Antioqueño travelers until the settlement of the Quindío basin in the 'eighties, but Humboldt's description of it in 1801 provides a faithful picture of the hardships of travel on these *caminos de herradura,* even at a much later date:

> The mountain of Quindiu [*sic*] is considered as the most difficult passage in the Cordillera of the Andes. It is a thick, uninhabited forest which in the finest season cannot be traversed in less than ten or twelve days. Not even a hut is to be seen, nor can any means of subsistence be found. Travellers at all times of the year furnish themselves with a month's provisions since it often happens that, by the melting of the snows and the sudden swell of the torrents, they find themselves so circumstanced that they can descend neither on the side of Cartago, nor on that of Ibagué.... The pathway which forms the passage of the Cordillera is only 3 or 4 decimeters in breadth and has the appearance in several places of a gallery dug, and left open to the sky.... The streamlets, which flow down the

mountains, have hollowed out gullies six or seven meters deep. Along the crevices, which are full of mud, the traveller is forced to grope his passage, the darkness of which is increased by the thick vegetation that covers the opening above. The oxen, which are the beasts of burden commonly made use of in the country, can scarcely force their way through these galleries, some of which are 200 meters in length...."[19]

The bulk of Antioquia's commerce during the nineteenth century was with Great Britain, France and Germany following in that order. In 1879 the United States commercial agent in Medellín wrote that scarcely 1 per cent of the imports there originated in the United States.[20] Shipping charges on imported merchandise were, of course, high. River freight on the eight-day trip from Barranquilla to Islitas for one load (two 70-kilogram bales) was $3.20 (U.S.), whereas the cost of overland transport from Islitas to Medellín varied from 10 to 12 dollars a load plus another dollar for warehouse services. Pianos, machinery, and other out-size objects were swung on long bamboo poles and borne on the backs of a number of men over " a wretched bridle path that does not go over three consecutive kilometers of relatively level ground." The average time to Medellín for a loaded mule train was twelve to fifteen days, although travelers with light luggage made the trip in five.

Proper packing, the agent pointed out, had been an important factor in giving the European countries their trade advantage:

> The weight of each case or bale destined for Antioquia... should be between 65 and 70 kilogrammes; if packages weigh too little, as they are conveyed overland by muleback and a pair of packages constitutes a mule-load, full freight is charged on them, thus needlessly increasing the cost of conveyance; and if packages weigh more than 70 kilogrammes muleteers refuse to take them.
>
> American packing cases are generally made of one-inch and three-quarter inch boards and are in consequence a great deal too heavy. It must be borne in mind that goods imported into Antioquia are subject to two sets of specific duties on gross weight; one to the national and another to the state government.
>
> Another important point is to protect packages properly from the tropical rains to which they are exposed for several days before they reach their destinations. This again is scrupulously attended to in Europe and is either not attempted at all, or attempted ineffectually by American exporters...."[21]

Human carriers still compete with animals in the transport of freight in some parts of Colombia, especially during the rainy seasons, when the poorer pack trails became almost impassable for mules and oxen. In colonial Antioquia, especially, many of the major roads were considered passable only for human carriers. Since the average weight carried by a peon was from 75 to 100 pounds or about one-third of a mule load, they were referred to on tax and toll records as *peones con tercio*. Humboldt had heard that a few years before his visit to New Granada a project to improve the route from Nare to the interior for mules had had to be abandoned in the face of formal remonstrances by the carriers against mending the road.[22] Peñol, Guatapé, and Canoas were all miserable clusters of houses inhabited by poor peons who worked the road to Nare.

Neither asses nor horses have ever been popular among Antioqueños, the former especially being almost unknown in Antioquia and Caldas except for a few breeding farms, in contrast to the Caribbean coast and the upper Magdalena Valley where the ass is used almost exclusively as a beast of burden. Even the wealthiest Antioqueño ranchers prefer saddle mules to horses, for their surefootedness and stamina give them a decisive advantage on the rough mountain bridle trails.

At the end of the rainy seasons the mules may have to be replaced by oxen on routes where the shallow, heavy soils turn into a particularly sticky quagmire. Since oxen place their forefeet straight ahead (i.e., together), the mules which follow in their steps, find this an unnatural gait, and tire easily and stumble.[23] Such ox roads have always been avoided by travelers who would go on muleback.[24]

To be a *caporal* or pack-train owner was a respected profession in nineteenth-century Antioquia, and more than one of Medellín's leading families are said to descend from muleteers. Envigado was known as the leading horse and mule market of the region, but excellent mules also came from Bello and Barbosa, below Medellín, and from the higher *vegas* of El Retiro, which also supplied many of the oxen for the Manizales trade. Roadside inns (*tambos*) were unknown in Antioquia despite the great importance of pack transport, and muleteers and travelers alike carried their own tents or *bihao* leaves from

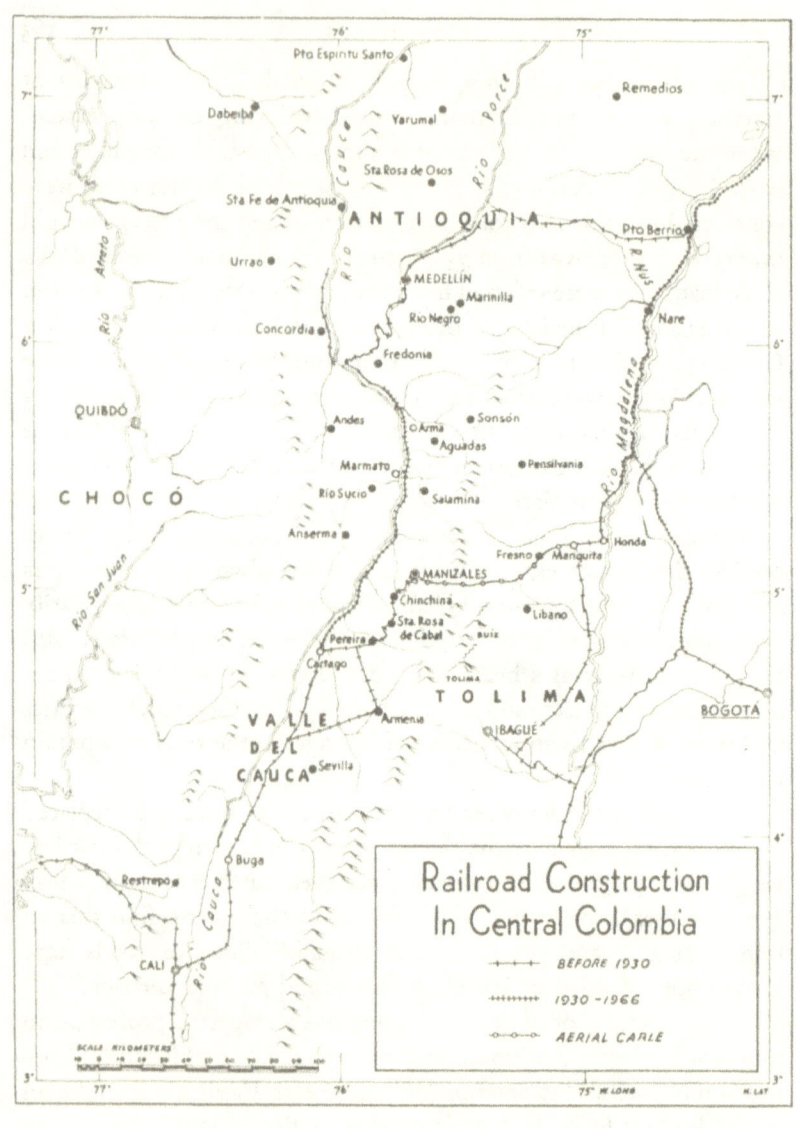

Map 11. Railroad Construction in Central Colombia.

which they constructed lean-tos for protection against the rains. Small areas of cleared, leveled earth lined with stones marked the traditional camping spots along the trail.

Canalization of the Río Cauca to provide Antioquia with an independent waterway to the Caribbean has been a project since colonial times. Although it is a broad, placid stream navigable by paddle wheelers both in its upper reaches, through the Valle, and again below Cáceres, its 160-mile middle course through the Antioqueño country is impeded by rapids, whirlpools, and submerged rocks as it knifes through the volcanic beds and the tremendous gorge below Santa Fé de Antioquia. The stretch between the Río Arma and the old capital can sometimes be navigated by rafts in periods of high water, as was done in the sixteenth century when Arma hogs were sent downstream to market "in five or six hours, but with great risk from the rapids."[35] Above and below, from La Virginia to the mouth of the Arma, and from the rapids of Juan García (Liborina) to Puerto Espíritu Santo, passage by any means is impossible.

Although the steamship *Santa Marta* reached Cáceres from Barranquilla in 1864, submerged sand bars and lack of a guaranteed outbound cargo discouraged others from following. Privileges and subsidies granted in the 'nineties to develop steam navigation on the lower Cauca below Puerto Valdivia had disappointing results.[36] Plans to link the head of navigation on the Río Cauca at Puerto Antioquia with Bolombolo and Medellín by rail (*Troncal de Occidente*) never materialized. Although funds were cut off in 1930, a 44-kilometer section, Bolombolo to Anzá, which was eventually to have joined with rails coming upstream from the Bajo Cauca, was completed. It operated occasional freights for some years despite the necessity of ferrying the Cauca at Bolombolo. Plans for its extension along the Cauca gorge and across the plains of Bolívar to Cartagena have long since been abandoned in the face of competition from highway and air traffic.

Following the launching of the first steamboat in the early 'nineties, commerce on the upper Cauca, between Cali and Cartago, reached very considerable proportions. Most of the coffee exported from Caldas before 1925 moved by water from La Virginia or Puerto Caldas to Cali (Puerto Isaacs), where it was transshipped by rail to Buenaventura. The Mariquita to Manizales aerial cable, and the extension of the Ferrocarril del Pacífico to Pereira and Manizales put the last of the eight paddle-wheelers out of business in the depression of the early 'thirties.

The upper Cauca is today again quiet, but from Cáceres, Caucasia, Margento, and Zaragoza gasoline launches, most of them operated out of Magangué, carry rice and plantains to the lower Magdalena ports, and a few larger barges move heavy mining equipment to Pato, Zaragoza, and Cáceres. For most products freight costs to Cartagena and Barranquilla from central Antioquia are much lower by truck than by the combined rail-river route. Indeed, by the 1960's Puerto Berrío had almost ceased to exist as a river port although it continued to play the role of regional marketplace and railroad junction. A petroleum products pipeline that links the Barranca Bermeja refinery with the Medellín market, following the railroad right-of-way, passes through the town.

The peculiar problems of transportation in these rugged mountains and the sudden demand for improved facilities which came with the coffee boom were met in Caldas by the construction of high-line aerial cables. Manizales' ridge-top site and the broken nature of the terrain surrounding it suggested some such device. Aerial cables ran out from the city in four directions by 1930.

Only the 73-kilometer Mariquita cable, begun in 1912 by an English company under contract with the national government, has survived until the present day. It is reputedly the longest aerial cable in the world. From its completion in 1922 until the arrival of the railroad six years later the aerial cable provided Manizales' only alternative to pack-train transport. Other cables were strung northwards to Aranzazu (Cable Aéreo del Norte) and from Manizales across the Río Chinchiná to Villamaría. A fourth, planned to link Manizales with the distant Chocó, was constructed for 10 kilometers before work was halted by the depression of the 'thirties, but it served as a local distribution line to the coffee regions below Manizales for several years before its abandonment in the face of trucking competition.[17] Other cables planned for Aguadas, Marsella, and Manzanares were never constructed.

The railroad from Puerto Berrío, which was to break down the isolation of Antioquia and revolutionize its commercial and industrial orientation, was fifty years in arriving. An American engineer of Cuban birth, Francisco J. Cisneros, had been summoned in 1874 by the government of Antioquia which, aided by a National Congress grant of money and public lands, contracted with him for the construction of a yard-gauge, single-track railroad from Puerto Berrío to Barbosa, exactly 100 miles, at a cost of $61,599 (U.S.) a mile. The job was to be completed in eight and a half years, with a maximum permissible grade of 6 per cent.[*]

TABLE 14

FREIGHT MOVED BY THE MARIQUITA AERIAL CABLE
(Both directions)

1923	28,765 tons
1925	36,944 tons
1935	35,132 tons
1945	50,921 tons

It was recognized that some sort of export agriculture must be developed to provide a pay load on the return trip to the river. Cisneros correctly saw the answer to this problem in the incipient coffee industry. Moreover, he was confident that by opening up these new and fertile lands along the valleys of the Nus and Porce the steady drain of Antioqueño emigrants to Cauca, Tolima, and Cundinamarca could be diverted.

Following his Antioquia operations, Cisneros contracted for construction of the Girardot, La Dorada, and Buenaventura-Cali railways as well as a Barranquilla streetcar line and various improvements at Magdalena river ports.[*] Civil war in 1885 forced the temporary abandonment of all of these projects and he disposed of his interests in them to the departmental and national governments. Cisneros is still honored throughout Colombia as the father of the railroads, having provided the initial impetus and overcome the formidable obstacles of malaria and politics.

In Antioquia the railroad had reached the valley of the Nus at Pavas (50 km.) on the border of the tierra caliente when the department took over in 1885. Already traffic over this completed sector

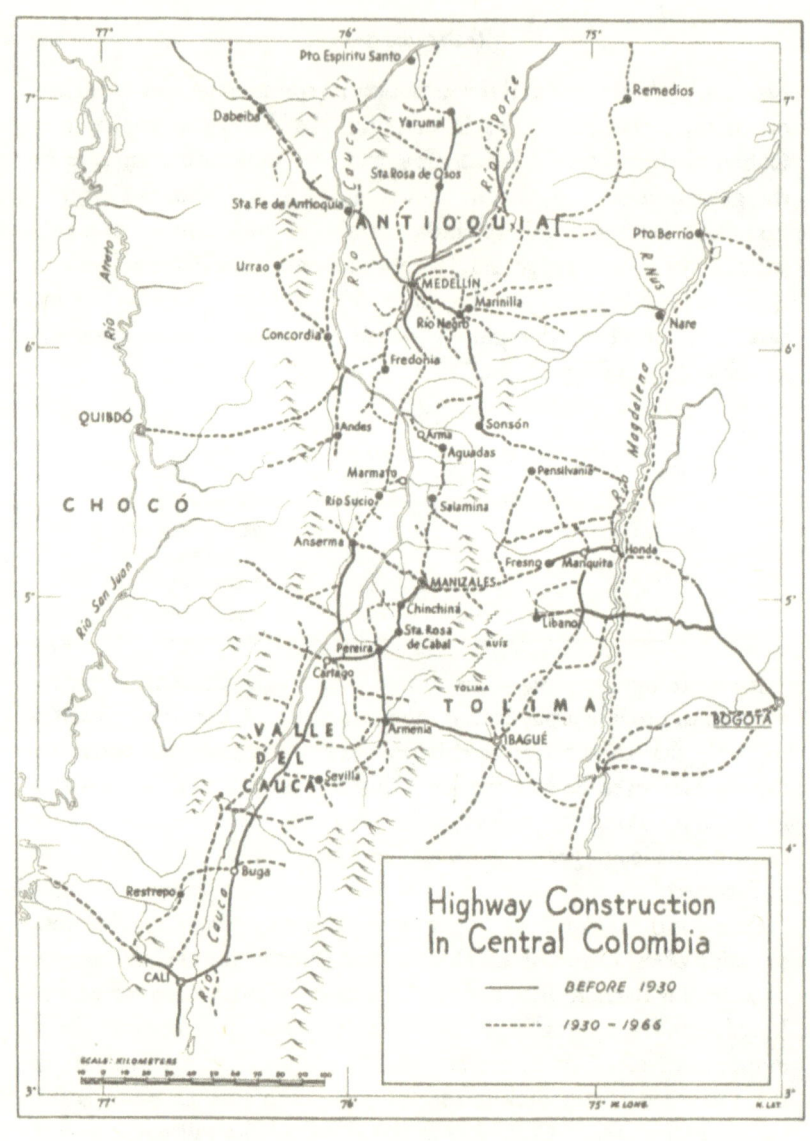

Map. 12. Highway Construction in Central Colombia.

exceeded that going through Islitas, cargo being transferred to the backs of mules at the railhead to continue the journey to Medellín. After one contract with an English construction company had resulted in a costly fiasco, the department, in 1892, established a three-man *junta* composed of the governor and two citizens to drive the line through to completion. Under this direction, and using local engineers and labor, the rails were continued on up the valley of the Nus to the new terminus of Cisneros (108 km.) from where a 27-kilometer motor road over the Quiebra de Santo Domingo joined with the 58-kilometer Porce section from Santiago to Medellín.

La Quiebra's 1,650-meter granitic barrier split the Ferrocarril de Antioquia into two separate sections for almost twenty years while engineers argued the relative merits of tunnels, aerial cables, funiculars, and highways. In 1926 a contract was finally awarded to a British company, Fraser, Brace Ltd., for the construction of a tunnel from Estación Limón to Santiago. The first train passed through the 3,742-meter tunnel on August 7, 1929, to set off celebrations throughout the department. Medellín was now only eight hours distant from the Río Magdalena.

Meanwhile a second railroad was under construction from Medellín westward toward the Río Cauca, work having been started in 1907 by an Antioqueño company, the Ferrocarril de Amagá. It was purchased by the department of Antioquia for integration with the Puerto Berrío line when work had reached a distance of 58 kilometers, at the head of the Quebrada Sinufaná, and a foreign firm contracted to extend the rails on to the Cauca over one of the toughest routes of any railroad in the country. In 1942 the tracks were linked at La Pintada to those of the national government's Ferrocarril del Pacífico to provide through, single-gauge track from Medellín to Cartago, Cali, Popayán, and Buenaventura.

From 1890 on surveys were conducted on several lines designed to link Medellín with the Chocó, Urabá, Anorí, and Cáceres, and for a time it looked as though the department would be webbed with rails.[20] A narrow-gauge line for gasoline-powered cars (Tranvía del Oriente) was actually constructed up the difficult scarp of the valley of Medellín, via Guarne, to Ríonegro and Marinilla and plans called for its extension to Peñol, Corcorná, Granada, Abejorral, Sonsón, and the Río Magdalena. The depression and the new highway (*carretera*) to Ríonegro doomed the project almost before operations had gotten under way, leaving the municipios of the Oriente saddled with debt.

In Caldas the topography was even less favorable for railroad development than in Antioquia. Work had been commenced by the department on the line running from the Río Cauca to Manizales in 1911, but it was eighteen years under construction before the last section of the zigzag climb from the Río Chinchiná bridge to the top of the Manizales hogback had been completed, providing an all-rail outlet to the Pacific. The Ferrocarril del Pacífico constructed a branch to Armenia which, linked with Ibagué by a new truck road over the Quindío, became the main trunk line between Bogotá and Buenaventura.

Completion of the controversial Ferrocarril del Atlántico in 1961, between La Dorada and the port of Santa Marta, gave the interior population centers of Colombia direct rail outlets to the Caribbean coast for the first time. This much-heralded axial route down the Magdalena valley followed the left bank of the river from La Dorada to Puerto Berrío, where it crossed to the right side over a handsome new trestle. At Puerto Berrío it linked up with the Ferrocarril de Antioquia, thus providing Medellín with direct rail connections with both Bogotá and a port on the Caribbean. By this time, however, highway transport linkages were already well established between the Antioquia capital and these same terminuses and the expected volume of rail freight movement failed to materialize. Completion of the petroleum products pipeline from Barranca Bermeja to Medellín in 1955 had further reduced the cargo potential of the Antioquia section of the line.

With Medellín securely linked by road and rail with ports on both the Pacific and Caribbean coasts the Magdalena river, long the lifeline of Antioquia and the rest of interior Colombia, has been all but abandoned for dry-cargo movements. The last paddle-wheel passenger boat was destroyed by fire some years ago. Puerto Berrío's once crowded wharves are today empty, despite the enormous increase in economic activity in the highland area it was built to serve.

Cargo handled at Puerto Berrío declined more than 50 per cent in the decade 1955–1965 and there have been further drops since.[31] The river had been at best an uncertain avenue of transit, with low-water interrupting navigation in the middle and upper courses for increasingly long periods of time. Shippers complained of inventory tie-ups, high losses through pilferage, and the costly cargo transfer at Puerto Berrío.

The sale in 1962 of the departmentally-owned Ferrocarril de Antioquia (Puerto Berrío-Medellín) to the nation, then bent on the development of an integrated rail net, could not have been more opportune from Antioquia's point of view. Since then its traffic has continued to decline and its roadbed and rolling stock to deteriorate.[32] Today it is in a dilapidated condition, fast becoming a relict of another era. The Antioquia economy is truck, air, and pipeline based, with a sturdy assist from the mule. Proceeds from the sales of the Medellín-Puerto Berrío railroad, engineered by then-Governor Ignacio Vélez Escobar, have been employed to set up an Instituto para el Desarrollo de Antioquia (IDEA), to provide low-interest loans to departmental municipios and other civic entities. The self-liquidating fund is managed by a semiautonomous corporation responsible directly to the governor of the department.

What the Colombians call *la revolución carretera* has had an even more profound and far-reaching effect on the internal economy of the Antioqueño country than did the coming of the railroad. Beginning in 1920 outlying markets, one by one, were linked by motor roads with Medellín or Manizales. Transport costs for moving crops to market dropped as much as 400 per cent.[33] Whereas the pack trails had generally followed in the wake of Antioqueño colonization in the nineteenth century, today the new motor roads pushing into the margins of the settled land (e.g., Dabeiba-Turbo, Sonsón-La Dorada, Bolívar-Quibdó, Cocorná-San Carlos) have become the axes of most active settlement, as the valley of the Nus had been during the construction of the Ferrocarril de Antioquia from Puerto Berrío.

In 1967 only three of Antioquia's 106 municipios lacked a road link with the departmental capital. Yet it was only 27 years earlier that the first highway had been pushed through the ring of mountains to give Medellín access to Manizales and the outside world by truck.

The decade of the fifties was one of tremendous advances in transportation everywhere in Colombia, but perhaps especially in Antioquia. In 1955 Medellín was linked to Cartagena and Barranquilla by the Troncal del Occidente, relieving Antioquia of its dependence on the Río Magdalena for the important Atlantic trade. The pipeline from the Magdalena oil fields was completed the same year and the Carretera al Mar, after three decades of intermittent work, was finally completed to Turbo on the Gulf of Urabá. A shortcut to Bogotá, by way of Sonsón and La Dorada, was also opened, obviating the more circuitous route through Manizales and across the flanks of the Volcán de Ruíz. On the west Quibdó, capital of the department of Chocó, had also been linked to Medellín by a road that may eventually be pushed through to the Pacific Coast at Bahía Solano. Every one of these involves tortuous mountain driving with a generous quota of slides, dust, and mud, but for the Antioqueño trucker, heir to the earlier *arriero* (mule-driver) tradition, that is the norm. Road maintenance is costly, and progress in paving is slow, but most of the routes are kept open through all but the worst of the rainy seasons. Work on a modern freeway (*autopista*) that would knife across the mountains of the Oriente to Bogotá was initiated in 1966, but its completion is many years away. Meanwhile, Bogotá lies 18 hours distance away by truck from Medellín, Cartagena perhaps 14 hours, Cali 8 hours.[14]

Air transport, even more than the truck, has opened the doors of Antioquia to the outside world. Although the first aircraft landed on the Medellín municipal airfield in 1932, the constricted form of the valley of Aburrá excluded four-engined planes until 1947. Twenty years later it was receiving jets and Bogotá had become just 24 minutes away. Medellín's handsome new Aeropuerto Olaya Herrera is the second busiest in the country after that of Bogotá (table 15). It was handling some 50 scheduled domestic flights per day in 1967, with direct international connections to Miami (twice a week) and Panamá (once a week). Tourist departures to the remote island of San Andrés in the Caribbean from Medellín exceeded 100 a day.

With the new highway links with the outside world the former movement of such low value cargo as raw cotton, lumber, meat, and milk has become a thing of the past, but industrial machinery

TABLE 15
Principal Colombian Airports

	Total paying passenger departures, 1966		Total paying passenger departures, 1966
Bogotá	690,325	Cartagena	82,416
Medellín	345,986	San Andrés I	66,743
Cali	248,594	Barrancabermeja	47,255
Barranquilla	213,422	Santa Marta	44,429
Cúcuta	94,907	Neiva	30,631
Pereira	87,196	Montería	27,643
Bucaramanga	86,579		

Other airports within Antioqueño zone of influence: Armenia, 18,621; Turbo, 15,257; Manizales, 8,579; Quibdó, 7,118; El Bagre (Pato), 6,010; Planeta Rica, 6,877; Puerto Berrío, 5,168; Caucasia, 2,994; Arboletes, 2,021; Otú, 1,217.

SOURCE: *Boletín Mensual de Estadística* (DANE), No. 193, April 1967, p. 63.

and other high value imports are still flown in directly from North America or Europe.[35] Local cow-pasture airfields were first confined to the mining centers such as Amalfi, Pato, and Otú (Segovia). By 1967 there was "Aerotaxi" service to more than a dozen strips within the department, including Andes, Urrao, Puerto Berrío, Nare, Caucasia, Ituango, and a handful of new communities in the Urabá area. In addition there was daily DC-3 service to Turbo and to the mining camp of El Bagre (Pato).[36]

XII. THE NEW INDUSTRIAL ERA

THE FIRST pride and wealth of Antioquia today is no longer its gold or its coffee but its manufacturing industries. In the last few decades the factory has replaced the frontier finca as the absorbent for the vigorous natural increase of population.

Home industry had played a very subsidiary role within the framework of the colonial mining economy. Of the imports passing through Nare and Puerto Espíritu Santo clothing was by far the most important, both by weight and value. For the wealthy the clothes came from Castile, for the masses either from Quito or the manufacturing cities of Santander and Boyacá (e.g., Socorro, Pamplona, Ocaña, Girón), where an independent freeholder economy had developed in sharp contrast to the colonial feudalism of Bogotá and Popayán.[1] Later, in the nineteenth century, Antioquia was to turn to England for cheap textiles, paid for in gold from mines often controlled by London interests.

The first Antioquia export industry was the weaving of fine, hand-plaited, *iraca* (Panamá) hats from the bleached leaves of the low-growing *Carludovica palmata*. Introduced from Ecuador during the early days of the republic, the skill became localized in half a dozen Antioqueño communities including Antioquia, Sopetrán, Buriticá, Aguadas, and Santa Rosa de Cabal. During the late nineteenth century thousands of bales of hats were exported to Cuba and the United States, as well as to other departments of the republic. Today only Aguadas has maintained its hat-making industry and traditions. Here, every evening, women weavers still congregate on the plaza to sell the products of their hands to professional buyers at ridiculously low prices. Twenty years ago the entire population of Aguadas was dedicated to this activity but today the industry is in deep depression. The Antioqueño countryman is gradually abandoning the traditional white straw hat with its wide black band for factory-made felt hats.

Toward the end of the last century ceramics and glassware made in the town of Caldas (Antioquia) began to be exported in quantity to other parts of the republic. Another center of pottery production is

---

[1]For notes to chap. xii, see pp. 210–212.

the valley of Carmen de Viboral in the cool uplands near Ríonegro where common tableware has long been made by more than twenty independent, small potteries using local clays and primitive, wooden cog-driven wheels for mixing and molding.

Demand for agricultural implements which followed the introduction of commercial coffeegrowing brought the establishment of small foundries manufacturing coffee-, cane- and cabuya-processing machinery and light mining equipment at Amagá, La Estrella, Caldas, and Robledo, near Medellín. By 1898 the department was already exporting hundreds of coffee pulpers to Cundinamarca, Santander, and Cauca where the coffee industry was much older. Most of the coffee of Colombia is still processed and cleaned by machinery manufactured in the valley of Medellín.

The transformation from such small machine shop and craft industry to modern, corporate manufacturing enterprise was earlier and more successful in Antioquia than elsewhere in Colombia or for that matter in most of Latin America. For this reason the "case of Medellín" has attracted the attention of a growing number of students of economic development. A recent report by the National Planning Association* places special emphasis on the role of a youthful group of Antioqueños ("the Group of the 1920's") which, with relatively modest personal savings, turned to collective venture to acquire sufficient investment capital to enter industry. This Medellín group, composed of persons of varied backgrounds, attained early successes, it is suggested, through sound finance, integrity, and the spirit of association and soon attracted financing from other Colombians and from Germans and British.

Among the principal businesses promoted by the group were some of today's largest private enterprises. They included Colombia's two largest textile companies (Fabricato, Coltejer), its largest tobacco manufacturer, the largest chocolate company, the number two brewery, the country's second bank (Banco Commercial Antioqueño), and its leading motion picture distributor. Other entrepreneurs established what have become the nation's two leading department store chains (Tia, Ley) and a leading retail food chain (Mercados Candelaria).

EXPLANATION OF MAP 13

MAJOR INDUSTRIAL ESTABLISHMENTS IN THE VALLEY OF ABURRÁ, 1966

Map legend	Name and product	Approximate number of employees
(1)	Cía. Colombiana de Tejidos, "Coltejer" (cotton textiles, synthetics)	8,100
	a. Itagüí plant 4,200	
	b. Rosellón plant 2,300	
	c. Medellín plant 1,600	
(2)	Fábrica de Hilados y Tejidos del Hato, "Fabricato" (cotton textiles, synthetics)	5,400
(3)	Tejidos El Condor, "Tejicondor" (cotton textiles, synthetics)	2,200
(4)	ªTextiles Panamericana, "Pantex" (rayon, acetate, polyester fibers)	1,200
(5)	Cía. de Empaques (coffee sacks, fique products)	1,200
(6)	Textiles Pepalfa (ladies' wear, textile products)	1,190
(7)	Confecciones Colombiana, "Everfit"–"Indulana" (men's suits)	1,140
(8)	Cervecería Unión (beer)	1,030
(9)	Tejidos Leticia	900
(10)	Locería Colombiana (earthenware, porcelain)	800
(11)	Cristalería Peldar (glassware)	800
(12)	Cía. de Productos Caucho Grullo (rubber products)	720
(13)	Empresa Siderúrgica (structural steel)	700
(14)	Shellmar de Colombia (containers)	590
(15)	Cía. Textil Colombiana, "Satexco" (cotton thread and yarn)	580
(16)	Cía. Nacional de Chocolate, "Luker" (candies, chocolate)	550
(17)	Enka de Colombia (synthetic fibers)	520
(18)	Paños Vicuña "Santa Fe" (woolens)	500
(19)	Industrias Metalúrgicas Apolo (farm machinery, cement mixers)	500
(20)	Landers Mora y Cía. (pressure cookers, milling equipment)	450
(21)	Cía. Colombiana de Tobaco (cigarettes, cigars)	440
(22)	Gaseosas Posada Tobón, "Postobón" (soft drinks)	410
(23)	Cía. de Tejidos Unión (textiles)	400
(24)	Calox Colombiana (pharmaceuticals)	400
(25)	ᵇFundiciones y Repuestos, "Furesa" (textile machinery, parts)	400
(26)	Haceb (stoves, furnaces, washing machines)	385
(27)	Textiles Modernos (textiles)	370
(28)	Industrias Metalúrgicas Unidas, "Imusa" (aluminum ware, plastics)	360
(29)	Procesadora de Leche, "Proleche" (milk, milk products)	350
(30)	Fábrica Textil de los Andes, "Fatelares" (towels, sheets, etc.)	330
(31)	Industrias Estra (plastics)	300
(32)	Calcetería Helios (hosiery)	265
(33)	Pinturas Colombiana, "Pintura" (paint)	260
(34)	Manufacturas de Cuero, Ltd. (leather goods)	220
(35)	Nylon Colombiana (synthetic fibers, plastics)	200
(36)	ᵇ Fundiciones Técnica (foundry)	200
(37)	ᵇPolímeros Colombiana (synthetic fibers)	—
(38)	Fábrica de Sombreros de Fieltro (hats)	200
(39)	Manufactura de Cerámica, "Mancera" (sanitary ware)	—
(40)	Hijos de Eleazar Ospina (metal furniture)	—
(41)	Cía. de Cementos Argos (cement)	—
(42)	Rentas Departmental de Antioquia (liquors)	—
(43)	Larco (air conditioning equipment)	160
(44)	Colcafé (coffee products)	190
(45)	Sintéticos, S.A. (plastics)	—
(46)	Gaseosas Lux (soft drinks)	—
(47)	Industrial de Gaseosas (Coca Cola)	—
(48)	Confecciones Primavera (men's shirts, underwear)	—
(49)	Fábrica de Galletas y Confites Noel (crackers)	—

ª Controlled by "Fabricato."
ᵇ Controlled by "Coltejer."

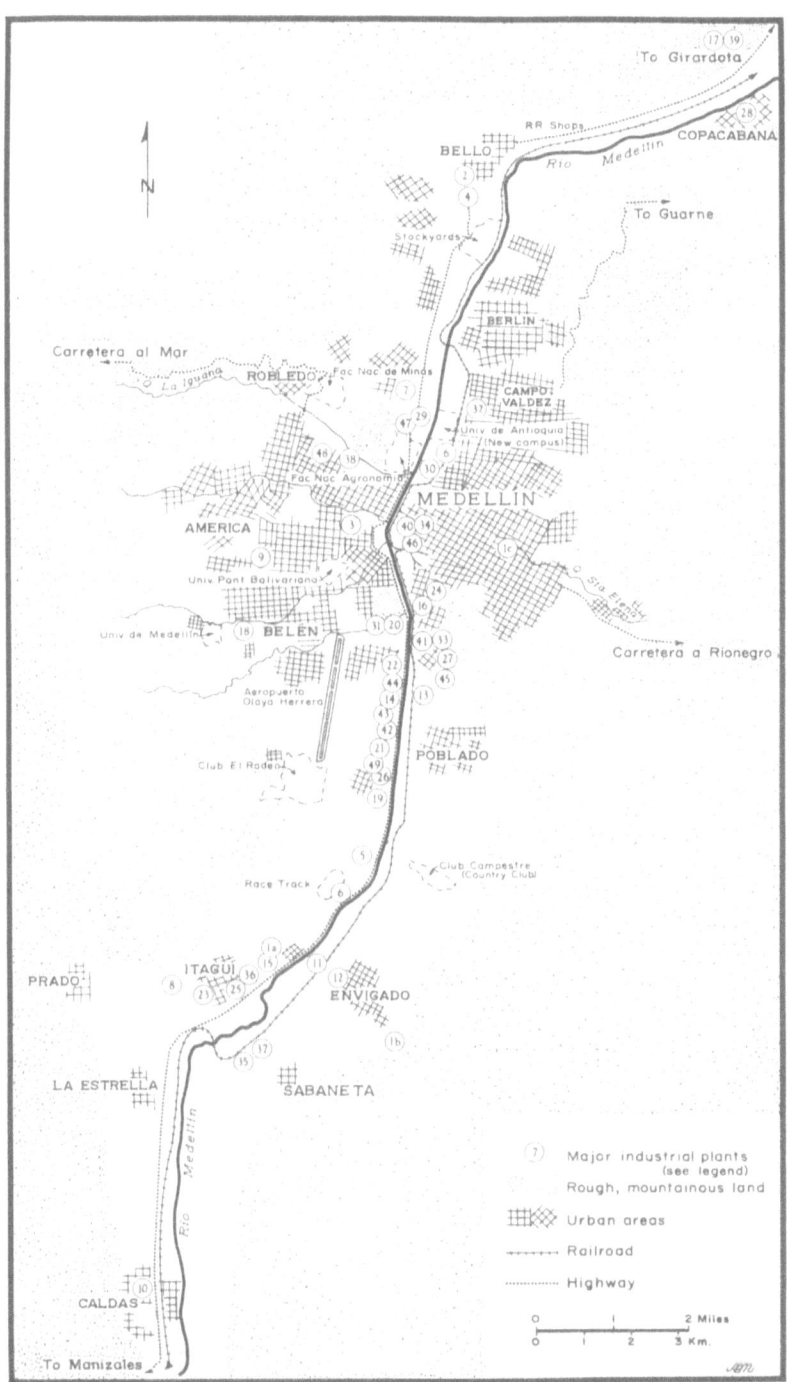

Map 13. Major Industrial Plants in the Valley of Aburrá, 1966.

Medellín has the oldest industrial tradition in Colombia. The early development of commercial and banking institutions, the technologic experiences associated with gold mining, and the contacts with foreign tradesmen and engineers that these induced, all helped establish the necessary conditions under which the new manufacturing ventures might flourish. These were supported, at the appropriate time, by a protective tariff policy. Most importantly, they were reinforced by what Luis Ospina Vásquez[2] has termed "the peculiar cast of the [Antioqueño] *modo de ser*," fostered and sharpened by the experience in mining ventures and the successful development of a major export trade in coffee. Their vigor and business acumen and their attitudes toward innovation, risk-taking, and capital accumulation brought out what he terms "a not-quite-to-be-expected response" to a certain set of circumstances. Although actively participated in by a few persons, the movement toward industrialization had the collaboration of many others. This positive attitude in regard to industry led first to small successes and then to larger ones, as the local and regional market expanded. Jorge Rodríguez A. aptly refers to the process as "el contagio de la mentalidad industrial."

Everett E. Hagen, in his work, *On the Theory of Social Change*,[4] devotes considerable attention to the Antioquia example of successful early industrialization in a predominantly peasant society. In attempting to explain why the Antioqueños so successfully seized the opportunities to industrialize he emphasizes, as did others before him, their particularistic history and culture, the existence of an incipient commercial and technologic infrastructure afforded by coffee and mining, and the circumstance of abundant coal and hydroelectric power potential. But he also adds another, more specifically psychological, element in the strong impulse to industrialize that existed in Antioquia in the first years of this century. This derives from presumed social tensions arising from the attitudes of other Colombians who reputedly considered the Antioqueños their social and cultural inferiors. The latter, according to the Hagen thesis, reacted to this "status deprivation" by a search for recognition in other channels, and this led them to turn to trade and industry.

The Hagen thesis, which has attracted wide attention both within and without Colombia, has been challenged in a highly convincing way by the North American scholar Frank Safford of Northwestern University.⁵ Safford argues that gold mining and the capital accumulation and entrepreneurial enterprises it induced, rather than condescension and disparagement,.were the principal enabling factors in the precocious economic development of Antioquia. He insists that other Colombians did not look on Antioqueños as their inferiors, as has so often been affirmed, but rather that they were respected for their *laborosidad,* integrity, and their often substantial economic power. Wealthy Antioqueños, for example, were readily accepted into Bogotá's upper, ruling class.⁶

Gold mining in Antioquia, and the commerce it engendered, facilitated the accumulation of large amounts of liquid capital in the hands of a few. Thus, Safford points out, the government in 1852 ceded the tobacco monopoly at Ambalema to Francisco Montoya, an Antioqueño, because he was the largest, and most secure, capitalist in the country. There were few landed aristocrats in Antioquia but a surprising number of merchants (*rescatantes*), mine owners, and mule-train operators who became involved in the money market. Antioqueño control of the tobacco trade and Río Magdalena transport at the time meant effective control of the commercial life of the country. Loans and direct investments also supported many a Bogotá merchant and more than one Bogotá government. From 1820 to 1870, he avers, Medellín was Bogota's banker. The experience so gained seems to have been a crucial precondition to the industrial development that was initiated in Antioquia in the first years of the twentieth century.

In this development the cotton textile industry was the bellwether. It dates from 1902 with the founding of the Compañía Antioqueño de Tejidos of Pedro Nel Ospina who had studied the industry in Mexico and Lancashire.⁷ The first plant was established near a small waterfall at Bello, some kilometers northeast of Medellín, thus setting a pattern of decentralization toward the small towns of the valley which has continued to the present day. The heavy textile machinery was all brought in on muleback from the railhead at Carocolí with extensive loss and damage from breakage that almost wrecked the project. After a series of reorganizations and combinations, which involved important shifts of technical and management personnel with Coltejer, the Bello mills emerged in 1939 as Fabrica de Hilados y Tejidos del Hato, S.A., better known as "Fabricato." Its cotton textile section included some 180,000 spindles and 3,440 looms in 1967.[8] In recent years Fabricato has moved importantly into polyester fibers and fabrics, too. Its three plants at Bello employ some 5,400 workers, providing almost the entire economic base of that town. A branch plant is being established in Nicaragua.

Of the Big Three that dominate Colombian textiles, the largest today is the aggressive Compañía Colombiana de Tejidos ("Coltejer"), one of the corporate giants of Latin American industry. Its widely advertised name is a household word. Established in 1907 by a wealthy coffee merchant, Alejandro Echavarría, on Quebrada Santa Elena in the upper part of Medellín, the first plant was patterned closely after Bello. Real expansion did not get under way until the depression years of the thirties, which were to see the beginning of many of Antioquia's major industrial concerns. In 1942 it absorbed the Rosellón Company (2,800 wage earners), which had been established in 1911 near a waterfall site behind Envigado with the assistance of the same foreign technicians who had set up Bello and Coltejer.[9] In 1967 Coltejer was operating 233,000 spindles and 4,800 looms, employing a total of 8,500 persons at four plants (Medellín, Envigado, Itagüí, Rionegro) and an additional 800 in related machine and parts shops and starch mills. Sales in 1966 totaled 738 million pesos ($50 million U. S.). More than 37,000 stockholders held a stake in the company, making it one of the most broadly held corporations in Latin America.

Coltejer and Fabricato are the pacesetters among the 460 concerns that constitute Colombia's textile industry, the most efficient and modern in Latin America.[10] Its gross production in 1966 amounted to 200 million pesos, representing 15 per cent of the total value of all Colombian manufacturing. The big Medellín companies, in particular, have set the example for others by their enlightened management practices. Textile exports have been increasing and now rank fourth among all Colombian exports. In 1965 foreign sales totaled 27 million yards of cloth valued at nearly $6 million U. S. Two-thirds of all shipments went to the United States. The related garment industry nationwide employs two-thirds as many persons as textiles; in Medellín it accounts for 20 per cent of all industrial employment. These two industries combined account for one of every three persons employed in manufacturing in Colombia, one half of those so employed in Antioquia.

The dominant position of textiles in Antioquia was already well indicated by the Industrial Census of 1945.[11] The value of textile products alone was more than double that of the coffee exported from the department in that year. Some 43 per cent of all wage earners in industry (excluding gold mining) were employed in textile mills. Twenty years later, in 1964, textiles employed only 26 per cent of all Antioquia manufacturing workers in spite of the fact that total employment in textiles had nearly doubled, to 25,300 (table 16).[12] Medellín and its satellite industrial communities in that year accounted for 22 per cent of the value added by manufacturing in all of Colombia and for 70 per cent of the value added in textiles.

TABLE 16
Principal Manufacturing Industries in Antioquia
1964[a]

Industry	Number of establishments[b]	Number of employees	Value of product[c]	Value added by manufacture[c]
Textiles.................	112	25,300	1,820	947
Clothing.................	445	7,800	300	138
Food and beverages[d]........	363	7,100	1,055	380
All metal products[e].........	246	7,600	310	174
Nonmetallic minerals........	200	7,200	251	118
Chemicals................	101	2,600	244	103
Tobacco products..........	26	600	162	122
All industry.............	1,864	68,800	4,761	2,258

[a] Departamento Administrativo Nacional de Estadística, *Boletín Mensual de Estadística*, No. 183, July 1966.
[b] Including all businesses with five or more paid workers.
[c] In millions of pesos (peso = .06 U.S.).
[d] Including coffee *trilladoras*.
[e] Includes electrical and nonelectrical machinery and transportation equipment.

At an earlier time young girls from the country provided the most important reservoir of cheap labor to operate the looms and spindles of Medellín. As late as 1945 half of the textile mill operatives in Antioquia were women and 65 per cent of them were from rural sections of the department.[13] Today the proportion of women is much reduced. A kind of benevolent paternalism, however, still marks the relations between employer and employee among the large textile companies. At Bello, Fabricato maintains a dormitory under the supervision of nuns where single girls are given board and lodging on a payroll deduction plan. Within the well-kept building is a chapel, dining hall, auditorium, library, and lounge. Schooling is provided to workers who desire it as well as to their children. The company also maintains a modern clinic. Coltejer long provided married workers with low-cost rental housing in company *barrios* near the mills, but these have been sold to workers in recent years on very favorable terms. Today more than three-quarters of the married workers at both Fabricato and Coltejer own their own homes. Job stability is accordingly high. A third of the work forces at both companies has been employed for more than twelve years at the same place. Wages are adjusted to the cost-of-living index and labor disputes have been few. Social benefits provided by the larger establishments include nonprofit cooperative stores, free medical and dental services and hospitalization, social welfare counseling, relief to needy families, special schools for children of workers, and free transportation to and from work. Solemn religious processions, festivals, and Masses frequently interrupt factory routine, and images and paintings of Jesus and Mary are everywhere in evidence in plants and offices. Management here has been remarkably successful in investing factory work with an esteem not common in older industrial lands.

Here, in the Valley of Aburrá, has been repeated an evolutionary process of industrialization strikingly parallel in many ways to that which made England and New England the world's spinning and weaving centers in the last century.

In its earlier years Antioquia's textile industry was supplied largely by imported raw materials,[14] but today it is close to self-sufficient. Ginned cotton comes from the Sinú and César valleys on the north coast, either by truck or rail, and by truck from the Tolima plains.

Caustic soda, soda ash, dyestuffs, sulfuric acid, and polyester fibers come from factories in Cali, Bogotá, and Barranquilla as well as in Medellín. Wool, part of which is imported, plays a relatively minor role. In 1967 a German-Swiss consortium and Dutch-owned Enka were both constructing major facilities in outlying communities near Medellín to supply polyester fibers and plastic resins to the local industries. Coltejer had its own polyester fiber plant (Sadeco) at Itagüi, the pioneer producer of synthetic yarns in Colombia.

Other major manufacturing industries that have been established in Medellín (map 13) include building materials, tanneries, plastic and light metal goods, sulfuric acid, chemical fertilizers, rubber goods, cigarettes, patent medicines, beverages, and foodstuffs. According to the Asociación Nacional de Industrias (ANDI),[16] Medellín in a recent year produced the following percentages of total Colombian production: cotton cloth 90, phonograph records 80, aluminum ware, hardware and cutlery 70, woolens 63, electrical apparatuses 56, industrial machinery 51, sulfuric acid 50, glass 47, ceramics 42, leather goods 40. The Empresa Siderúrgica produces structural steel and bars for Medellín industry from scrap iron. Investigations have been carried on from time to time on the possibilities of establishing a blast furnace for the reduction of residual limonite ores in the area.

TABLE 17
POPULATION OF THE VALLEY OF MEDELLÍN (METROPOLITAN AREA)
BY MUNICIPIOS, CENSUSES OF 1938, 1951, AND 1964
(in thousands)

	1938	1951	1964
Medellín.	168	358	778
Bello.	13	34	91
Envigado.	14	29	68
Itagüi.	7	20	65
Caldas.	9	12	25
La Estrella.	6	9	20
Copacabana.	7	11	21
Girardota.	9	11	13
Totals.	233	484	1,081

The stepped-up tempo of manufacturing has been accompanied by an increasing urban congestion both in Medellín and in such satellite valley communities as Bello, Itagüi, Envigado, and Sabaneta. The 1964 census showed the population of Greater Medellín (the capital and its five suburban valley municipios) to have reached more than one million (table 17) or 40 per cent of the population of the department of Antioquia. This represents an increase of more than 100 per cent since the 1951 census, or an annual growth rate of better than 9 per cent. The largest share of this increase must be attributed to the inward shift of campesinos from outlying municipios, attracted largely by new industrial jobs, educational opportunity, and welfare.

As the valley of Medellín has filled up, attention has been directed increasingly to the need for decentralization of future industrial growth. To this end two major new plants recently have been built some 20 kilometers down the valley at Girardota (Mancesa, Enka de Colombia) and production of women's wear has been initiated near Rionegro, in the Oriente, at branch plants of both Coltejer and Pepalfa. At the latter place an industrial park is being planned to accommodate future growth. Elsewhere there is no manufacturing of significance anywhere within Antioquia save for the cement mills at Nare and Santa Barbara. One day, however, the plantings of pines, cypress, and eucalyptus being made on the thin soils of the uplands may support a paper-making industry.

As the second Antioqueño city Manizales, capital of Caldas, has partaken to a modest extent of this industrial development but its location with regard to transportation is disadvantageous. It is the seat of one of the larger cotton textile producers, Tejidos Unidos, specializing in poplins and twills. Pereira, the fast-growing capital of the new department of Risaralda, is an important manufacturer of men's shirts. Total industrial employment in Caldas in 1964 (including Risaralda and Quindío) was 13,100 persons, with nearly one-fourth of this figure represented by the clothing industry.

In contrast to other Colombian manufacturing centers where branch plants of United States or European concerns are common, most Medellín industry is home-owned. Foreign technicians have often been invited to install new machinery and to instruct in its operation, but have then usually been hurried home by employers anxious to proclaim their independence from outsiders. Perhaps the most important exception to this has been Fabricato's working agreement with Burlington International, with which it jointly owns Pantex of Medellín (Textiles Panamericana) and a synthetic fiber plant in Bogotá (La Esmeralda). Other Antioquia industry in which there is significant foreign participation includes Cristales Peldar (Owens-Illinois), Shellmar (Continental Can), Sintéticos Proco (W. R. Grace), Mancesa (American Radiator-Standard Sanitary), Landers Mora (Landers, Frary and Clark), Enka de Colombia (Dutch), Satexco (French), and Nylon Colombiana (25 per cent German capital). Of the North American colony of some 400 in Medellín probably fewer than 20 are there in connection with manufacturing activities. Protestant missionaries and Peace Corps workers are more numerous.

The relatively low level of foreign investment in Medellín industry, as compared with Bogotá, Cali, or Barranquilla, has been a source of pride in Antioquia. But recently it has also become a cause for concern as the area's early lead in industry has lessened. New plant investment in the 'sixties was not keeping pace with the earlier growth rate, nor with that of rival centers. Between the 1945 and 1964 industrial censuses Antioquia's share of the country's manufacturing employment dropped from 25 to 16 per cent, its share of the value added by manufacturing from 25 per cent to 22.4 per cent. This is in part inevitable, as other centers and other industries, starting later, catch up to Medellín and textiles. But it is also suspected that Medellín may have developed a reputation as an attractive city, but one with a closed, inner-oriented society and that this may have influenced the locational decision of some foreign firms negatively. Recently a movement has been afoot to reverse this image.

A plentiful supply of cheap hydroelectric power has facilitated Medellín's industrial growth. The Empresas Públicas de Medellín, acclaimed throughout Latin America as a model public service organization, has been responsible for its development, along with water, telephone and sewer service.[16] Between 1932 and 1966 the waters of the Río Grande and Río Guadalupe north of the Valley of Aburrá were developed to a capacity of 440,000 kilowatts, distributed to Medellín and adjacent communities at the lowest rates of any power in Colombia. In 1970 additional energy supplies will be required. To provide for these projected demands the 700,000 kilowatt Río Nare project has been undertaken on the Oriente plateau. It will consist of a dam and power house on the Río Nare at Guatapé and, eventually, the diversion of part of the Nare flow southward into the Río Samaná, where other generating units will be installed to take advantage of a 280-meter difference in elevation. Studies of the Samaná itself have suggested the possibility of developing another million kilowatts or more on that stream. The first stage in the Nare project, the *Central* at Guatapé (70,000 kilowatts) has been scheduled for completion in 1969. The second stage (1973-1975) will involve completion of the Nare dam and the flooding of the town of El Peñol and part of Guatapé. The resettlement of some 5,000 persons as a result of this project has recently been a major concern of government and private planning agencies in Antioquia." It is hoped that the Nare development, lying as it does on the route of the projected new highway (*autopista*) from Medellín to Bogotá, may provide a much-needed fillip to the presently depressed economy of the Oriente municipios. The Nare project is one of Latin America's most ambitious power developments. It will make Antioquia a major power exporter. Plans for interconnections with Bogotá, Manizales, and Cali are under study.

Industrialization has brought a new way of life to the Valley of Aburrá. Today, although there are no figures to prove it, Medellín undoubtedly has a middle class and upper class more numerous relative to its total population than almost any other Latin American city. The lush country estates of El Poblado and Envigado, the vast expanses of upper middle class homes that comprise the well-kept suburbs of América, Belén, and Prado, and the mushrooming 20- and 30-story downtown condominium apartments, demonstrate far better than words or figures the broad base of this successful democracy. The heart of the city, centering on Parque Berrío and Plaza Nutibara, is in the process of being rebuilt under a *Plan Piloto* adopted in 1948 and an ingenious and much-copied system of special assessments on landowners (*impuestos de valorización*) for the construction of wide new *avenidas* and the enlargement of public parks.[18] But with this burgeoning growth has come a proliferation of urban slums (*turgurios*), especially on the northern outskirts of the city. The municipio of Medellín estimated in 1966 that some 180,000 persons were living in "subnormal" housing in 74 distinct nuclei (*barrios piratas*) within the metropolitan area.[19] Such slum housing, nevertheless, poses a lesser problem in Medellín than in other major Colombian cities. An active program is afoot to eliminate those that exist and to control their future development. But the chronically high unemployment rate in the Valley of Aburrá (12.4 per cent of the labor force in January, 1967) does not promise an early end to the problem.[20]

The strong regional pride and sense of identification of the Antioqueños is reflected in the new *Acción Communal* programs and the activities of such civic and charitable planning groups as the influential Corporación Patriotica de Antioquia, "Codesarrollo," Incoplan, "Los Barrios de Jesus" (a church-sponsored housing venture), and the new Instituto para el Desarrollo de Antioquia (IDEA). The last, a kind of departmental development bank set up with proceeds from the sale of the Ferrocarril de Antioquia, makes loans to rural municipios for such internal improvements as roads, sanitary facilities, and schools. In 1967 it set aside 10 million pesos for the establishment of a departmental tourist board (Corporación de Desarrollo Turistica de Antioquia, S.A.) designed to attract to Antioquia some of the travellers' dollars that have for so long passed it by. Some of the railroad money has gone, too, for construction of the handsome new Ciudad Universitaria of the well-regarded Universidad de Antioquia, a rambling red-tile roofed, adobe complex on a large tract of riverside land immediately north of the city center.[21]

Yet despite the vigor of the Antioqueño culture and economy there is still a certain sense of frustration and even bitterness directed against the central government in Bogotá which, it is claimed, has more or less systematically excluded the *paisas* from their rightful share of government expenditures. Sentiment for decentralization,

TABLE 18
LEADING MANUFACTURING DEPARTMENTS, COLOMBIA, 1964*

Department and capital	Percentage value added by manufacturing	Percentage manufacturing workers	Percentage installed energy (KW)	Percentage total population
Antioquia (Medellín)....	22.4	16.0	25.5	14.2
Cundinamarca (Bogotá).	29.1	28.4	24.7	16.1
Valle del Cauca (Cali)...	20.8	14.9	15.2	10.0
Atlántico (Barranquilla).	8.1	5.9	8.0	3.9
Other departments......	19.6	26.9	26.6	55.8

* Computed from Census of Manufacturing, 1964, in *Boletín Mensúal de Estadística* (DANE), various issues, 1966.

always strong in Antioquia, has become increasingly vocal. A collection of Medellín newspaper editorials directed to this sensitive point was recently published under the revealing title *Antioquia: Olvidada, Marginada y Resentida*." The department, it is continually being pointed out, pays much more in taxes to the national government than it receives in benefits. It is, in effect, carrying much of the rest of the country on its back. But it is also extending its influence increasingly and in subtle ways into the farthest corners of the republic. Antioqueño values, speech, and money may be quietly effectuating a second conquest of Colombia, a cultural and economic one, as surely as the enterprising and prolific *colonos,* surging forth from the spent soils of the granitic batholith, achieved a spatial one in the last century and in the first years of this century."

Urbanization and industrialization are imposing new strains on the Antioqueño economy of a nature and magnitude not previously known. Today this sober, vigorous, vital culture group, product of four centuries of geographic isolation, constitutes close to one-third of Colombia's population, grows three-fourths of its great export coffee crop, and controls the lion's share of its industry and commerce. Its capital city, in a picture-book setting in a mile-high Andean valley, has become one of the most dynamic and prosperous urban centers in all of Latin America. But that quality of cultural particularism that has given the land its distinctive personality remains essentially undisturbed.

NOTES

NOTES TO CHAPTER I

THE PEOPLE

[1] Luís Eduardo Nieto Arteta, *Economía y Cultura en la Historia de Colombia* (Bogotá, 1942).
[2] Gabriel Arango Mejía, *Geneologías de Antioquia y Caldas*, 2 vols. (Medellín, 1942), contains the results of a lifetime of genealogical research by the director of the Biblioteca y Archivo de Antioquia in Medellín.
[3] Francisco Silvestre, "Relación del Estado de la Provincia de Antioquia cuando la entrego a Don Cayetano Buelta" [December 1, 1776], *Archivo Historial* (Manizales), July, 1919, pp. 569–605.
[4] Tulio Ospina, "El Oidor Mon y Velarde, Regenerador de Antioquia" [1901], *Repertorio Histórico* (Medellín), September, 1918, p. 412. After leaving his Antioquia assignment Mon y Velarde served briefly as president of the Real Audiencia of Quito until named, in 1790, to the Royal Council of the Indies at Seville, but he died of poisoning en route to his new post. See also, Emilio Robledo, *Bosquejo Biográfico del Señor Oidor Juan Antonio Mon y Velarde* (Bogotá, 1954).
[5] Quoted in Ramón Franco, *Antropogeografía Colombiana* (Manizales, 1941), p. 177.
[6] Ferdinand von Schenck, "Risen in Antioquia," *Petermanns Mitteilungen* (1883), vol. 29, p. 89. Another German observer of the Antioqueño character in this period was Ernst Röthlisberger, *El Dorado...* [1897] (Bogotá, 1963), pp. 346–348.

NOTES TO CHAPTER II

THE NATURAL SETTING

[1] The name Aburrá has currency today only as a literary form, applied to the flared-out section of the valley of the Río Porce (Río Medellín) above Bello. In the seventeenth century, however, it was in common usage. Documents of that period also refer to another Río Aburrá (de Sopetrán), today the Río Aurrá, the deep canyon of which is followed by the modern highway from Medellín to Antioquia. The Río Porce at Medellín was commonly referred to as the Río Nechí in colonial times. The original Porce (or "Poroze") was the right-bank tributary, 60 kilometers below Medellín, known today as the Río Porcecito. The modern Río Nechí above Dos Bocas may have been the Río Tenche of an earlier day.
[2] The level floor of the upper valley of the Río Cauca is known simply as El Valle in local usage. The department of Valle del Cauca, carved from the old province of Gran Cauca in 1910, comprises a much larger area, extending from the Pacific to the crest of the Central Cordillera.
[3] A. Hettner, "Die Anden des westlichen Columbiens," *Petermanns Mitteilungen* (1893), vol. 39, pp. 129–136.
[4] Emil Grosse, *Estudio Geológico del Terciario Carbonífero de Antioquia. ...* (Berlin, 1926), contains a geologic map in 4 sheets, scale, 1:50,000. The results of recent geological investigations have been published in *Compilación de los Estúdios Geológicos Oficiales* (Bogotá, 1933–1947). An important geological and topographical summary is in P. Schaufelberger, *Apuntes Geológicos y Pedológicos de la Zona Cafetera de Colombia* (Manizales, Federación Nacional de Cafeteros, 1944).
[5] Fray Pedro Simón, *Noticias Historiales de las Conquistas de Tierra Firme en las Indias Occidentales*, 5 vols. (Bogotá, 1882–1892), vol. 4, p. 186.
[6] J. B. Boussingault, *Mémoires* (Paris, 1898–1903), vol. 3.

[7] Joaquín Acosta, "Relation de l'éruption boueuse sortie du volcan de Ruiz et de la catastrophe de Lagunilla," *Comptes Rendus, Acad. Sci.* (Paris, 1846), vol. 22, pp. 709–710.

[8] Most early aneroid readings indicated that the cone of Tolima was about 5,600 meters in height; thus some 200 meters higher than the Nevado del Ruiz. Following the ascent of Erwin Krauss in 1943 the Oficina de Longitudes corrected its height to 4,810 meters, thus making Tolima the lowest of the snow-capped peaks of the Central Cordillera. "Relatos de un Excursionista por las Cimas Nevadas de Nuestros Cordilleras," *Boletín de la Sociedad Geográfica de Colombia* (May, 1944), pp. 331–333. The American Geographical Society's Millionth Map gives Tolima's height as 5,210 meters. In this matter see especially the detailed section on the physical geography of the Central Cordillera in Gonzalo Paris Lozano, *Geografía Económica de Colombia, VII: Tolima* (Bogotá, 1946); also, E. Krüger, "Eine Besteigung des Tolima," and Immanuel Friedländer, "Ueber Einige Vulkane Columbiens," in *Zeitschrift für Vulkanologie*, Band X.

[9] Gerardo Botero Arango, "Sobre el Ordiviciano de Antioquia," *Proc.*, Eighth American Science Congress (Washington, 1940), vol. 4, pp. 19–25; "Contribución al Conocimiento de la Geología de la Zona Central de Antioquia," *Anales*, Facultad de Minas, No. 57 (Medellín, 1963). The limits of the batholith are mapped in *Informe del Ministerio de Minas y Petróleos* (Bogotá, 1942), map facing p. 202.

[10] Robert Blake White, "Brief Notes on the Glacial Phenomena of Colombia," *Scottish Geographical Magazine* (1899), vol. 15, pp. 470–479.

[11] R. D. O. Johnson, "Placer Mining in Colombia," *Engineering & Mining Journal* (1911), vol. 92, pp. 1137–1141.

[12] Grosse, *op. cit.*, p. 342.

[13] These plugs are located on a sketch map by Dr. White Uribe reproduced in Antonio García, *Geografía Económica de Colombia, IV: Caldas* (Bogotá, 1937), p. 165.

[14] A small "volcano" has been reported in the municipio of Buriticá by Tulio Ospina, *Reseña Geológica de Antioquia* (2d ed., Medellín, 1939), p. 57.

[15] The highest temperature ever recorded in Medellín is 33.5° C. (92° F.), and the all-time low is 7.5° C. (45.5° F.). For Manizales comparable extremes are 25.4° C. (77.7° F.) and 7.0° C. (44.6° F.), the lesser range here undoubtedly is due to its ridge-top site which enjoys superior air drainage.

[16] In 1966 the Empresas Públicas de Medellín, with the aid of a five million dollar loan from the Bank for International Development, completed an 8½-kilometer tunnel to bring water from the upper Río Negro to the city. Its daily capacity of 100,000 cu.m. is to be enlarged to 345,000 cu.m. within ten years.

[17] Alberto Machado S., "Fomento de la Industria Cafetera en el Valle del Cauca," *Revista Facultad Nacional Agronomía* (Medellín, 1942), pp. 488–552.

[18] In Antioquia the January-February dry season is known as the Verano de San Martín and that of July-August as the Verano de San Juan.

[19] Both Yarumal (6°59′N) and Remedios (7°02′N) have a pronounced January-March dry season but their ten-year records reveal no summer verano. These stations seem to be the southernmost in Antioquia with a single dry season and a single wet season.

[20] Southward toward the equator the summer dry season becomes increasingly long and the winter dry season more and more abbreviated. Quito, astride the equator, has a subtropical rainfall regime with a single maximum and minimum. A. Hettner, "Regenverteilung, Pflanzendecke und Besiedelung der tropischen Anden," *Festschrift Ferdinand Freiherr von Richthofen zum sechzigsten Geburtstag* (Berlin, 1893), pp. 199–233.

[21] Lucio Chiquito, "Apuntes sobre Lluvias en Medellín," unpublished thesis, Escuela de Minas, Medellín, 1941.

[22] A "destructive hurricane," for instance, is reported to have hit Manizales on May 7,

1910. Emilio Robledo, *Geografía Médica y Nosología del Departmento de Caldas* (Manizales, 1916).

[22] Manuel Uribe Angel, *Geografía General y Compendio Histórico del Estado de Antioquia* (Paris, 1885), p. 45.

[24] Alexander von Humboldt and Aimé Bonpland, *Essai sur la géographie des plantes* (Paris, 1805).

[25] Francisco José de Caldas, "Memoria sobre Nivelación de las Plantas que se cultivan en la vecindad del Ecuador," [1803] *Obras de Caldas* (Bogotá, 1912), pp. 85-95.

[26] O Führmann and E. Mayor, "Voyage d'Exploration Scientifique en Colombie," *Mémoires de la Société Neuchateloise des Sciences Naturelle* (1914), vol. 5, pp. 1-116.

[27] Otto Bürger, *Reisen eines Naturforschers in tropischen Amerika* [1900] 2 vols. (Leipzig, 1923). The most recent and detailed vegetation study (with map) is Luis Espinal, "Formaciones Vegetales del Departamento de Antioquia," *Revista Facultad Nacional Agronomía*, No. 60 (Medellín, 1964).

[28] Teodoro Wolf, *Geografía y Geología del Ecuador* (Leipzig, 1892).

[29] Frank M. Chapman, "The Distribution of Bird-Life in Colombia," *Bulletin American Museum of Natural History* (1917), vol. 36.

[30] Optimum conditions for coffeegrowing in Antioquia and Caldas are found between 1,200-1,800 meters elevation, but individual plantations may extend as low as 700 meters (e.g., Caracolí) and as high as 2,200 meters (e.g., Caicedo). High-grown coffee is of superior quality, but yield is so low as to become uneconomical above 2,000 meters. Successful plantings at this elevation are generally on the steep slopes of deep canyons where insolation is high. Agronomists of the Federación Nacional de Cafeteros are currently urging 1,900 meters as the upper limit of plantings in Antioquia. At low elevations quality drops off, and insect and fungus infestations become increasingly prevalent.

[31] Juan Antonio Mon y Velarde, "Sucinta Relación de la Visita de Antioquia" [1788], *Anales de la Instrucción Pública* (Bogotá, 1890), vol. 16, p. 27.

[32] Archivo de Antioquia, Estadístico y Censo, tomo 5, fol. 25.

[33] Juan Enrique White, "Disertación sobre los indígenes de Occidente," *Repertorio Histórico* (Medellín, 1919), p. 585.

[34] *The Travels of Pedro Cieza de León, A. D. 1532-50*, translated and edited by Clements R. Markham (London, Hakluyt Society, 1864), p. 89.

[35] At the beginning of the nineteenth century the Ríonegro region was producing 50,000 pounds of this wax annually. José Manuel Restrepo, "Ensayo sobre la Geografía: Producciones, Industria y Población de la Provincia de Antioquia en el Nuevo Reino de Granada," *Semanario del Nuevo Reino de Granada* (Bogotá, 1808-1810). Reprinted in 3 vols. (Bogotá, 1942), vol. 1, pp. 243-286.

[36] Restrepo, *op. cit.*, p. 253, estimated in 1808 that of the Province of Antioquia's 2,200 square leagues "scarcely 250 are in grass and another 70 continuously under cultivation."

[37] *The Travels of Cieza de León*, p. 69.

NOTES TO CHAPTER III

ORIGINAL INDIAN INHABITANTS

[1] Wendell C. Bennett, *Archeological Regions of Colombia: A Ceramic Survey* (New Haven, 1944). Evidence accumulating in other areas, however, suggests a much greater population density for pre-Columbian America than has heretofore been admitted. See, for example, Henry F. Dobyns, "Estimating Aboriginal American Population: An Appraisal of Techniques, with a New Hemispheric Estimate," *Current Anthropology*, 7:395-449 (1966), and Woodrow Borah and S. F. Cook, *The Aboriginal Population of Central Mexico on the Eve of the Spanish Conquest*, University of California: Ibero-Americana, vol. 45 (1963).

[2] Tulio Ospina, "El Oidor Mon y Velarde, Regenerador de Antioquia," *Repertorio Histórico* (Medellín), September, 1918, pp. 413–415. The most recent review of the question, by Jaime Jaramillo Uribe, "La Población Indígena de Colombia en el Momento de la Conquista...," *Anuario Colombiano de História Social y de la Cultura*, vol. 1, pp. 239–293 (Bogotá, 1964) leans toward a more conservative interpretation. For Antioquia he suggests an original population of 100,000, citing Trimborn (*Señorio y Barbarie en el Valle del Cauca*, Madrid, 1949, p. 140). The wide discrepancy stems largely from uncertainty as to whether the chroniclers' figures referred to total population or only to adult *tributarios*. Both Ospina's and Jaramillo's estimates may well have been based on Fray Jeronimo Escobar's figure of 100,000 Indians (families?) for Antioquia in 1540. He estimated another 115,000 within the upper Río Cauca drainage in modern Caldas and Valle. Assigning six persons per family, Escobar's estimate would have given a population of 600,000 for Antioquia, nearly a million and a half for the entire Cauca drainage. R. B. White had earlier estimated a pre-Colombian population ranging between two and three million for Antioquia and the Cauca Valley (quoted in Robert C. West, *Colonial Placer Mining in Colombia*, Louisiana State University Press, Baton Rouge, 1952, pp. 91–92).

[3] *The Travels of Cieza de León*, p. 50.

[4] Cieza wrote of the country around Cali: "All this valley...was formerly very populous and covered with large and beautiful villages, the houses being close together and of great size. These Indian settlements have wasted away and been destroyed by time and war...." *Ibid.*, pp. 93–94.

[5] Pedro de Aguado, *Recopilación Historial* [ca. 1568–1578] (Bogotá, 1906).

[6] *Revista del Archivo Nacional*, Bogotá, Jan.–Feb. 1937, pp. 52–68.

[7] Juan Enrique White, *op. cit.*, p. 588.

[8] The best surveys of the native tribes of western Colombia are in Jacinto Jijón y Caamaño, *Sebastián Benalcázar* (Quito, 1938), vol. 2, app., pp. 1–201, and Hermann Trimborn, *Señorio y Barbarie en el Valle del Cauca*.

[9] Juan Friede, *Los Quimbayas Bajo la Dominación Española* (Bogotá, 1963), a study based on the extensive materials in the Archivo de las Indias in Sevilla. See also, Ernesto Restrepo Tirado, *Ensayo Etnográfico y Arqueológico de la Provincia de los Quimbayas* (Bogotá, 1892).

[10] Hermann Trimborn, "Der Kannîbalismus im Caucatal," *Zeitschrift für Ethnologie* (1938), vol. 70, pp. 310–330.

[11] Roberto Pineda Giraldo, "Material Arqueológico de la Zona Calima," *Boletín de Arqueología* (Bogotá, 1945), vol. 1, pp. 491–518. See also, Henry Wassén, "An Archeological Study in the Western Colombia Cordillera," *Etnologiska Studier* (Stockholm, 1936), vol. 2, pp. 30–67.

[12] *El Colombiano* (Medellín), August 25, 1946. By present Colombian law treasure found by guaqueros on private property must be divided equally with the owner.

[13] Luís Arango C., *Recuerdos de la Guaquería en el Quindío*, (Bogotá, 1941), p. 17.

[14] Pineda Giraldo, *op. cit.*, has reported graves as deep as 35 varas (28 m.) in the parishes of Los Cedros and San Salvador near Restrepo (Valle).

[15] *The Travels of Cieza de León*, p. 89. From this evidence he shrewdly notes that a very long time must have elapsed since the Indians first peopled the Indies.

[16] James J. Parsons and William Bowen, "Ancient Ridged Fields of the San Jorge River Floodplain, Colombia," *Geographical Review*, 56:317–343 (1966).

NOTES TO CHAPTER IV

Spanish Mines and the Labor Supply

[1] The location of the valley of Guaca (or Guacá) has long been in dispute, but Hermann Trimborn, *Vergessende Königreich* (Braunsweig, 1948) seems to have established beyond doubt that it was in the upper Río Sinú. See also the map accompanying Emilio Robledo, *La Vida del Mariscal Jorge Robledo* (Bogotá, 1945).

[3] In a footnote to his Hakluyt Society translation of Cieza's travels Clements Markham observed (p. 52): "The province of Antioquia, in New Granada, including the lower course of the great river Cauca, is still the least known part of Spanish South America. Even now the account of this region given by Cieza de León ... is the best that has been published. Humboldt was never there, nor is this country described by such modern books of travels as those of Captain Cochrane, Mollien or Holton. Some of these travellers, as well as General Mosquera in his pamphlet, give accounts of Cartago, Cali and other places in the upper part of the valley of the Cauca; but none of them ever visited or described the lower course of the valley of that river nor the province of Antioquia."

[3] Quoted in Robledo, *op. cit.*, p. 95.

[4] *Ibid.*, p. 99.

[5] West, *Colonial Placer Mining* ..., p. 45; Trimborn, *op. cit.*, map p. 122.

[6] José María Restrepo Sáenz, *Gobernadores de Antioquia, 1579–1819* (2d ed., Bogotá, 1944), vol. I, pp. 17–19, 30–31.

[7] A part of the title referred to is quoted by Restrepo Sáenz, *op. cit.*, p. 3: "Primeramente os hazemos merced de la dha. gobernación poblazon e rehedificaciones de las dhas. provincias de Antiocha, Ytuango, Nibe y Brenunco y otras entre los rrios que dicen en todo se llama e titula la provincia de Antiocha y se extiende a la dha. desde la dha. provincia de Antiocha y sus provincias comarcanas hasta la mar del norte e puerto de Uraba con que no entre la dha. gobernación ningun lugar de los poblados al presente de españoles ni de yndios que esten pacificados en nra. obediencia ..."

[8] Antonio Vásquez de Espinosa's detailed description of "the city of Cáceres and the rich gold mines in its districts," although written about 1628, clearly refers to Cáceres as still being on or near the site mentioned (Loma de Nohava). Its removal to its present location, on the flood plain of the lower Cauca, must have come much later. *Compendium and Description of the West Indies* [1628] (Washington, 1942). West, *op. cit.*, p. 39, shows that the move had been made prior to 1720.

[9] Antioquia's isolation is evidenced in its long struggle to obtain its own bishopric. Demands for the creation of a diocese of Antioquia had been heard as early as 1597 when a royal cédula ordered an investigation of the question, but it was not to be granted for more than two hundred years. Although subordinate *visitadores* from Popayán visited the province every two or three years, the long muleback trip was seldom undertaken by presiding bishops. Francisco Luís Toro, "Obispos de Popayán que visitaron a Antioquia," *Antioquia Histórica* (Antioquia, 1925–1926), pp. 174–181, 252–263, 320–328, 361–371. This same ephemeral periodical of the old capital contains an "Informe del Virrey Espeleta al Gobierno Real de la Península sobre la Necessidad de la Creación de un Obispado en la Provincia de Antioquia" [1790], p. 462.

More serious for the economy was the 8 to 16 thousand pesos of gold which left the province annually for Church taxes (*diezmos* and *cuartas episcopales*). The Oidor Mon y Velarde ("Sucinta Relación ...") suggested that this drain had been largely responsible for the retarded development of the province. He listed remissions of *diezmos* outside the province during the biennium 1777–1778 as follows:

Antioquia	6,160 castellanos
Medellín	6,200 "
Ríonegro	6,000 "
Cancán-Yolombó	615 "
Remedios	180 "
San Bartolomé	750 "
Zaragoza	160 "
Cáceres-Nechí	200 "
	20,595 "

[10] According to Oviedo they found here "muchos crisoles e otros aparejos para fundir oro." He speaks of veins of white rock which were worked to a depth of 3 estados (15 feet). Quoted in Jijón y Caamaño, *op. cit.*, app. pp. 65–66.

[11] Uribe Ángel wrote in 1885 that the remains of an aqueduct, built by the slaves of the legendary criolla Doña María Centeño to bring water a distance of more than 3 leagues to her mines, could still be observed near Buriticá. The exact site of the mines, however, was lost to the memory of the inhabitants. (*Op. cit.*, p. 249.)

[12] Francisco Guillén Chaparro, "Memoria de los Pueblos de la Gobernación de Popayán ..." [c. 1582] *Archivo Historial* (Manizales), May, 1919, pp. 451–501.

[13] Vicente Restrepo, *A Study of the Gold and Silver Mines of Colombia*, translated from the Spanish by C. W. Fisher (New York, 1886), p. 26. This exhaustive work is rich in historical information. It was first published in Bogotá in 1884 and reissued in 1888 as *Estudio Sobre las Minas de Oro y Plata de Colombia*.

[14] Archivo Nacional, Bogotá, Minas de Antioquia, tomo 1, fol. 436 ff.

[15] Archivo de Antioquia, Medellín, Fundiciones, tomo 3.

[16] Mon y Velarde, *op. cit.*, p. 273.

[17] J. B. Boussingault, "Informe sobre las Minas de Antioquia" [*ca.* 1830] *Dyna*, Facultad Nacional de Minas, Medellín, June, 1946, pp. 16–23.

[18] The census of 1964 gave the municipio of Buriticá a population of 5,600. In 1947 the municipio was accessible only by pack trail, but a vehicular road has since been built in from Manglar on the Antioquia-Cañasgordas road.

[19] Simón, *op. cit.*

[20] Published as an appendix to Vicente Restrepo, *op. cit.* (2d ed., 1888). Among other things it stipulated that each miner was to have the image of the Virgin in his rancho and a high cross over the door. Fine for noncompliance, 10 pesos. Likewise there was to be no gambling. Anyone selling wine, ham, tobacco, cheese, or clothes to escaped Negroes was subject to a 100-peso fine and, if a slave, 200 lashes.

[21] Vásquez de Espinosa, *op. cit.*

[22] Restrepo Sáenz, *op. cit.*, p. 85.

[23] Simón, *op. cit.*, vol. 5, p. 322.

[24] Illustrative of the wealth of the lower Nechí was the famous pineapple-shaped nugget which was sent to the King of Spain as an example of its riches. As recompense the Crown awarded Zaragoza its own coat of arms.

[25] The classical account of this entrada is in Fray Pedro de Aguado, *op. cit.*

[26] Simón, *op. cit.*, vol. 3, p. 215.

[27] "Autos sobre la Fundación y Población y Apuntamiento de los Naturales de la Ciudad de Remedios," *Revista del Archivo Nacional* (Bogotá) January–February, 1937, pp. 52–68.

[28] According to the Oidor Guillén Chaparro there were in his time only three vecinos left in Victoria. He recommended that 1,000 Negro slaves be brought in if the settlement was to survive. (*Op. cit.*, pp. 451–501.)

[29] This epidemic, one of the worst ever known in those lands, is described by Simón (*op. cit.*, vol. 3, p. 271) as "... so universal for all types of peoples, natives and Spaniards alike, that, having commenced in the city of Mariquita in this New Kingdom in a single Negro woman who arrived in the city infected with this disease, bringing it from Guinea without having informed the inspectors, ... it infested all the New Kingdom and ran from the coast to the borders of Perú and to Chile and, in the north, to Caracas, destroying more than one-third of the population, both natives and Spaniards. In the New Kingdom only the city of Pamplona escaped, owing to the vigilant care of the corregidor of Tunja ... who guarded carefully against the entry of those from the outside."

[30] Simón, *op. cit.*, vol. 3, pp. 216–217.

[31] *Ibid.*

[32] It is locally held that the first settlers of Marinilla were Remedianos, perhaps dissident elements from earlier sites of Remedios in the San Carlos region.

Notes

[33] Archivo Nacional, Bogotá, Minas de Antioquia, tomo 4, fol. 990.
[34] Francisco Luís Toro, *op. cit.*, p. 177.
[35] Archivo Nacional, Bogotá, Visitas de Antioquia, tomo 2, fols. 393–398. Documents from the Herrera y Campuzano visita of 1614–1615 are also in Visitas de Antioquia, tomos 1 and 3; Visitas de Antioquia y Cundinamarca, tomo 1; Virreyes, tomo 6; Encomiendas, tomo 10.
[36] In 1631 the income of the Real Hacienda in Madrid from taxes on New World encomiendas was 966,228 ducats, of which Antioquia contributed only 4,000. Other figures included Popayán, 10,000; New Kingdom of Granada, 50,000; New Spain, 150,000; Yucatán, 100,000; Cuzco, 130,000. Silvio A. Zavala, *La Encomienda Indiana* (Madrid, 1935), p. 329.
[37] Tulio Ospina, in introduction to Mesa Jaramillo, *Catálogo de Minas* (Medellín, n.d.), pp. vii–viii.
[38] Simón, *op. cit.*, vol. 5, p. 322.
[39] The first recorded epidemic, which Padre Simón wrote had killed a third of the population in these provinces in 1546, was probably influenza. The smallpox epidemic of 1588 had a comparable mortality rate.
[40] Census of 1797, published in *El Guardian* (Medellín), October 22, 1878.
[41] Archivo de Antioquia, Bogotá, Estadístico y Censo, tomo 7, fol. 40.
[42] Mon y Velarde, *op. cit.*, p. 28.
[43] Archivo de Antioquia, Medellín, Visitas, tomo 2, expediente 14.
[44] Archivo de Antioquia, Medellín, Estadístico y Censo, tomo 5, fol. 25.
[45] In Caldas the disappearance of the Indian communities was less complete than has popularly been supposed. Besides the present-day native population living within the Río San Juan (Pacific) drainage in the municipio of Pueblorrico there is a considerable Indian element remaining in the vicinity of Ríosucio and Quinchía. Although the area east of the Cauca has generally been described as an unpeopled wilderness at the arrival of the first Antioqueño settlers, it is recorded that one of their number established cordial relations with "numerous groups of Indians" in the upper Río Pozo region near Salamina between 1827–1833, and that he recorded a vocabulary of their language. As late as 1860 there remained a few survivors on a hill above the valley of San Lorenzo "who were well appreciated by the inhabitants of Salamina," being distinguished for their capacity for hard work. Juan B. López, *Salamina; de su História y de sus Costumbres*, 2 vols. (Manizales, 1944).
[46] According to Simón (*op. cit.*, vol. 5, p. 367) 4,000–5,000 Negro slaves from Angola and other parts of Guinea arrived annually in Cartagena to be distributed in Perú, the New Kingdom of Granada, and other sections.
[47] *The Travels of Cieza de León*, p. 58.
[48] Vásquez de Espinosa, *op. cit.*, p. 341.
[49] Eduardo Posada, *La Esclavitud en Colombia* (Bogotá, 1933).
[50] Simón, *op. cit.*, vol. 3, pp. 217–218.
[51] Quoted in Tulio Ospina, *op. cit.*, pp. 415–416.
[52] Posada, *op. cit.*, p. 26.
[53] Quoted in Vicente Restrepo, *op. cit.*, p. 37.
[54] Posada, *op. cit.*, p. 18.
[55] Archivo de Antioquia, Medellín, Estadístico y Censo, tomo 5, expedientes 40–42.
[56] *Ibid.*, tomo 1, expediente 6.
[57] *Ibid.*, tomo 5, expediente 29.
[58] *Ibid.*
[59] Ernesto Estarita C., *Monografía de Zaragoza* (Medellín, 1941), p. 83.
[60] R. D. O. Johnson, "Native Placer Mining in Colombia," *Engineering & Mining Journal* (1912), vol. 94, pp. 741–744; West, *op. cit.*, pp. 52–77.

⁶¹ A provision in the charter of the new villa of Medellín (1675) provided that the proceeds from the sale of certain offices should be expended in draining the river which flowed through the valley. Vicente Restrepo, *op. cit.*, p. 31.
⁶² *Dyna*, Escuela de Minas, Medellín, June, 1946, pp. 16-23.
⁶³ Padre Joaquín de Finestrad, *El Vasallo Instruido*, quoted by Rufino Gutiérrez, *Monografías*, 2 vols. (Bogotá, 1920-1921), vol. 1, p. 413.
⁶⁴ For a review of d'Elúyar's work at Mariquita, see Vicente Restrepo, *op. cit.*, pp. 253-279.
⁶⁵ *Ibid.*, p. 251.
⁶⁶ José Manuel Restrepo, *op. cit.*, p. 257.
⁶⁷ Vicente Restrepo, *op. cit.*, pp. 280-282.
⁶⁸ Grosse, *op. cit.*, pp. 314 ff.
⁶⁹ B. L. Miller and J. T. Singewald, *The Mineral Deposits of South America* (New York, 1919).
⁷⁰ William F. Ward, "Nechí River Placer Mining," *Engineering & Mining Journal* (1913), vol. 96, pp. 297-299.
⁷¹ International Mining, which absorbed Pato's former owners, South American Gold and Platinum Co., in 1963, currently holds 66 per cent of Pato's stock. The remainder is in the hands of some 2,000 Pato stockholders. The stock is listed on the American Stock Exchange. International operates some dozen other dredges in South America and has the largest gold dredging fleet outside of the U.S.S.R.
⁷² Vicente Restrepo, *op. cit.*

NOTES TO CHAPTER V

COLONIAL AGRICULTURAL SETTLEMENT

¹ Luís Latorre Mendoza, *Historia e Historias de Medellín* (Medellín, 1934), p. 12.
² Aguado, *op. cit.*, p. 376.
³ Vásquez de Espinosa, *op. cit.*, p. 335.
⁴ Miguel Martínez, "Este Día," *El Colombiano* (Medellín), November 2, 1946. A group of the principal vecinos who met with the governor and the curate in 1649 to discuss plans for the construction of a tile church included men from the following places in Spain: Almendralejo (Extremadura), Albacete (Murcia), San Lucar de Barrameda (Andalucía), Castropol (Asturias), Burgos (Old Castile), Villalba de Ríoja (Galicia ?), and three each from Toledo and Jérez de la Frontera.
⁵ Ramón Franco R., *op. cit.*, p. 169.
⁶ *Antioquia Histórica* (Antioquia), November 1925, p. 206.
⁷ Archivo Central del Cauca, Popayán, signatura 1633.
⁸ Later disputes occurred between the curates of Antioquia and Medellín over rights to diezmos and other taxes collected from parishes as far away as Ayapel and Cáceres. Although is was claimed that the curacy of Medellín already contained most of the wealthy residents of the province so that little remained for the city of Antioquia, the above-mentioned parishes were in the end ordered to turn over their collections to Medellín. Archivo Central del Cauca, Popayán (documents dated 1695-1705).
⁹ Latorre Mendoza, *op. cit.*, pp. 14-15.
¹⁰ *Ibid.*, p. 36.
¹¹ In the preface to Gabriel Arango Mejía, *Genealogías de Antioquia y Caldas* (2d ed., Medellín, 1942), vol. 1.
¹² Manuel Antonio del Campo y Rivas, *Compendio historial sobre la fundación y estado actual de la Ciudad de Cartago* ... (Guadalajara, 1803).
¹³ Enrique Otero d'Acosta, "El Semitismo Antioqueño," *Archivo Historial* (Manizales), October, 1921, pp. 252-262.
¹⁴ M. F. Suárez, *Sueños de Luciano Pulgar*, 12 vols., (Bogotá, 1925-1940), vol. 10, p. 284.

[15] Emilio Robledo, *Vida del Mariscal Jorge Robledo*, p. 113.
[16] Antonio Gómez Campillo, "Erección del Municipio de Ríonegro," *Repertorio Histórico*, Medellín, pp. 643–645.
[17] The decree of the governor, authorized by the archbishop of Popayán and the viceroy of New Granada, was published in the *Repertorio Histórico*, March, 1924, pp. 194 ff. The old city of Arma, founded in 1542 near the junction of the Cauca and the Arma rivers, fell into early decay and had served principally in later years as a way station for the pack trains traveling between Antioquia and Popayán. It had originally twenty-eight Spanish encomenderos, one of whom was Cieza de León, the chronicler.
[18] Francisco Silvestre, *op. cit.*, p. 577.
[19] Mon y Velarde, *op. cit.*, p. 224.
[20] Gabriel Arango Mejía, "Algo sobre Orígenes de los Antioqueños," *IV Centenario de la Raza* (Medellín, 1941), p. 21.
[21] Silvestre, *op. cit.*, p. 578.
[22] Mon y Velarde, *op. cit.*, p. 58.
[23] Archivo de Antioquia, Medellín, Tierras, tomo 53 (unnumbered leaves).

NOTES TO CHAPTER VI

Modern Antioqueño Colonization

[1] Archivo de Antioquia, Medellín, Tierras, tomo 26, fol. 423. The boundaries of the grant included parts of the present-day municipios of La Ceja, Abejorral, and Sonsón.
[2] Manuel F. Calle G., "El Fundador de Abejorral," *Archivo Historial* (Manizales), October, 1920, pp. 469–470.
[3] Francisco Silvestre, "Relación que se cita presentada al Excelentísma Sr. Virrey de Sta Fé" [1776], *Archivo Historial* (Manizales), July, 1919, pp. 556–557. This road was finally opened by Spanish Loyalists using imprisoned patriots as laborers in 1817.
[4] Benigno A. Gutiérrez, *Sonsón en 1917* (Sonsón, 1917), p. 11.
[5] Archivo de Antioquia, Medellín, Fundaciones: Sonsón, 1789–1809, unnumbered leaves.
[6] Archivo Nacional, Bogotá, Poblaciones Varias, tomo 3, fols. 385 ff.
[7] Gutiérrez, *op. cit.*
[8] Archivo Nacional, Bogotá, Poblaciones Varias, tomo 2, fols. 449 ff.
[9] Archivo de Antioquia, Medellín, Fundaciones: Sonsón, 1789–1809. Another document gives a Church census figure of 2,080 for the same year but excluding "the 48 families which have arrived since the distribution of the lands." Archivo Nacional, Bogotá, Poblaciones Varias, tomo 2, fol. 749 f.
[10] Archivo de Antioquia, Medellín, Fundaciones: Sonsón, 1789–1809.
[11] Archivo de Antioquia, Medellín, Estadístico y Censo, tomo 1, fols. 1 ff. In this census document the families are listed as either "Familías Agregadores" or "Dueños de Posesión." The former, who served as hired hands to the latter, were in the majority by a 3-to-1 ratio.
[12] Manuel F. Calle G., *op. cit.*, pp. 436–444.
[13] Mon y Velarde, *op. cit.*, p. 35.
[14] Lázaro Villegas E., *Geografía e História de Aguadas* (Manizales, 1945). The first houses were built on the site of Aguadas in 1808.
[15] On October 12, 1832, the provincial *Cámara* "decreed Arma moved to the Pácora region." A total of 1,172 inhabitants moved on, taking some of the Church furnishings with them, and 584 remained in Arma. Delio Gómez García, *Santiago de Arma* (Aguadas, 1941), p. 53.
[16] Archivo de Antioquia, Medellín, Fundaciones, tomo 11, unnumbered leaves. The

place of origin of the signators suggests the role that the early nineteenth-century Antioqueño settlements were to play in feeding the later immigrant stream to the south. Of the one hundred and forty-five signers there were eight from Abejorral, five from Arma Viejo, five from the valley of Medellín, one from Ríonegro and the remaining one hundred and twenty-six from Sonsón. Others, of course, were arriving at Sonsón to take their places. Some, undoubtedly, were transients for whom Sonsón, the jumping-off place for the south, was the last address.

[17] Following a trip through these lands in 1801, Don José María Aranzazu had filed a petition for the grant. Delays in the proceedings were further extended by the War of Independence until Juan de Díos Aranzazu, as heir to his father's claim, asked, and surprisingly received, confirmation of the title from the court of primera instancia at Ríonegro in 1824.

[18] The principal stockholders of this company were Elias González, a relative of Aranzazu, and Luís Gómez de Salazar, resident of Ríonegro. Luís Londoño O., *Manizales* (Manizales, 1936), p. 198.

[19] The government decree founding Salamina seems to have assumed that the Aranzazu grant did not exist. The ratification of the latter by the Supreme Court three years later simply added to the confusion. Similiar cases of towns decreed on private lands by the colonial government were Yarumal, Carolina, Sonsón, and San Carlos.

[20] Of these the type example is Fermín López, who had come to Sonsón from Ríonegro in 1804 to win his fortune. Attracted by the tales of the "fertile, inexhaustible lands to the south," he sold out after a few years and went to Salamina. When the courts ruled his hacienda the property of González, Salazar y Cía. in 1833 he packed up once more and, with "a brother, sons, nephew and a considerable number of peones and oxen," started his classic trek southward. Selecting the site, later occupied by Manizales, for a town, he returned to Salamina seeking additional companions. But, informed that he had mistaken the Río Guacaica for the Chinchiná and that he was still within the bounds of the company's claim, he moved on with his party to Cartago for supplies and obtained permission to found the new town of Santa Rosa de Cabal. López died in 1846 at the age of eighty-two, having opened the road for the thousands of land-hungry Antioqueños who were to follow him. His three sons returned from Santa Rosa to Salamina. Juan B. López O., *op. cit.*, vol. 1, p. 98.

[21] *Repertorio Histórico* (Medellín), October, 1924, p. 376.

[22] Manizales means literally "place of the granites"; it is derived from the Antioqueño word for "granite," *maní*.

[23] The first business of these settlers, according to a later account by one of their numbers, was the planting of maize and the fattening of pigs for the Ríonegro market. Wild cattle, which had originally belonged to a religious order at Mariquita, were also hunted on the flanks of the Nevado del Ruiz. Enrique Otero d'Acosta, "Reportaje con Don Alejandro Echeverri," *Archivo Historial* (Manizales), March, 1919, pp. 388–392.

[24] Ferdinand von Schenck, "Reisen in Antioquia," *Petermanns Mitteilungen* (1883), vol. 29, p. 217.

[25] Rufino Gutiérrez, *Monografías*, vol. 2, p. 36. Gold production in the municipio of Manizales has fallen off sharply in recent years.

[26] Ferdinand von Schenck, *op. cit.*

[27] Juan Pinzón, "Apuntes Históricos y Crónicas de Manizales," *Archivo Historial* (Manizales), March, 1920, pp. 263–267.

[28] Law 37 of 1871.

[29] Archivo del Congreso Nacional, Bogotá, Leyes (1849), tomo 2, 174–175.

[30] Cartago had been founded in 1540 and named after the Carthagenians in Badillo's party. By 1570 it had become an important city "of 82 blocks, with a large temple and

a *fundición*. Indian raids eventually forced its removal to the city's present site near the Cauca in 1690. Carlos Echeverri Uribe, *Apuntes para la Historia de Pereira* (Medellín, 1921). An extraordinary urban history, Luis Duque Gómez et al., *História de Pereira* (Pereira, 1963) was published by the city's Club Rotario to commemorate the 400th anniversary of its first founding. It was not available for consultation at the time this study was made.

[81] A 12,000-hectare grant was made to the new cabildo of Pereira in 1870. Any shortage of land was to be made up from the lands of Condina, a town established in 1851 a few miles south of Pereira on a high plain between the Consota and Barbas rivers. Condina had been abandoned shortly thereafter, "its inhabitants dispersing within the limits of the 24,000 fanegas of land which the government had ceded its founders in 1853." Carlos Echeverri Uribe, *op. cit.*, pp. 48–51, and Heliodoro Peña, *Geografía é Historia de la Provincia del Quindío* (Popayán, 1892), p. 108.

[82] Carlos Echeverri Uribe, *op. cit.*, p. 45.

[83] See, for example, Jaime Buitrago, *Hombres Transplantados* (Manizales, 1943), and Antonio J. Arango, *Quindío: Epopeya de la Colonización Antioqueña* (Manizales, 1940), both historical novels on the settlement of the Quindío.

[84] *La Tribuna* (Medellín), September 25, 1880.

[85] Heliodoro Peña, *op. cit.*, pp. 20–21.

[86] Roberto Restrepo, "El Quindío y su Colonización," *Archivo Historial* (Manizales, July, 1921, pp. 228–231.

[87] *Ibid.*

[88] *Ibid.* A further factor, according to one contemporary editor, was the pressure of the loan sharks and moneylenders (*gamonales*) of Ríonegro against the emigrants. *Los Ecos del Ruiz* (Manizales), October 24, 1880.

[89] Antonio García, *Geografía Económica de Colombia, IV: Caldas* (Bogotá, 1937), p. 237.

[40] Buitrago, *op. cit.*, p. 109.

[41] Named in honor of the St. Louis (Mo.) Exposition of 1903. The town had originally been laid out in 1885 at a place known as La Mesa. After its formal founding in 1903 it remained a corregimiento of Bugalagrande until 1914 when the district of Sevilla was established. Caicedonia, founded with the support of the Empresa Burila in 1905, did not become a separate municipio until 1923. Porfirio Díaz del Castillo, *El Valle del Cauca: Historia y Realidades de sus Municipios* (Cali, 1937), p. 245.

[42] *Diario Oficial* (Bogotá), May 22, 1940.

[43] Mon y Velarde, *op. cit.*, p. 30.

[44] Archivo de Antioquia, Medellín, Fundaciones, tomo 1.

[45] Uribe Ángel, *op. cit.*, p. 153.

[46] *Ibid.*, pp. 158–159. It is interesting to compare the very meager historical data available on the founding of such towns as Fredonia (today one of the largest centers in Antioquia) with the voluminous material on earlier colonial foundations. The tireless and artistic scriveners of colonial Spain were replaced by drab legalists in the time of the republic. Nor have the historians of later years been concerned significantly with nineteenth-century settlement history. Political and military heroes and their exploits dominate the literature of republican Colombia.

[47] Uribe Ángel, *op. cit.*, p. 154.

[48] Archivo del Congreso Nacional, Bogotá, Senado, 1835, tomo 5.

[49] *Memoria del Ministerio de Industrias al Congreso Nacional*, (Bogotá, 1931), vol. 3. The original grant was for 12,000 fanegas. A second cession of additional lands "in the mountains of Comía" was apparently made in 1837. *Ibid.*, vol. 4, p. 32.

[50] Uribe Ángel, *op. cit.*, pp. 154–155.

[51] Archivo de Antioquia, Medellín, Baldíos, 1847–1859, tomo 3, fols. 45 ff.

[52] Rufino Gutiérrez, *Monografías*, vol. 1, p. 322.
[53] Uribe Ángel, *op. cit.*, pp. 389–394.
[54] Archivo del Congreso Nacional, Bogotá, Leyes, 1839, tomo 3, fol. 28.
[55] Cervecería Union, S.A., *Monografías de Antioquia* (Medellín, 1940 ?), pp. 112 ff.
[56] *Ibid.*, p. 222.
[57] Von Schenck, *op. cit.*, vol. 29, p. 215.
[58] Fray Jerónimo de Escobar, "Relación sobre el Cáracter e Costumbres de los Indios de la Provincia de Popayán," in J. Jijon y Caamaño, *Sebastián Benalcázar*, vol. 2, appendix.
[59] Guillén Chaparro, *op. cit.*, p. 492.
[60] Boussingault, *op. cit.*, vol. 4.
[61] The bewildering succession of names by which many Colombian towns have been known in recent epochs is well illustrated by Ríosucio, which at one time or another has been called Bolívar, Polonia, and Hispania, as well as the earlier names of Quiebralomo and La Montaña. The latter was actually a separate parish until 1819 when it was joined to Quiebralomo. Their combined population was more than 3,000 in 1843 and by 1870 had reached 5,689. In 1938 the town of Ríosucio alone had a population of 5,801, making its the largest Antioqueño settlement west of the Río Cauca, whereas the municipio, with 27,684, was the seventh largest in Caldas.
[62] The Cámara de Comercio of Cali, in opposing a proposed boundary change between the Chocó and Valle, pointed to the fact that these new Antioqueño settlements of the last forty years are in a formerly unproductive area which today yields more than 700,000 sacks of coffee annually. *El Tiempo* (Bogotá), October 22, 1946.
[63] Alberto Machado S., "Fomento de la Industria Cafetera en el Valle del Cauca," *Rev. Fac. Nac. Agr.*, 1942, vol. 19, pp. 448–452.
[64] Roberto Pineda Giraldo, "Colonización e Inmigración y el Problema Indígena," *Boletín de Arqueología* (Bogotá), October–December, 1946, vol. 2, pp. 361–379.
[65] The curious occurrence of this North American place name here traces back to the popularity at this time of the Spanish novel, *Eusebio*, by Pedro de Montengón (1745–1825). It is the story of a Spanish boy shipwrecked on the Atlantic Coast of the United States and brought up by a Quaker family. According to Emilio Robledo of Medellín the name of the Antioqueño settlement of Filadelfia, in Caldas, was suggested by the same source.
[66] *Pensilvania* (Pensilvania, Antioquia), 1906, p. 66.
[67] Archivo del Congreso Nacional, Bogotá, Cámara, 1890, tomo 2, fols. 77 ff.
[68] Rufino Gutiérrez, *op. cit.*, vol. 2, p. 199.
[69] This 2,980-meter saddle, at the point where the three departments of Caldas, Tolima, and Valle del Cauca join, has curiously been neglected by government engineers who have chosen the 3,280-meter Depresión de Calarcá for the route of the highway and proposed railroad linking the Magdalena and Cauca valleys. Gonzalo Paris Lozano, *Geografía Económica de Colombia; VII: Tolima*, pp. 32, 110–111.
[70] Julio C. Cubillos, "Arqueología de Ríoblanco (Chaparral, Tol.)," *Boletín de Arqueología* (Bogotá), November–December, 1945.
[71] Uribe Ángel, *op. cit.*, p. 266, wrote of the Urrao-Quibdó trade in 1885: "... it is a slight commerce consisting of the sale of some cheese and a little salted meat, carried on the shoulders of peones through the middle of almost impassable mountains."
[72] International Railway Commission, *Report of Surveys and Explorations made by Corps No. 2 in Costa Rica, Colombia and Ecuador, 1891–93* (Washington, 1896), William F. Schunck, engineer in charge, vol. 2, pp. 75–76.
[73] *Informe que el Secretario de Hacienda presenta al Sr. Gobernador del Departamento para la Asamblea de 1898* (Medellín, 1898), p. 20.
[74] For a more detailed treatment and references for material in the following paragraphs see James J. Parsons, *Antioquia's Corridor to the Sea: An Historical Geography of the Settlement of Urabá*, Univ. Calif.: Ibero-Americana, vol. 49 (1967).

[75] B. L. Gordon, *The Human Geography and Ecology of the Sinú Country of Colombia*, Univ. Calif.: Ibero-Americana, vol. 39 (1957); James J. Parsons, "The Settlement of the Sinú Valley, Colombia," *Geographical Review*, 1952, vol. 42, pp. 67–86.

[76] G. Reichel-Dolmatoff, "Apuntes Etnográficos Sobre los Indios del Alto Sinú," *Revista Acad. Col. Ciencias Físicas...*, 12:29–40 (1963).

[77] Among schemes that failed have been the Albernia colony in Amazonia "where 200 Antioqueño families were sacrificed in an almost inhuman manner," the Patiburrú penal colony near Puerto Berrío, and the Ciudad Mutís (Bahía Solano) colony on the Chocó coast. *Informe del Fondo de Fomento Agrícola e Industrial de Antioquia* (Medellín, 1946).

NOTES TO CHAPTER VII

Public Land Policies

[1] For a description of the disastrous effects of this policy upon the watershed of Manizales see José Royo y Gómez, "El Territorio de Manizales y la Estabilidad de su Suelo," *Revista de la Academia Colombiana de Ciencias Exactas, Físicas y Naturales* (Bogotá, 1943), pp. 337–343.

[2] *Memoria del Ministerio de Industrias*, 1931, vol. 5, pp. 249 ff.

[3] The government of the province of Antioquia was at first more concerned with the problem of colonization than was Bogotá. In 1843 the governor wrote: "... with the new town of Neira ... it will be possible to open communications with the province of Cauca which will be shorter and easier than that which is presently used through the canton of Supía. ... These colonizing enterprises demand the preferential attention of the legislature because they are to the admitted advantage of all the province. ... Lack of funds to transport the settlers ... and to survey the lands has been an almost insuperable obstacle up to now. ... Settlement for much time to come must remain a matter of individual initiative. ... A new town is urgently needed on the Gulf of Urabá ... and a road is being built." *Memorial del Gobernador de Antioquia a la Cámara Provincial* (Medellín, 1843).

[4] The Colombian fanega (or fanegada) of 1.59 acres was used until the 1850's in delimiting adjudications, after which they were made in hectares (2.47 acres). The Federación Nacional de Cafeteros stilll uses fanegadas in its coffee census. The cuadra, used by cattlemen, is comparable to the fanega.

[5] For a review of this problem, see Diego Mendoza, *Ensayo sobre la Evolución de Propriedad en Colombia* (Bogotá, 1897), and, more recently, Juan Friede, *El Indio en Lucha por la Tierra* (Bogotá, 1944).

[6] *Memoria del Ministerio de Industrias*, 1931, vols. 4, 6.

[7] *Ibid.*, vol. 4.

[8] Estanislao Gómez Barrientos, "Extranjeros Benemeritos de Antioquia," *Repertorio Histórico* (Medellín), September, 1924, pp. 311–345.

[9] Law 13 of 1937 authorized the president of the republic to forbid denouncement of alluvial mining claims in important agricultural zones by executive decrees. In Antioquia the valleys of the Río Negro (1939) and the Río Grande (Entrerríos, 1944) have been so exempted.

NOTES TO CHAPTER VIII

Population Growth

[1] An account of one group of Swedish adventurers who came to Antioquia in 1826 is Rosa Nisser's *Guld och gröna skogar* (Stockholm, 1939).

A colony of sixteen refugee Polish families recently settled in the municipio of La

Unión. Within two months all but one had abandoned their new fincas "owing to the sterility of the soil and the attitude of the local population." *Mensaje del Gobernador de Antioquia a la Hon. Asamblea* (Medellín, 1940), p. 153. The London-published *Colombian Trade Review*, September, 1927, advertised "An Opportunity for Small Farmers on the Property Known as 'Alaska,' three miles from Salento, Caldas." There seems to have been no response.

[2] Uribe Angel, *op. cit.*, pp. 113–114.
[3] Führmann and Mayor, *op. cit.*, p. 43.
[4] Jorge Rodríguez, "La Fecundidad en Antioquia," *Boletín de Estadística* (Medellín), September, 1927, pp. 29–33.
[5] Gastroenteritis is the single most common cause of death in both Antioquia and Caldas; pneumonia is second. (In 1965 some 120,000 cases of diarrhea and enteritis were reported in the two departments among children of less than two years of age.)
[6] Dysentery was reportedly unknown in Titiribí before coffee began to be washed in the local springs and streams and its pulp left to decay. Rufino Gutiérrez, *op. cit.*, vol. 1, p. 307.
[7] Statistics on disease and mortality in this chapter are from the Dirección Departamental de Estadística, Medellín, and the Departamento Administrativa Estadística Nacional, Bogotá, or from U. S. Department of Commerce, 1944.
[8] At the Pato mines near Zaragoza a malaria incidence of 67 per cent in 1937 was reduced to 6–7 per cent in three years as a result of control measures instituted by foreign engineers.
[9] Virginia Gutiérrez de Pineda, *La Familia en Colombia*, vol. 1, Bogotá, 1962 makes reference to the role of prostitution in colonial Antioquia, pp. 265, 358. A second volume of this remarkable sociological study (in press) considers the contemporary situation.
[10] *El Colombiano* (Medellín), January 18, 1947.

NOTES TO CHAPTER IX
THE AGRICULTURAL BASIS OF OCCUPANCE

[1] José Manuel Restrepo, *op. cit.*, pp. 267 ff.
[2] Even on the lands of earlier occupance closer to Medellín and Ríonegro much of the arable land is held in small parcels. The rolling, 4,632-hectare watershed of the upper Q. Piedrasblancas (El Mazo), less than two hours climb by trail from Medellín, was held, until recently, by 222 separate owners. The two largest blocks of land were 350 and 175 hectares, respectively. This is an average of 20.9 hectares (52 acres) to a family for generally Grade C red upland soils near the tierra fría boundary where scratching out a living means hard work and minimal returns. Recently this valley has been growing carnations to be flown to markets in the Canal Zone, but the lands are gradually being bought up by the municipio of Medellín to be placed under a watershed conservation program. A reforestation program to replace the native bracken and scrub oak and to heal the old scars of former mining operations is being vigorously pressed.
[3] Acknowledgment is gratefully made to Dr. Edgar Anderson of the Missouri Botanical Gardens who has inspected our collection of Antioquia maizes. His comments on their general significance and relationships have been incorporated in the paragraphs which follow.
[4] Despite frequent denials by authorities, overzealous Antioqueños have persisted in the apochryphal claim that the Latin binomial for maize (*Zea mays*) honors the Antioqueño statesman, Francisco Zea.
[5] Antioqueño mazamorra is entirely distinct from the stew formed from corn meal, beans, potatoes, and meat which is known by that name in Bogotá.
[6] José Manuel Restrepo, *op. cit.*, p. 270.
[7] J. B. Montoya y Flores, "Titiribíes y Sinufanáes," *Repertorio Histórico* (Medellín), August, 1922, p. 560.

Notes 205

[8] Although I did not encounter it, Joaquín Antonio Uribe, *Flora de Antioquia* (Medellín, 1941), p. 128, has recorded a podcorn for Antioquia. Earlier viewed as a very primitive type, geneticists now know that podcorn is due to a single gene mutation which is likely to turn up in any kind of corn. Its occurrence seems not to be of particular significance. The relative scarcity of native sweet corn may be related to the curiously minor role of chicha and other fermented drinks in Antioquia, for sweet corn is most commonly used among native peoples as the base for superior alcoholic beverages.

[9] Kaj Birket-Smith, "The Origin of Maize Cultivation," *Det Kgl. Danske Videnskabernes Selskab, Historisk-Filologiske Meddelelser* (Copenhagen, 1943), vol. 30, no. 3. Birket-Smith believed that the wide distribution of Colombian words for maize (from Nicaragua to Uruguay) supported this interpretation. For the critical Antioquia-Quimbaya region, however, the Indian words for maize were not considered; his evidence all came from the Bogotá Cordillera and Amazonia. Several terms still current in Antioquia are of Peruvian Indian origin, including *choclo* (green corn), *capio* (flour corn), *tusa* (cob) and *pisingallo* (popcorn).

[10] C. O. Sauer, "The Cultivated Plants of South and Central America," *Handbook of South American Indians, Bull. 143*, Bureau of American Ethnology, vol. 6, in press.

[11] S. M. Bukasov, "The Cultivated Plants of Mexico, Guatemala and Colombia," *Bulletin Applied Botany, Genetics and Plant Breeding* (Leningrad), suppl. 47, pp. 1–553 (manuscript translation in Department of Geography, Univ. of California, Berkeley).

[12] Montoya y Flores, *op. cit.*, pp. 556–571.

[13] In the department of Antioquia in 1938 the 3,810 trapiches in operation were distributed as follows: animal-driven, 1,656; hand-operated, 1,256; waterwheels, 838; motor-driven, 80.

[14] In some parts of Colombia sugar cane is cultivated above 2,000 meters. Caldas reported having seen it growing at 2,230 meters near Ibarra, Ecuador, in the same field with wheat. Nearby, under a single roof, was a flour mill and a trapiche. Francisco José de Caldas, "Memoria sobre la Nivelación de las Plantas ... ," pp. 85–95.

[15] Carlos E. Chardón, *Viajes y Naturaleza* (Caracas, 1941).

[16] The items listed are taken from the cost of living index published each year in the *Anuario Estadístico de Antioquia*.

[17] José Manuel Restrepo, *op. cit.*

[18] *Ecos del Ruiz* (Manizales), December 5, 1880.

[19] Probably the highest grown cacao in either Antioquia or Caldas is that in the Q. Chinchiná above the coffee experiment station where a criollo-pajarito hybrid plantation prospers at 1,400 meters above sea level.

[20] National Archives (Washington, D.C.), Consular Letters: Medellín, no. 32, from Nestro Castro, May 4, 1882.

[21] Locally grown anise, he observed, would keep the royal distillery at Medellín operating during the rainy seasons when imports from Bogotá over the Nare road were either interrupted or too costly to permit maintenance of operations. Mon y Velarde, *op. cit.* In 1788, the year in which he wrote, the administration of the aguardiente monopoly in Antioquia purchased 746 arrobas of anise seed of which most came from local "cosecheros." The remainder was brought in from Nare. In the same year the administration purchased 3,118 mule loads of molasses (*miel*) and 1,866 mule loads of fuel wood. Archivo de Antioquia, Medellín, Libros de Aguardiente, 1788.

[22] The production of anise has fallen off sharply in the last few years. In 1945 less than 10 per cent of the anise purchased by Rentas Departamentales de Antioquia was grown in the department, the rest coming from the Pasto-Popayán area and from Perú, Argentina, and México. Antioquia's anise production at the end of the nineteenth century had averaged close to 100,000 kilograms a year.

[23] Rice is a major dietary item only in the lowlands. Elsewhere maize is preeminent.

[24] Simón, op. cit., vol. 3, p. 131.
[25] The 246 mule loads (cargas) of imports declared to Crown officials at Santa Fé de Antioquia between February 1, 1685 and September 15, 1687, included: clothes and goods from Castile, 52; clothes and goods from Quito, 20; clothes and goods from New Granada, 9; tobacco, 45; wine, 37; cacao, 27; wax (for candles), 19; iron, 8; aguardiente, 8; flour, 4; olive oil, 2; wool, 2; other miscellaneous, 13. Archivo de Antioquia, Medellín, Caminos, tomo 1, expediente 1.
[26] The municipios of Santa Bárbara, Venecia, and Bolívar are the leading producers.
[27] Mon y Velarde, op. cit.
[28] Ecos del Ruiz (Manizales), October 31, 1880.
[29] Antonio J. Restrepo, *El Moderno Imperialismo* (Barcelona, 1919).
[30] *Informe del Gobernador a la Asamblea* (Medellín, 1892), vol. 2, pp. 33–42.
[31] In 1922 the abnormally high price of raw silk on the international market caused a brief flurry of interest in Caldas. Production there reached a peak of 2,500 pounds in 1925, but a soaring coffee market soon brought an end to the business. Antonio García, *Geografía Económica de Colombia, IV: Caldas*, p. 504.
[32] Lester H. Dewey, *Fiber Production in the Western Hemisphere*, United States Department of Agriculture Misc. Publ. 518 (Washington, 1943), contains excellent illustrations of the Colombian cabuya.
[33] Aurelio Mejía, "La Ganadería en Antioquia," *Revista Nacional de Agricultura* (Bogotá), March, 1944, p. 47.
[34] Archivo de Antioquia, Medellín, Tierras, tomo 37, expediente 645.
[35] Mejía, op. cit., p. 49.
[36] Archivo de Antioquia, Medellín, Minas, sec. 2, tomo 19, no. 4350.
[37] Although the average milk production for unimproved native stock is one and a half liters a day, a selected herd at the department's Granja Ganadera del Nus at San Roque produces close to two and a half liters a day with 3.7 per cent butter-fat. Crossings with European breeds have brought highly promising results.
[38] The declining numbers of blanco oreji-negro may be in part attributable to the increase in cattle rustling associated with the *violencia* of recent years. The *criollo* cattle are slow moving, phlegmatic, and easy to handle while the zebu is *muy bravo*.
[39] Alvin H. Sanders, "The Taurine World," *National Geographic Magazine*, December, 1925, pp. 591–710.
[40] Charles Darwin, *The Variation of Animals and Plants under Domestication* (2d ed., New York, 1876), vol. 1, pp. 82 ff.
[41] John Storer, *The Wild White Cattle of Great Britain* (London, 1881). Of the better preserved Park herds, that of Chillingham Castle (Northumberland) had had the same black ears, muzzle, and hooves in the seventeenth century, but through the agency of human selection the ear color later became a brownish red. The Hamilton herd of Cadzow Park, Lanarkshire, Scotland, still has black ears. Storer also gives references to several descriptions of white cattle with black points in southeastern Europe (Hungary, Serbia) from whence he surmised came the urus progenitors of the Chillingham and other Park herds.
[42] Francisco Silvestre, "Informe sobre la Apertura del Camino desde Antioquia hasta Ayapel ..." [June 4, 1776], *Archivo Historial* (Manizales), July, 1919, pp. 560–566.
[43] In 1945 the movement of cattle to the interior from the Sabanas de Bolívar was reported as follows:

To Antioquia:
    via "La Trocha" 30,859
    via Puerto Berrío 34,726
To Caldas:
    via La Dorada 35,000

[44] An overland stock trail was first opened between the Sinú and Turbo in 1915. Another trail led from the Alto Sinú to Chigorodó, from which stock were driven overland to Dabeiba.

⁴⁵ The *Feria* is administered by the Empresas Públicas de Medellín; it earns the city several million pesos a month. It covers 30,000 square meters and has a capacity of 11,000 head. See E. Livardo Ospina, *op. cit.*, pp. 124–125.

⁴⁶ Letter from Eusebio A. Jaramillo quoted in José Domingo Sierra S., *Estudios sobre los Pastos de Antioquia* (Medellín, [1916]).

⁴⁷ Carlos E. Chardón, *Reconocimiento Agro-pecuario del Valle del Cauca* (San Juan, Puerto Rico, 1930), p. 70.

⁴⁸ Letter written in 1907 by General Uribe Uribe, quoted in *Boletín Agricola* (Bogotá), May–June, 1931, p. 586.

⁴⁹ The confusion over terminology has been furthered in Enrique Pérez Arbelaez, *Plantas Utiles de Colombia* (Bogotá, 1947), p. 118.

⁵⁰ José Domingo Sierra S., *op. cit.* Writing of Medellín in 1916 he says: "Today we have magnificent finishing pastures on these lands which by reason of their temperate climate and little fertility had only been usable by a few small herds.... It has doubled and tripled milk production."

⁵¹ Rufino Gutiérrez, *op. cit.*, vol. 2, p. 49.

NOTES TO CHAPTER X
COFFEE

¹ Nicolas Sáenz, *Memoria sobre el Cultivo del Cafeto* (3d ed., Bogotá, 1895), p. 9.

² Robert C. Beyer, "The Colombian Coffee Industry: Origins and Major Trends, 1740–1940," Ph.D. thesis, University of Minnesota, 1947.

³ Quoted in Nicolas Sáenz, *op. cit.*, p. 8.

⁴ Diego Monsalve, *Colombia Cafetera* (Barcelona, 1927), p. 237. Other references name Pedro Sáenz as owner of the first cafetal at Ríonegro.

⁵ Quoted *ibid*.

⁶ Francisco Javier Cisneros, *Report on the Construction of a Railway from Puerto Berrío to Barbosa, Antioquia* (New York, 1878), p. 38.

⁷ Estanislao Gómez Barrientos, "Don Tulio Ospina," *Repertorio Histórico* (Medellín), April, 1923, pp. 243–280.

⁸ *Memoria que el Secretaria de Hacienda y Fomento presenta al Ciudano Presidente del Estado* (Medellín, 1883), p. xviii.

⁹ *Informe que el Secretaria de Hacienda Presenta al Sr. Gobernador del Departamento* (Medellín, 1898), p. 35.

¹⁰ Rudesindo Ocampo and Tulio Londoño J., "Reseña Histórica de la Industria de Café en el Departamento de Caldas," *Revista Cafetera Colombiano* (Bogotá), May–June, 1932, pp. 1454–1459.

¹¹ *Ecos del Ruiz* (Manizales), December 19, 1880. The editor of this short-lived periodical, Frederico Velásquez C., had a clear, sharp eye for agricultural development which delights the historical geographer.

¹² The 1932 census data is in the Federation's *Boletín Extraordinario* No. 5, March, 1933; the later one for Tolima and Cundinamarca in *Revista Cafetera de Colombia*, May, 1942, pp. 2865–2872. More recent figures, probably of less reliability, appear in Fundación para el Progreso de Colombia, *La Industria Cafetera en la Agricultura Colombiana*, 1962, p. 18.

¹³ In 1960 some 66 per cent of all coffee fincas in Colombia were of less than 10 hectares, 26 per cent from 10 to 50 hectares, and 8 per cent larger than 50 hectares.

¹⁴ *La Industria Cafetera en la Agricultura Colombiana*.

¹⁵ Estanislao Gómez Barrientos, "Informe sobre la Industria Cafetera Antioqueña," *Boletín Agricola* (Bogotá), December, 1916, p. 102.

¹⁶ Experiments in southern Florida have shown that coffee requires shade for fruiting and normal growth there. Many of the tropical crop plants have the ecological status of *hylophytes*, that is, being especially adapted to forest undergrowth conditions where sun and wind do not reach the soil surface, which explains why so many tropical seeds such as coffee and cacao are viable only in the fresh state and do not withstand drying. Their shade tolerance is also high. O. F. Cook, "Coffee and Cacao in Southern Florida," *Science*, n.s., 1936, pp. 55–56.

[17] See, e.g., Feliz Rawitscher, "Die Erschöpfung tropischer Boden infolge der Entwaldung," *Acta Tropica* (Basle), 1946, vol. 3, no. 3, and Pierre Gourou, *Les Pays Tropicaux* (Paris, 1947).

[18] Chardón, *op. cit.*, p. 254.

[19] Mariano Ospina Rodríguez had recognized the erosion problem in his 1880 pamphlet, *El Cultivo del Café*, when he wrote: "Coffee grows and produces well on very steep slopes, but the plantation cannot last long for, owing to the necessity of maintaining the soil free from grass and weeds, the copious tropical rains will wash away the earth and uproot the trees."

[20] Some of the abandonment is due to fungus diseases, most of which have only recently become serious. *Gotera*, a fungus leaving white spots on leaves and fruit, has destroyed many Caldas fincas. A root rot (*llaga*) and iron rust (*hierra de mancha*) have also become virulent. The failure of the cafetales of the Fresno region has been attributed to *palomilla*. The Old World leaf blight, *Hemelia Vasatrix*, has never gained a foothold. Between diseased coffee and steep slopes there is a distinct correlation, suggesting that a weakened plant condition induced by erosion may favor such mass infections.

[21] Hugh Bennett, "Soil Conservation in Latin America," in *Plants and Plant Science in Latin America*, Franz Verdoon, ed. (Waltham, Mass., 1945), pp. 165–169; see also William Vogt, *Road to Survival* (New York, 1948).

[22] Visitors are likely to get an extreme view of the destruction by erosion in Colombia, for the Bogotá region and the easily accessible uplands along the surfaced highway to Pamplona have been the most cruelly exploited of all. The 20-mile drive between Bogotá and the spectacular Salto de Tequendamá passes through an area of almost complete soil destruction. The municipios of Bosa and Soacha are erosional skeletons.

NOTES TO CHAPTER XI
Transportation

[1] *Colección de Documentos Inéditos sobre la Geografía y la Historia de Colombia*, ed., Antonio B. Cuervos, 4 vols. (Bogotá, 1891–1894), vol. 2, p. 253.

[2] From the Gulf of Urabá to Antioquia was rated a twenty to twenty-two day trip, with twelve to fourteen days for poling or paddling to the head of navigation on the Río León and eight days overland. Joaquín F. Fidalgo, "Derrotero de las Costas de la América Septentrional desde Maracaibo hasta el Río de Chagres," Cuervos' *Colección de Documentos ...*, vol. 1, pp. 188 ff.

[3] Archivo de Antioquia, Medellín, Caminos-Colonia, tomo 1, expedientes 10, 11.

[4] The first governor of Antioquia, Andres de Valdivia, apparently entered the province from Cartagena by this route in 1570. José María Restrepo Sáenz, *op. cit.*, Gobernadores de Antioquia, p. 6.

[5] Archivo Nacional, Bogotá, Caciques y Indios, tomo 3, fols. 1–211. This interesting volume contains depositions relating to the *bodegas* of Puerto Espíritu Santo from 1756–1761. The testimony indicates that considerable contrabrand passed through the port and that it was notorious "that the vecinos of San Andrés and Junco live on the contraband trade."

[6] Mon y Velarde, *op. cit.*, p. 49.

[7] The destinations of the merchandise imported into Antioquia during the five-year period, 1773–1778, were:

	Goods from Castile	Goods of the New Kingdom
To: Antioquia	451 cargas	701 ¾ cargas
Medellín	259 cargas	2,394 cargas
Ríonegro	301 ½ cargas	2,147 ¾ cargas
	1,011 ½ cargas	5,243 ½ cargas

The report, signed at Santa Fé de Antioquia September 1, 1778, does not, of course, include contraband goods. Archivo de Antioquia, Medellín, Caminos-Colonia, tomo 1, expediente 9.

[8] A small amount of cargo, primarily destined for Remedios, entered the province through San Bartolomé, a *bodega* on the Magdalena a few miles north of modern Puerto Berrío. A report on the opening of this road in 1778 is found in Archivo de Antioquia, Medellín, Caminos-Colonia, tomo 1, expediente 8.

[9] The Oidor Mon y Velarde reported to the Viceroy in 1788: "The administration of the bodegas of Nare, usurped many years by intriguers and profiteers in prejudice to the King and the people, has unfortunately been one of the greatest obstacles to the development of the wretched province of Antioquia." (*Op. cit.*, p. 48.)

[10] Francisco Silvestre, "Relación que se cita presentada al Excelentismo Sr. Virrey de Santa Fé" [May 8, 1776], *Archivo Historial* (Manizales), July, 1919, pp. 551–560.

[11] Archivo de Antioquia, Medellín, Caminos-Colonia, tomo 1, expediente 9.

[12] An alternative route slightly to the north passed through San Rafael and was known as the Muños Road. José Manuel Restrepo observed that it was less popular than the Juntas route but equally good and capable of improvement. But most travelers during the nineteenth century followed the more southerly route through the valley of San Carlos.

[13] Antonio J. Duque, "Nare, el más antiguo y el primer Puerto de Antioquia," *Repertorio Histórico* (Medellín), March, 1937, pp. 440–455.

[14] Mules seem always to have been preferred to oxen in the Río Magdalena trade, although the latter were extensively employed in other parts of the province. Schenck observed that many oxen were being used at the time of his journey (1880) because an epidemic was raging among the mules and many dead beasts lay along the road, especially the first two days out of Islitas. The epidemic had caused a great shortage of mules and an accumulation of merchandise in the bodegas. A saddle mule to Medellín, normally costing 8 to 10 pesos, then brought 20 to 25 pesos. Ferdinand von Schenck, *op. cit.*, vol. 29, p. 87.

[15] Francisco Silvestre, "Relación que se cita ... ," p. 555.

[16] José Manuel Restrepo, *op. cit.*, pp. 275 ff.

[17] Archivo de Antioquia, Medellín, Estadístico y Censo, tomo 2, expediente 7, contains depositions of arrieros on the condition of the Popayán road.

[18] Alexander von Humboldt, *Researches Concerning the Institutions and Monuments of the Ancient Inhabitants of America* ... , translated by Helen María Williams, 2 vols. (London, 1814), vol. 1, p. 67.

[19] *Ibid.*, vol. 1, pp. 63–64.

[20] National Archives (Washington, D.C.), Consular Letters–Medellín, no. 6, from Thomas Herran, U. S. Commercial Agent in Medellín, August 4, 1879.

[21] *Ibid.*

[22] Alexander von Humboldt, *op. cit.*, vol. 1, p. 68.

[23] Von Schenck, *op. cit.*, vol. 29, p. 213.

[24] W. F. Shunk, engineer for the Intercontinental Railway Commission, heard, while he was in Medellín in 1892, that 130 loaded mules were stuck in the mud and perishing on the road to Puerto Berrío.

[25] Guillén Chaparro, *op. cit.*

[26] *Los Ecos del Norte* (Yarumal), May 12, 1894, and *Informe que el Secretaria de Hacienda presenta al Sr. Gobernador* (Medellín, 1898), p. 28.

[27] García, *op. cit.*, *Caldas*, pp. 417 ff.

[28] Cisneros, *op. cit.*

[29] Alfredo Ortega, *Ferrocarriles Colombianos*, vol. 26 of *Biblioteca de Historia Nacional* (Bogotá, 1920), p. 26. This work on the history of the railroads of Colombia,

together with volume 47 of the same series published in 1932 and relating to the intervening decade, has been extensively employed in the pages which follow.

[20] For example, Intercontinental Railway Commission, *Report of Surveys and Explorations* (Washington, 1896).

[21] Raul Aguilar Rodas, Secretaria de Hacienda de Antioquia, quoted in *El Colombiano*, Nov. 7, 1966.

[22] One of the principal causes of the persistent financial difficulties of the Ferrocarril de Antioquia had always been the imbalance between incoming and outgoing traffic. In 1945, on the Puerto Berrío line, for every ton carried toward the Magdalena 2.57 tons moved toward Medellín; on the Cauca division 3.45 tons moved toward Medellín for every ton carried in the opposite direction. F. C. de A., *Informe a la Honorable Asamblea* (Medellín, 1946), p. 22.

[23] García, *op. cit.*, p. 396.

[24] A few truck roads in Antioquia have been privately constructed. The English company, Frontino Mines, Ltd., finished the road from Zaragoza, at the head of navigation on the Río Nechí, to Segovia in 1940. Earlier a French company had constructed a 50-kilometer carretera from Dos Bocas on the Nechí to the Madre Seca mine near Anorí. Later abandoned, it has since been repaired by the Pato interests as far as Providencia, about halfway to Anorí.

[25] Between 1950 and 1965 passenger-miles flown by Colombian airlines increased fivefold while ton-miles of air freight flown remained constant. Medellín's share of combined inbound and outbound air cargo traffic (10 per cent) is significantly less than its share of all passenger traffic (14 per cent).

[26] Colombia is one of the most air-minded and air-transport-conscious nations of the world. It ranks third in number of passengers transported by air in proportion to population. Avianca, the principal carrier, handles about two million passengers yearly, ranking seventh among the world's airlines in this category. In 1962 it acquired the controlling interest in SAM (Sociedad Aeronautica de Medellín), a Medellín-based company that had been founded in 1946 to haul cargo to and from Miami. SAM did not become a passenger carrier until 1958.

NOTES TO CHAPTER XII

THE NEW INDUSTRIAL ERA

[1] In the first years of the republic Bogotá continued to be a trade emporium, especially for Socorro clothing, but the competition of cheaper English goods spelled an end to the business. Bogotá's trade in 1830 amounted to some $820,000, of which $200,000 was with Antioquia. There were already many Antioqueños residing in the capital to handle the trade as well as the coinage of money from Antioquia gold. Guillermo Wills, *Observaciones sobre el Comercio de la Nueva Granada* (Bogotá, 1831), with appendix on the trade of Bogotá.

[2] Frank Brandenburg, *The Development of Latin American Private Enterprise*, National Planning Association, Planning Pamphlet No. 121 (Washington, D.C., 1964), pp. 30–31.

[3] Personal communication. Ospina Vásquez' brilliant analysis of the development of the Colombian economy, *Industria y Protección en Colombia, 1810–1930* (Medellín, 1955) gives special attention to the politics of tariff legislation and to the role of Antioquia in the country's industrial evolution.

Notes 211

⁴ Everett E. Hagen, *On the Theory of Social Change* (Homewood, Ill., 1962). Chapter 5, "The Transition in Colombia," has been published in Spanish translation as *El Cambio Social en Colombia* (Ediciones Tercer Mundo, Bogotá, 1963), translation and introduction by Jorge Vélez García.

⁵ Frank Safford, "Significación de los Antioqueños en el Desarrollo Económico Colombiano, un Examen Crítico de las Tesis de Everett Hagen," *Anuario Colombiano de Historia Social y de la Cultura*, Bogotá, 1965 (1967), no. 3, pp. 49–69.

⁶ *Ibid.* Safford contends further that the isolation of Antioquia, socially, politically and culturally, has also been exaggerated. It derived, Safford argues, as much from its political conservatism as from geography. Antioquia could more or less go it alone financially, and involvement in civil wars had little appeal. The recurrent disturbances of the 19th century were looked upon more as costly plagues sapping Antioquian wealth rather than as opportunities for gaining any regional advantage. Some Medellín leaders could even suggest annexation to the United States in the 1860's as possibly a desirable stabilizing move in an essentially rudderless economy. The legend of Jewish origin of the Antioqueños, Safford argues, was created and sustained by the people of the weaker provinces who were envious of Antioquia's increasingly superior economic position. If there were few Antioqueños who became rich from mining and commerce, they at least demonstrated the potentialities for wealth that existed and thus, perhaps, their superiority over other Colombians without such hopes. From such origins may have sprung much of the pride and regional identity which marks the self-confident, loquacious *paisa of* today, and the "achievement drive" of an earlier group of entrepreneurial leaders.

⁷ Enrique Echavarría, *Historia de los Textiles en Antioquia* (Medellín, 1943). This source has been used for much of the material in the paragraphs that follow.

⁸ This figure for a single company compares with a total of 22,000 spindles which were reported installed in the valley of Medellín forty years ago. Arno Pearse, *Colombia, with Special Reference to Cotton* (London, 1926).

⁹ Rosellón was completely destroyed in 1927 by a landslide that buried not only the factory but many employees. It was later rebuilt. Like most of the other mills in Antioquia it works three shifts.

¹⁰ *Colombia Today*, April, 1967, vol. 2, no. 2 (Colombian Information Service, New York).

¹¹ *Premer Censo Industrial de Colombia, 1945* (Bogotá, 1947).

¹² *Boletín Mensual de Estadística* (DANE), no. 183, July, 1966, p. 46.

¹³ *Anuario Estadística*, Municipio de Medellín (Medellín, 1946), p. 126.

¹⁴ Of raw materials consumed by Antioquia textile mills July 1944–June 1945, the following percentages were imported: ginned cotton 77%, cotton yarn 18%, raw wool 93%, wool yarn 73%, rayon yarn 52%, caustic soda 100%, sulfuric acid 2%, soda ash 100%, aniline dyes 100%. Source: *Primer Censo Industrial*, 1945.

¹⁵ *Medellín y su Area Circundante* (Medellín, 1961), p. 66.

¹⁶ E. Livardo Ospina, *Una Vida, Una Lucha, Una Victoria* ... (Medellín, 1966).

¹⁷ *Estudio sobre el Municipio de El Peñol y la Incidencia del Proyecto Nare* ("Codesarrollo," Medellín, 1966), and *Primer Plan Regional de Desarrollo para el Oriente Antioqueño, 1963–1970* ("Codesarrollo"-"Incoplan," Medellín, 1963). These two studies contain extraordinarily detailed data on the economy of the Oriente of Antioquia, the basis for a definitive human geography. They are representative of the noteworthy contribution to regional planning being made by the Corporación Social de Desarollo y Bienestar ("Codesarrollo") established in 1960 with the support of private industry and banks.

¹⁸ The budget of the municipio of Medellín in recent years has been about half derived from *valorización*. Its most impressive achievement has been the widening

of the Carrera Bolívar and related works, cutting a wide swath through the heart of the city and linking the airport with the Plaza Nutibara. It had involved expenditures of 100 million pesos ($7 million U.S.) to 1966. Juan Restrepo Uribe, "La Valorización está haciendo al Medellín Futuro," *El Colombiano*, Mar. 2, 1966 (Edición Especial).

[19] *El Correo* (Medellín), February 11, 1967.

[20] Calculation by the Centro de Investigaciones Económicas, Facultad de Economía, Universidad de Antioquia, based on those in the labor force 14 years of age or over.

[21] The Bank for International Development and the Ford Foundation have also contributed heavily to the financing of the new University of Antioquia. The new campus near the Río Medellín is expected to accommodate 15,000 students by 1970.

[22] Jorge Restrepo Uribe, *Antioquia: Olvidada, Marginada y Resentida* (Medellín, 1964). This animosity towards Antioquia, he writes, dating from the 19th century, must undergo a marked modification lest the department, becoming tired of this aberrant situation, find itself obliged to establish *"su rancho aparte."*

[23] This has been suggested to me by my friend Dr. Virginia Gutiérrez de Pineda. And it may eventually reach even farther. A colony of Antioqueños is said to have recently settled in northern Ecuador. In 1959 an Antioqueña from Manizales was named "Miss Universe."

BIBLIOGRAPHY

UNPUBLISHED DOCUMENTS

Archivo Central del Cauca, Popayán
　Signaturas 178, 1633
Archivo del Congreso Nacional, Bogotá
　Cámara
　Senato
　Leyes
Archivo Nacional, Bogotá
　Caciques e Indios
　Encomiendas
　Minas de Antioquia
　Minas de Antioquia y Cundinamarca
　Poblaciones Varias
　Virreyes
　Visitas de Antioquia
　Visitas de Antioquia y Cundinamarca
Archivo de Antioquia, Medellín
　Baldíos
　Caminos
　Censos
　Diezmos
　Estadístico y Censo
　Fundiciones
　Fundaciones
　Indios
　Libros de Aguardiente
　Minas
　Reales Cédulas
　Tierras
　Visitas
National Archives, Department of State, Washington, D.C. "Consular Letters—Medellín, I, July 25, 1859–January 18, 1902."

Books, Articles, and Published Documents

Acosta, Joaquín. "Relation de l'eruption boueuse sortie du volcan de Ruiz et de la catastrophe de Lagunilla ... ," *Comptes-rendus,* Académie des Sciences, Paris, 1846. Vol. 22, pp. 709–710.
Aguado, Pedro de. *Recopilación Historial* [*ca.* 1570]. Bogotá, 1906.
Arango, Luís C. *Recuerdos de la Guaquería en el Quindío.* 2d ed., Bogotá, 1941.
Arango Mejía, Gabriel. "Algo Sobre Orígenes de los Antioqueños." *IV Centenario de la Raza,* ed., Alfonso Villegas Montoya. Medellín, 1941.
———. *Geneologías de Antioquia y Caldas.* 2 vols. 2d ed., Medellín, 1942.
"Autos sobre la Fundación y Población y Apuntamiento de los Naturales de la Ciudad de Remedios" [1572], *Revista del Archivo Nacional,* Bogotá, 1937. Pp. 52–68.
Bennett, Hugh, "Soil Conservation in Latin America," *Plants and Plant Science in Latin America,* ed., Frans Verdoon. Waltham, Mass., 1945. Pp. 165–169.
Bennett, Wendell C. *Archaeological Regions of Colombia: A Ceramic Survey.* New Haven, 1944.
Beyer, Robert C. "The Colombian Coffee Industry: Origins and Major Trends, 1740–1940." Ph.D. thesis, University of Minnesota Library, 1947.
Birket-Smith, Kaj. "The Origin of Maize Cultivation," *Det Kôngliche Danske Videnskabernes Selskab,* Historisk-Filologiske Meddelelser. Copenhagen, 1943. Bind XXX, No. 3.
Botero Arango, Gerardo. "Sobre el Ordiviciano de Antioquia," *Proceedings of Eighth American Science Congress.* Washington, 1940. Vol. IV, pp. 19–25.
Boussingault, J. B. *Mémoires.* 5 vols. Paris, 1892–1903.
———. "Informe sobre las Minas de Antioquia," *Dyna.* Facultad Nacional de Minas, Medellín. June, 1946.
Buitrago, Jaime. *Hombres Transplantados.* Manizales, 1943.
Bukasov, S. M. *The Cultivated Plants of Mexico, Guatemala and Colombia.* Translated by M. H. Bylweld from the Russian (manuscript in Department of Geography, University of California, Berkeley). *Bulletin of Applied Botany, Genetics and Plant Breeding.* Leningrad, 1930. Suppl. 47, pp. 1–553.
Bürger, Otto. *Reisen Eines Naturforschers im Tropischen Amerika.* 2 vols. Leipzig, 1923.
Caldas, Francisco José de. "Memoria Sobre la Nivelación de las Plantas que se cultivan en la Vecindidad del Ecuador" [1803], *Obras de Caldas,* ed., E. Posada. Bogotá, 1912.
———. "Estado de la Geografía del Virreinato de Santa Fé de Bogotá" [1807]. *Obras de Caldas,* ed., E. Posada. Bogotá, 1912.
Calle G., Manuel F. "El Fundador de Abejorral," *Archivo Historial.* Manizales, 1920. Pp. 469–470.
Castellanos, Juan de. *Historia de la Gobernación de Antioquia y de la del Chocó* [*ca.* 1570]. Bogotá, 1942.
Cathcart, James K. "Résumé of Gold and Silver Production in Colombia." U. S. Department of the Interior, Bureau of Mines. *Mineral Trade Notes.* Washington, 1946. Special Supplement No. 11.
Cervecería Unión, S. A. *Monografías de Antioquia.* Medellín [1940].
Chapman, F. M. "The Distribution of Bird Life in Colombia." *Bulletin of the American Museum of Natural History,* XXXVI, 1917.
Chardón, Carlos E. *Reconocimiento Agro-pecuario del Valle del Cauca.* San Juan, Puerto Rico, 1930.
———. *Viajes y Naturaleza.* Caracas, 1941.
Chiquito, Lucio. "Apuntes Sobre Lluvias en Medellín." Tesis de Grado, Escuela de Minas. Medellín, 1941.

CIEZA DE LEÓN, PEDRO DE. *The Travels of Pedro Cieza de León, A.D. 1532–50*, contained in the First Part of his Chronicle of Perú. Translated and edited by C. R. Markham. Hakluyt Society. London, 1864. Ser. 1, Vol. XXXIII.

CISNEROS, FRANCISCO J. *Report on the Construction of a Railway from Puerto Berrío to Barbosa (Ant.).* New York, 1878.

Colección de Documentos Inéditos sobre la Geografía y Historia de Colombia, ed., Antonio B. Cuervo. 4 vols. Bogotá, 1891–1894.

COOK, O. F. "Coffee and Cacao in Southern Florida." *Science*. N.S., 1936. Pp. 55–56.

COOK, SHERBURNE F. and SIMPSON, LESLEY BYRD. *The Population of Central Mexico in the Sixteenth Century*. Univ. Calif. Ibero-Americana. Vol. 31, 1948.

CUBILLOS, JULIO C. "*Arqueología de Ríoblanco (Chaparral, Tol.).*" *Boletín de Arqueología*. Bogotá, 1945.

DARWIN, CHARLES. *The Variation of Animals and Plants under Domestication*. 2d ed., New York, 1876. Vol. 1.

DEWEY, LESTER A. *Fiber Production in the Western Hemisphere*. U. S. Department of Agriculture, Misc. Publ. 518. Washington, 1947.

DÍAZ DEL CASTILLO, PORFIRIO. *El Valle de Cauca: Historia y Realidades de sus Municipios*. Cali, 1937.

"Documentos Anotados que el Consejo Municipal de Río Negro presenta al Congreso de 1898 relativos a la patria del General José María Córdoba." *Repertorio Histórico*. Medellín, 1924. P. 194.

"Documentos Relativos a la Distribución de Terranos en Salamina, Neira y Manizales." *Repertorio Histórico*. Medellín, 1924. P. 376.

DUQUE, ANTONIO J. "Nare, el mas Antiguo y el Primer Puerto de Antioquia." *Repertorio Histórico*. Medellín, 1937. Pp. 440–455.

ECHAVARRÍA, ENRIQUE. *Historia de los Textiles en Antioquia*. Medellín, 1943.

ECHEVERRI URIBE, CARLOS. *Apuntes para la Historia de Pereira*. 2d ed., Medellín, 1921.

ESCOBAR, FRAY JERÓNIMO. "Relación sobre el cáracter e costumbres de los indios de la Provincia de Popayán," *in* J. Jijón y Caamaño, *Sebastián Benalcázar*. Vol. II, Appendix, pp. 149–176.

"Estado General de las Ciudades y Pueblos del Cauca en 1771." *Boletín Histórico del Valle*. Cali, 1941. P. 58.

ESTARITA, ERNESTO. *Monografía de Zaragoza*. Medellín, 1941.

FABO, P. *Historia de la Ciudad de Manizales*. Manizales, 1926.

FRANCO R., RAMÓN. *Antropogeografía Colombiana*. Manizales, 1941.

FRIEDE, JUAN. *El Indio en Lucha por la Tierra*. Bogotá, 1944.

FÜHRMANN, O., and MAYOR, E. "Voyage d'Exploration Scientifique en Colombie." *Mémoires de la Société Neuchateloise des Sciences Naturelles*. Vol. V, 1914. Pp. 18–116.

GARCÍA, ANTONIO. *Geografía Económica de Colombia, IV (Caldas)*. Contraloría General de la República, Bogotá, 1937.

GÓMEZ BARRIENTOS, ESTANISLAO. *Don Mariano Ospino y su Epoca*. 2 vols. Medellín, 1913.

———. "Don Tulio Ospina." *Repertorio Histórico*. Medellín, 1923. Pp. 243–280.

———. "Extranjeros Benemeritos de Antioquia." *Repertorio Histórico*. Medellín, 1924. Pp. 311–345.

———. "Informe sobre la Industria Cafetera Antioqueña." *Boletín Agrícola*. Medellín, 1916. P. 102.

GÓMEZ CAMPILLO, ANTONIO. "Erección del Municipio de Ríonegro." *Repertorio Histórico*. Medellín, 1922. Pp. 643–645.

GÓMEZ GARCÍA, DELIO. *Santiago de Arma*. Aguadas, Caldas, 1941.

GOUROU, PIERRE. *Les Pays Tropicaux*. Paris, 1947.

GROSSE, EMIL. *Estudio Geológico del Terciario Carbonífero de Antioquia en la Parte*

Occidental de la Cordillera Central de Colombia entre el Río Arma y Sacaojal. [Spanish and German texts] Berlin, 1926.
GUILLÉN CHAPARRO, FRANCISCO. "Memoria de los Pueblos de la Gobernación de Popayán ... " [1583]. *Archivo Historial.* Manizales, 1919. Pp. 451–501.
GUTIÉRREZ, BENIGNO A. *Sonsón en 1917.* Sonsón, Antioquia, 1917.
GUTIÉRREZ, RUFINO. *Monografías.* 2 vols. Bogotá, 1920–1921.
HETTNER, A. "Die Anden des westliches Kolumbiens." *Petermanns Mitteilungen,* Vol. XXXIX, 1893. Pp. 129–136.
———. "Regenverteilung, Pflanzendecke und Besiedelung der tropischen Anden." *Festschrift Ferdinand Freiherr von Richthofen zum sechzigsten Geburtstag.* Berlin, 1893.
HUMBOLDT, ALEXANDER VON. *Researches Concerning the Institutions and monuments of the Ancient Inhabitants of America, with Descriptions and Views of Some of the Most Striking Scenes in the Cordilleras.* Translated by Helen Maria Williams. London, 1814. Vol. I.
HUMBOLDT, ALEXANDER VON, and BONPLAND, AIMÉ. *Essai sur la géographie des plantes; accompagné d'un tableau physique des regions equinoxiales.* Paris, 1805.
INTERNATIONAL RAILWAY COMMISSION. *Report of Surveys and Explorations Made by Corps No. 2 in Costa Rica, Colombia and Ecuador,* by William F. Shunk, Engineer-in-Charge. Washington, 1896. Vol. II.
JIJÓN Y CAAMAÑO, JACINTO. *Sebastián de Benalcázar.* Quito, 1938. Vol. II.
JOHNSON, R. D. O. "Native Placer Mining in Colombia." *Engineering and Mining Journal.* Vol. 92 (1911), pp. 1137–1141; Vol. 94 (1912), pp. 741–744.
KRÜGER, E. "Eine Besteigung des Tolima." *Zeitschrift für Vulkanologie.* Berlin, 1927. Vol. 10, pp. 155–158.
LATORRE MENDOZA, LUÍS. *Historia e Historias de Medellín.* Medellín, 1934.
LONDOÑO, JUAN B. "Climas de Antioquia." *Anales de la Academia de Medicina de Antioquia.* Medellín, 1933–1934. Nos. 17–24.
LONDOÑO O., LUÍS. *Manizales: Contribución al Estudio de su Historia hasta el 75ᵉ Anniversario de su Fundación* ... Manizales, 1936.
LÓPEZ DE VELASCO, JUAN. *Geografía y Descripción Universal de las Indias, recopilada ... desde el año de 1571 al de 1574.* Madrid, 1894.
LÓPEZ O., JUAN B. *Salamina: de su Historia y de sus Costumbres.* 2 vols. Manizales, 1944.
MACHADO S., ALBERTO. "Fomento de la Industria Cafetera en el Valle del Cauca." *Revista Facultad Nacional de Agronomía.* Medellín, 1942. Pp. 488–552.
MEJÍA, AURELIO. "La Ganadería en Antioquia." *Revista Nacional de Agricultura.* Bogotá, 1944. P. 47.
MENDOZA, DIEGO. *Ensayo sobre la Evolución de la Propriedad en Colombia.* Bogotá, 1897.
MILLER, B. L. and SINGEWALD, J. T. *The Mineral Deposits of South America.* New York, 1919.
MON Y VELARDE, JUAN ANTONIO. "Sucinta Relación de la Visita de Antioquia" [1788]. *Anales de la Instrucción Pública de Colombia.* Bogotá, 1890. Vol. XVI, pp. 21–64; 216–224; 267–280.
MONSALVE, DIEGO. *Colombia Cafetera.* Barcelona, 1927.
MONTOYA Y FLORES, J. B. "Titiribíes y Sinufanáes." *Repertorio Histórico.* Medellín, 1922. Pp. 536–594.
NIETO ARTETA, LUÍS EDUARDO. *Economía y Cultura en la Historia de Colombia.* Bogotá, 1942.
NISSER, ROSA. *Guld och gröna skogar.* Stockholm, 1939.
OCAMPO, RUDESINO, and LONDOÑO, TULIO. "Reseña Histórica de la Industria de Café en el Departamento de Caldas." *Revista Cafetero Colombiano.* Bogotá, 1932. Pp. 1454–1459.

Ortega, Alfredo. *Ferrocarriles Colombianos.* 2 vols. Bogotá, 1920–1932.
Ospina, Tulio. "El Oidor Mon y Velarde, Regenerador de Antioquia" [1901]. *Repertorio Histórico.* Medellín, 1918.
———. *Reseña Geológica de Antioquia.* 2d ed., Medellín, 1939.
Ospina Rodríguez, Mariano. "Cultivo del Café: Nociones elementales al alcance de todos los labradores." Medellín, 1880.
———. *El Doctor José Felix de Restrepo y su Epoca.* 2d ed., Bogotá, 1936.
Otero d'Acosta, Enrique. "El Semitismo Antioqueño." *Archivo Historial.* Manizales, 1921. Pp. 252–262.
———. "Reportaje con Don Alejandro Echeverri." *Archivo Historial.* Manizales, 1919. Pp. 388–392.
Paris Lozano, Gonzalo. *Geografía Económica de Colombia, VII (Tolima).* Contraloría General de la República, Bogotá, 1946.
Peña, Heliodoro. *Geografía e Historia de la Provincia del Quindío.* Popayán, 1892.
Pérez, Filipe. *Jeografía física i política de los Estados Unidos de Colombia.* 2 vols. Bogotá, 1862.
Pérez Arbeláez, Enrique. *Plantas Útiles de Colombia.* Bogotá, 1947.
Pineda Giraldo, Roberto. "Colonización e Inmigración y el Problema Indígena." *Boletín de Arqueología.* Bogotá, 1946. Vol. 2, pp. 361–379.
———. "Material Arqueológico de la Zona Calima." *Boletín de Arqueología.* Bogotá, 1945. Vol. 1, pp. 491–518.
Pinzón, Juan. "Apuntes Históricos y Cronicas de Manizales." *Archivo Historial.* Manizales, 1920. Pp. 263–267.
Posada, Eduardo. *La Esclavitud en Colombia.* Bogotá, 1933.
Rawitscher, Felix. "Die Erschöpfung tropischer Boden infolge de Entwaldung." *Acta Tropica.* Basle, 1946. Vol. 3, No. 3.
Restrepo, Antonio J. *El Moderno Imperialismo.* Barcelona, 1919.
Restrepo, José Manuel. "Ensayo Sobre la Geografía: Producciones, Industria y Población de la Provincia de Antioquia en el Nuevo Reino de Granada." *Semanario del Nuevo Reino de Granada,* ed., Francisco José de Caldas, Bogotá, 1808–1810. Reprinted in 3 vols., Bogotá, 1942. Vol. I, pp. 243–286.
Restrepo, Roberto. "El Quindío y su Colonización." *Archivo Historial.* Manizales, 1921. Pp. 228–231; 311–313.
Restrepo, Vicente. *A Study of the Gold and Silver Mines of Colombia.* Translated by C. W. Fisher. New York, Colombian Consulate, 1886.
Restrepo Sáenz, José María. *Gobernadores de Antioquia, 1579–1819.* 2d ed., Bogotá, 1944. Vol. I.
Restrepo Tirado, Ernesto. *Ensayo Etnográfico y Arqueológico de la Provincia de los Quimbayas.* Sevilla, 1929.
Reyes, Rafael V. "La Ganadería en Antioquia." Contraloría General de la República, Bogotá, 1944. Pp. 286–291.
Robledo, Emilio. *Geografía Médica y Nosología del Departamento de Caldas.* Manizales, 1916.
———. "Un Millar Papeletas Lexicográficas relativas a los Departamentos de Antioquia y Caldas." *Repertorio Histórico.* Medellín, 1934. Pp. 1–164.
———. *La Vida del Mariscal Jorge Robledo.* Bogotá, 1945.
Rodríguez, Jorge. "La Fecundidad en Antioquia." Dirección de Estadística Departamental. Boletín de Estadística. Medellín, 1927. Pp. 29–33.
Royo y Gómez, José. "El Territorio de Manizales y la Estabilidad de su Suelo." *Revista de la Academia Colombiana de Ciencias Exactas, Fisicas y Naturales.* Bogotá, 1943. Vol. 5, pp. 337–343.

Bibliography

SÁENZ, NICOLÁS. *Memoria Sobre el Cultivo de Cafeto*. 3d ed., Bogotá, 1895.
SANDERS, ALVIN H. "The Taurine World." *National Geographic Magazine*. December, 1925. Pp. 591–710.
SAUER, CARL. *Colima of New Spain in the Sixteenth Century*. Univ. Calif. Ibero-Americana. Vol. 20, 1948.
———. "The Cultivated Plants of South and Central America." *Handbook of South American Indians*. Bureau of American Ethnology, Bull. 143. Vol. VI (in press).
SCHAUFELBERGER, P. *Apuntes Geológicos y Pedológicos de la Zona Cafetera de Colombia*. Manizales, 1944. Vol. I.
SCHENCK, FERDINAND VON. "Reisen in Antioquia." *Petermanns Mitteilungen*. Vol. 26 (1880), pp. 41–47; Vol. 29 (1883), pp. 81–93, 213–220, 441–453.
SIERRA, S., JOSÉ DOMINGO. *Estudios sobre los Pastos de Antioquia*. Medellín [1916].
SILVESTRE, FRANCISCO. "Informe sobre la Apertura del Camino desde Antioquia hasta Ayapel..." [1776]. *Archivo Historial*. Manizales, 1919. Pp. 560–568.
———. "Relación del Estado de la Provincia de Antioquia cuando la entrego a Don Cayetano Buelta" [1776]. *Archivo Historial*. Manizales, 1919. Pp. 569–605.
———. "Relación que se cita presentada al Excelentísmo Sr. Virrey de Santa Fé"[1776]. *Archivo Historial*. Manizales, 1919. Pp. 551–560.
SIMÓN, PEDRO. *Noticias Historiales de las Conquistas de Tierra Firme en las Indias Occidentales*. 5 vols. Bogotá, 1882–1892.
SIMPSON, LESLEY BYRD. *The Encomienda in New Spain: Forced Native Labor in the Spanish Colonies, 1492–1550*. Univ. Calif. Publ. Hist. Vol. XIX, 1929.
SORENSEN, HANS G. "Colombia's Plantation Rubber Program." *Agriculture in the Americas*, U. S. Department of Agriculture. Vol. 5, No. 6, 1943.
STORER, JOHN. *The Wild White Cattle of Great Britain*. London, 1881.
SUÁREZ, MARCO FIDEL. *Sueños de Luciano Pulgar*. 12 vols. Bogotá, 1925–1940.
TORO, FRANCISCO LUÍS. "Obispos de Popayán que Visitaron a Antioquia." *Antioquia Histórica*. Santa Fé de Antioquia, 1925–1926. Pp. 174–181, 252–263, 320–328, 361–371.
TRIMBORN, HERMANN. "Der Kannibalismus im Caucatal." *Zeitschrift für Ethnologie*. Vol. 70 (1938), pp. 310–330.
UNITED STATES DEPARTMENT OF COMMERCE, Bureau of the Census. *Colombia: Summary of Biostatistics*. Prepared in coöperation with the Office of the Coördinator of Inter-American Affairs. Washington, 1944.
URIBE, JOAQUIN. *Flora de Antioquia*. ed., Lorenzo Uribe Uribe, S.J. Medellín, 1941. 1941.
URIBE ÁNGEL, MANUEL. *Geografía General y Compendio Histórico del Estado de Antioquia*. Paris, 1885.
URIBE URIBE, RAFAEL. *Diccionario Abreviado de Galicismos, Provincialismos y Correcciones*. Bogotá, 1882.
VÁSQUEZ DE ESPINOSA, ANTONIO. *Compendium and Description of the West Indies* [1628]. Translated by Charles U. Clark. Smithsonian Misc. Collections. Vol. 102. Washington, 1942.
VERGARA VELASCO, FRANCISCO J. *Nueva Geografía de Colombia*. Bogotá, 1892.
VOGT, WILLIAM. *Road to Survival*. New York, 1948.
WARD, WILLIAM. "Nechí River Placer Mining." *Engineering and Mining Journal*. Vol. 96 (1913), pp. 297–299.
WASSÉN, HENRY. "An Archeological Study in the Western Colombia Cordillera." *Etnologiska Studier*. Stockholm, 1936. Vol. 2, pp. 30–67.
WHITE, JUAN ENRIQUE. "Disertación sobre los Indígenas de Occidente." *Repertorio Histórico*. Medellín, 1919. P. 585.

WHITE, ROBERT BLAKE. "The Andes of Western Colombia." *Scottish Geographical Magazine.* Vol. 9 (1893), 467-476.
———. "Brief Notes on the Glacial Phenomena of Colombia." *Scottish Geographical Magazine.* Vol. 15 (1899), 470-479.
WILLS, GUILLERMO. *Observaciones sobre el Comercio de la Nueva Granada con un Apéndice Relativo al de Bogotá.* Bogotá, 1831.
WOLF, TEODORO. *Geografía y Geología del Ecuador.* Leipzig, 1892.
WYLIE, KATHRYN. *The Agriculture of Colombia,* U. S. Department of Agriculture, Foreign Agriculture Bulletin, No. 1. Washington, 1942.
ZAVALA, SILVIO A. *La Encomienda Indiana.* Madrid, 1935.
ZULETA, EDUARDO. *Manuel Uribe Ángel y los Literatos de Antioquia.* Bogotá, 1937.

PUBLISHED OFFICIAL REPORTS, MEMORIALS, CENSUSES

ANTIOQUIA. *Memorial del Gobierno a la Cámara Provincial.* Medellín, 1843.
———. *Informe del Secretario de Despacho de Hacienda.* Medellín. 1847.
———. *Informe que el Secretaria de Hacienda presenta al Gobernador del Estado.* Medellín. 1859.
———. *Memoria que el Secretaria de Hacienda y Fomento presenta al Ciudano Presidente del Estado.* Medellín, 1883.
———. *Informe del Gobernador del Departamento a la Asamblea.* Medellín, 1892, 1894.
———. *Informe que el Secretaria de Hacienda presente al Sr. Gobernador.* Medellín, 1898.
———. *Mensaje del Gobernador a la Hon. Asamblea.* Medellín, 1940.
———. *Informe del Fondo de Fomento Agrícola e Industrial.* Medellín, 1946.
———. Ferrocarril de Antioquia. *Informe a la Honorable Asamblea.* Medellín, 1946.
COLOMBIA. *Memoria del Ministerio de Industrias al Congreso Nacional en las Sesiones Ordinarias de 1931,* ed., Francisco José Chaux. 7 vols. Bogotá, 1931.
———. *Informe de Ministerio de Minas y Petróleos al Congreso Nacional en sus sesiones ordinarias de 1942.* Bogotá, 1942.
———. Ministerio de Minas y Petróleos. Servicio Geológico Nacional. *Compilación de los Estudios Geológicos Oficiales en Colombia, 1917-1933.* 7 vols. Bogotá, 1933-1947.
———. Contraloría General de la República. *Censo General de Población.* Bogotá, 1938.
———. Contraloría General de la República. *Primer Censo Industrial de Colombia, 1945.* Bogotá, 1947.
Federación Nacional de Cafeteros. *Boletín de Estadística.* Bogotá, 1933-.
Municipio de Medellín. *Boletín de Estadística.* Medellín, 1911-1936.
———. *Anuario Estadística.* Medellín, 1937-.

NEWSPAPERS

Diario Oficial, Bogotá.
El Colombiano, Medellín, 1946-1947.
El Guardian, Medellín, 1878.
El Constitutional, Medellín, 1854.
El Tiempo, Bogotá, 1946-1947.
Gaceta de la Nueva Granada, Bogotá, 1836.
La Tribuna, Medellín, 1880.
Los Ecos del Ruiz, Manizales, 1881.
Los Ecos del Norte, Yarumal, 1894.
Pensilvania, Pensilvania, 1906-1907.

Supplementary Bibliography, 1949–1967

ANTIOQUIA. Archivo Histórico. *Indice del Archivo Colonial*. Vol. 1. Medellín, 1958 (?).
——. Secretaria de Agricultura. *La Agricultura en Antioquia*. Publicación Especial 14. Medellín, 1962 (mimeo.).
ASOCIACIÓN NATIONAL DE INDUSTRIAS. *Medellín y su Area Circundante*. Medellín, 1961.
BORAH, WOODROW, and S. F. COOK. *The Aboriginal Population of Central Mexico on the Eve of the Spanish Conquest*. Univ. Calif. Ibero-Americana. Vol. 45, 1963.
BOTERO ARANGO, GERARDO. "Contribución al Conocimiento de la Geología de la Zona Central de Antioquia." *Anales*, Facultad de Minas, No. 57. Medellín, 1963.
BRANDENBURG, FRANK. *The Development of Latin American Private Enterprise*. National Planning Association, Planning Pamphlet No. 121. Washington, 1964.
BUKASOV, S. M. *Las Plantas Cultivadas de Mexico, Guatemala y Colombia*. Instituto Interamericana de Ciencias Agrícolas, Dirección Regional de la Zona Andina, Misc. Publ. 20. Lima, 1963 (mimeo.).
"CODESARROLLO. "*Estudio sobre el Municipio de El Peñol y la Incidencia del Proyecto Nare*. Medellín, 1966 (processed).
——. *Primer Plan Regional de Desarrollo para el Oriente Antioqueño, 1963–1970*. Medellín, 1963 (processed).
COLOMBIA. Instituto Geográfico 'Agustín Codazzi.' *Laventamiento Agrológico de la Región Cafetera Central, Departamento de Antioquia*. Publ. LS-1. Bogotá, 1959.
COLOMBIA. Banco de la República. *Atlas de Economía Nacional*. 3 vols. Bogotá, 1959–1962.
COLOMBIA. Departamento Administrativo Nacional de Estadística. *XIII Censo Nacional de Población, 15 de junio de 1964*. Bogotá, 1965 (processed).
DOBYNS, HENRY F. "Estimating Aboriginal American Population: An Appraisal of Techniques with a New Hemispheric Estimate." *Current Anthropology*, 1966, vol. 7, pp. 395–449.
DUQUE GÓMEZ, LUIS et al. *Historia de Pereira*. Club Rotario, Pereira, 1963.
"El Pueblo Antioqueño." 2d ed. Ediciones de la *Revista Universidad de Antioquia*. Medellín, 1960.
ESPINAL, LUIS. "Formaciones Vegetales del Departamento de Antioquia." *Revista Facultad Nacional Agronomía*, No. 60. Medellín, 1964.
FLOREZ, LUIS. *Habla y Cultura Popular en Antioquia*. Instituto Caro y Cuevo, Publ. 13. Bogotá, 1957.
FRIEDE, JUAN (ed.). *Documentos Inéditos para la Historia de Colombia*. 10 vols. Academia de la Historia, Bogotá, 1955–1960.
——. *Los Quimbayas Bajo la Dominación Española*. Bogotá, 1963.
FUNDACIÓN PARA EL PROGRESO DE COLOMBIA. *La Industria Cafetera en la Agricultura Colombiana, 1962*. Banco Cafetero, Bogotá, 1962.
GÓMEZ, ANTONIO J. *Monografías de Todas las Parroquias y de Todos los Municipios de Antioquia*. Medellín, 1952.
GORDON, B. L. *The Human Geography and Ecology of the Sinú Country of Colombia*. Univ. Calif.: Ibero-Americana. Vol. 39, 1957.
GÜHL, ERNESTO. "Anotaciones sobre Población, Poblamiento, Posición y Estructura Demográfica en Colombia." *Revista de la Academia Colombiana de Ciencias Exactas, Físicas y Naturales*. Bogotá, 1966. Vol. 12, pp. 377–386.
——. "Aspecto Socio-geográfico de la Provincia Físcio-geográfico Formada por el Valle del Río San Juan y por el Codo de los Mellizos y sus Estribucaciones hacia el Río Cauca (Departamento de Antioquia)." *Revista Colombiana de Antropología*. Bogotá, 1954. Vol. 2, pp. 37–85.
——. "El Aspecto Económico-Social del Cultivo del Café en Antioquia." *Revista Colombiana de Antropología*. Bogotá, 1953. Vol. 1, pp. 197–258.
——. *Utilización de la Tierra en Colombia*. Escuela Superior de Administración Pública, Bogotá, 1963 (processed).

GUTIÉRREZ DE PINEDA, VIRGINIA. *La Familia en Colombia.* Vol. 1, "Trasfondo Histórico." Bogotá, 1962.
HAGEN, EVERETT E. *On the Theory of Social Change.* Homewood, Ill., 1962.
———. *El Cambio Social en Colombia.* Bogotá, 1963.
HARRISON, JOHN P. "The Colombian Tobacco Industry from Government Monopoly to Free Trade, 1778–1876." Ph.D. thesis, Univ. of California, Berkeley, 1951.
HAVENS, A. EUGENE. *Tamesis: Estructura y Cambio. Estudio de una Comunidad Antioqueña* (transl. by Jorge Zalamea). Facultad de Sociología, Universidad Nacional, Bogotá, 1966.
HODGE, W. H. "The Edible Arracacha—A Little-known Root Crop of the Andes." *Economic Botany,* 1954. Vol. 8, pp. 195–221.
JARAMILLO URIBE, JUAN. "Esclavos y Señores en la Sociedad Colombiana del Siglo XVIII." *Anuario Colombiano de Historia Social y de la Cultura.* Bogotá, 1963. Vol. 1, no. 1, pp. 3–55.
———. "La Población Indígena de Colombia en el Momento de la Conquista...." *Anuario Colombiano de Historia Social y de la Cultura.* Bogotá, 1964. Vol. 1, No. 2, pp. 239–293.
LALINDE BOTERO, LUIS. *Diccionario 'jilosofico' del Paisa.* Medellín, 1966.
LIVARDO OSPINA, E. *Una Vida, una Lucha, una Victoria: Monografía Histórica de las Empresas y Servicios Públicos de Medellín.* Empresas Públicas de Medellín, 1966.
MCGREEVEY, WILLIAM P. "Economic Development of Colombia." Ph.D. thesis, Massachusetts Institute of Technology, 1965.
MEDELLÍN (Municipio). *Crónica Municipal.* Edición Especial. August, 1963.
MÖRNER, MAGNUS. "El Comercio de Antioquia alrededor de 1830 según un Observador Sueco." *Anuario Colombiano de Historia Social y de la Cultura.* Bogatá, 1964. Vol. 1, No. 2, pp. 317–332.
OSPINA VÁSQUEZ, LUIS. *Industria y Protección en Colombia, 1810–1930.* Medellín, 1955.
PARSONS, JAMES J. *Antioquia's Corridor to the Sea: an Historical Geography of the Settlement of Urabá.* Univ. Calif. Ibero-Americana. Vol. 49, 1967.
———. "The Settlement of the Sinú Valley, Colombia." *Geographical Review,* 1952. Vol. 42, pp. 67–86.
———, and WILLIAM BOWEN. "Ancient Ridged Fields of the San Jorge River Floodplain, Colombia." *Geographical Review,* 1966. Vol. 56, pp. 317–343.
PATIÑO, VICTOR MANUEL. *Plantas Cultivadas y Animales Domésticos en América Equinoccial.* 2 vols. Cali, 1963–1964.
———. *Historia de la Actividad Agropecuaria en América Equinoccial.* Cali, 1965.
PINEDA GIRALDO, ROBERTO. *El Impacto de la Violencia en el Tolima: el Caso de El Líbano.* Bogotá, 1960.
POSADA, ANTONIO J. and JEANNE POSADA. *The CVC: Challenge to Underdevelopment and Traditionalism.* Bogotá, 1966.
REICHEL-DOLMATOFF, GERARDO. "Apuntes Etnográficos sobre los Indios del Alto Sinú." *Revista de la Academia Colombiana de Ciencias Exactas, Físicas y Naturales.* Bogotá, 1963. Vol. 12, pp. 29–40.
———. *Colombia* ("Ancient Peoples and Places"). London, 1966.
RESTREPO, VICENTE. *Estudio sobre las Minas de Oro y Plata* [1888]. Banco de la República, Archivo de la Economía Nacional No. 7 Bogotá, 1952.
RESTREPO URIBE, JORGE. *Antioquia: Olvidada, Marginada y Resentida.* Medellín, 1964 (processed).
ROBLEDO, EMILIO. *Bosquejo Biográfico del Señor Oidor Juan Antonio Mon y Velarde.* 2 vols. Bogotá, 1954.
———. *La Vida del General Pedro Nel Ospina.* Medellín, 1960.

Supplementary Bibliography

RÖTHLISBERGER, ERNST. *El Dorado, Estampas de Viaje y Cultura de la Colombia Suramericana* [1897]. Banco de la República, Archivo de la Economía Nacional No. 26. Bogotá, 1963.

SAFFORD, FRANK. "Foreign and National Enterprise in Nineteenth-Century Colombia." *The Business History Review*, 1965. Vol. 39, pp. 503–526.

———. "Commerce and Enterprise in Central Colombia, 1821–1870." Ph.D. Dissertation, Colombia University, 1965.

———. "Significación de los Antioqueños en el Desarrollo Económico Colombiano, un examen crítico de las tesis de Everett Hagen." *Anuario Colombiano de Historia Social y de la Cultura*. Bogotá, 1967. Vol. 3 (1965), pp. 49–69.

SAUER, CARL O. *The Early Spanish Main*. Univ. Calif. Press, 1966.

SCHAUFELBERGER, P. *Apuntes Geológicos y Pedológicos de la Zona Cafetera de Colombia*. Suplemento, tomo primero. "Genetica y Clasificación de los Suelos Tropicales." Federación Nacional de Cafeteros de Colombia. Chinchiná, 1962.

SCHENCK, FERDINAND VON. *Viajes por Antioquia en el Año de 1880*. Banco de la República, Archivo de la Economía Nacional No. 9. Bogotá, 1953.

SINGEWALD, QUENTIN D. *Mineral Resources of Colombia (Other than Petroleum)*. U. S. Geological Survey Bulletin 964-B. Washington, 1950.

SILVESTRE, FRANCISCO. *Descripción del Reyno del Santa Fé de Bogotá* [1789]. Biblioteca Popular de Cultura Colombiana. Bogotá, 1950.

SMITH, T. LYNN. *Colombia: Social Structure and the Process of Development*. Gainesville, 1967.

TRIMBORN, HERMANN. *Señorio y Barbarie en el Valle del Cauca*. Madrid, 1949.

———. *Vergessende Königsreich*. Braunsweig, 1948.

TROJER, HANS. *El Tiempo Reinante en Colombia*. Boletín Técnico No. 13. Federación Nacional de Cafeteros de Colombia. Chinchiná, 1954.

UNITED NATIONS. FOOD and AGRICULTURE ORGANIZATION. *Coffee in Latin America, I: Colombia and El Salvador*. New York, 1958.

WEST, ROBERT C. *Colonial Placer Mining in Colombia*. Baton Rouge, 1952.

———. *The Pacific Lowlands of Colombia: A Negroid Area in the American Tropics*. Baton Rouge, 1957.

WILGUS, A. CURTIS (ed.). *The Caribbean: Contemporary Colombia*. Gainesville, 1962.

NEWSPAPERS AND PERIODICALS

El Colombiano. Medellín. 1964–1967.
Colombia Today. Colombian Information Service, New York. 1966–1967.
Revista Mensual de Estadística. Departamento Administrativo Nacional de Estadística, Bogotá. 1964–1967.
Visión. New York. October, 1967.

INDEX

INDEX

Abejorral, 6, 71, 73, 85
Abibe, Serranía de, 16, 36
Aboriginal population. *See* Population
Aburrá valley. *See* Medellín valley
Achiote, 24, 117
Administrative divisions, colonial, 40
Aerial cables, 75, 147, 166–167
Agriculture: colonial, 60–68; modern, 79–80, 89, 95, 109 ff., 137 ff.
Aguadas, 71–72, 87, 137, 174
Aguardiente, 65, 120, 122, 152
Air transport, 7, 75, 172–173, 210
Amagá, 11, 14, 15, 82, 84
Amalfi, 14, 56, 74, 98, 135, 173
Ambalema, 20, 179
Aná, *sitio* of, 61, 62
Anderson, Edgar, 112
Andes (town), 10, 84, 85, 137, 173
Anise, 24, 122, 205
Anorí, 56
Anserma (province), 36–39 *passim*, 64, 86, 159
Anserma (town), 86, 159
Ansermanueva, 97
Antioquia la Vieja, 38–39
Antioquia (villa). *See* Santa Fe de Antioquia
Antioquia (department): topography, 10 ff.; establishment as *gobernación*, 39 ff; subdivision, 64; population, 93, 103–108; land grants, 98; agriculture, 109 ff.; coffee, 137 ff.; transportation, 154 ff.; industrial and urban development, 174 ff., 210–212
Antioqueños, cultural characteristics of, 1–9, 102, 104, 107–108, 175, 178–179, 187–188, 211–212
Añu, 115
Apía, 86
Aranzazu, 72, 166
Aranzazu land grant, 68, 72, 75, 98, 200
Arbi, 37–38
Arboletes, 93, 95, 173
Archeology, 31, 33–35, 37
Arma (city), 41, 63, 64, 69, 70–72, 127, 159, 165, 199
Arma (province), 23, 39, 41
Armenia, 7, 21, 80, 81, 90, 147, 148, 170, 173
Armero, 13
Arquí, quebrada, 84

Arracacha, 24, 35, 115, 116
Arrieros, 157, 172
Ash, volcanic, 11–14 *passim*, 34, 74, 91
Atrato river, 91, 92, 121, 131, 154
Aures quebrada, 70–71
Autopista to Bogotá, 172, 186
Ayapel, 16, 35, 63, 100, 130

Badillo, Oidor Juan de, 30, 36, 50
Bajo Cauca, 7, 35, 91–95 *passim*, 123, 131
Balboa, 86
Baldíos, 72–83 *passim*, 87, 91, 96 ff.
Bananas, 93
Barbosa, 47, 95, 163
Barequeros, 53 ff.
Basque immigration, 1
Batholith, Antioquia, 12–14, 192
Beans, kidney, 24, 60, 64, 109, 114–115
Belalcázar, Sebastián de, 37, 38, 71
Bello, 47, 61, 163, 179–180
Biblical place names. *See* Place names, Biblical
Birth rates, 102–105
Blanco oreji-negro cattle, 128–130, 206
Bogotá, 11, 33, 41, 46, 155, 158, 173, 179
Bolívar (Ant.), 85
Bolívar (department), 130
Bolombolo, 165
Boquerón de Toyo, 16
Boundaries, provincial, 39 ff., 75, 91, 202
Boussingault, J. B., 11, 43, 54, 86, 102
Bridges, 92, 161
Bukasov, S. M., 116
Bürger, Otto, 22
Burila land company, 81, 82, 201
Buriticá, 2, 16, 36, 41–43, 46, 48, 49, 92, 127, 196
Buenaventura, 16, 81, 145, 147

Cabuya, 24, 126–127
Cacao, 24, 74, 77, 110, 111, 120–121, 158, 159
Cáceres, 39–41 *passim*, 48, 63, 94, 95, 155, 165, 166, 195
Cajamarca, 90
Calarcá, 80, 81, 98
Caldas (Ant.), 47, 98, 174
Caldas (department), 1, 4, 6, 9, 14, 16, 27, 30, 33, 35, 45, 53, 72–80, 83, 88, 89, 98, 106, 141–142, 144, 147, 153, 165–166, 170, 184

[227]

Index

Caldas, Francisco José de, 22
Cali, 11, 15, 36, 37, 81, 145, 159, 165, 173
California miners, 57
Calima river, 33, 34, 87
Carmen de Viboral, 175
Campo y Rivas, Manuel del, 62
Cañabrava, 26
Cañasgordas, 16, 30, 49, 92
Cañaverales. See *Guadua*
Cancán, Lomas (Sabanas) de, 27–28, 41, 46
Cannibalism, 31
Capital accumulation, 179, 211
Caramanta, 26, 36, 84, 85, 97
Carolina, 5, 66–67
Cartagena (city), 50, 51, 154, 155, 166
Cartagena (province), 38, 39, 41, 63
Cartago, 10, 11, 13, 19, 37, 38, 62, 71, 77, 79, 80, 86, 94, 121, 159, 200–201
Carretera al Mar, 93, 172
Casabianca, 87, 98
Catholicism, 8
Catío Indians, 30, 92
Cattle. See Livestock
Cattle market, Medellín. See *Feria de Medellín*
Cattle drives, 131, 206
Caicedonia, 80, 81
Casabe, 94
Caturra coffee, 153
Cauca (state, department), 74–76, 79, 88, 91
Cauca (river), 6, 10, 35, 36, 41, 47, 53, 71, 72, 80, 82, 86, 100, 155, 161, 165
Cauca (valley), 11, 14–16, 19, 22, 23, 38, 64, 127, 130, 195. See Valle del Cauca
Caucasia, 93, 94, 166, 173
Cecropia, 28
Cedar, 25
Cement, 94, 184
Censuses, 4, 48–49, 52, 62, 70, 82, 103 ff., 183–184
Cerro Bravo, 15, 16, 82, 140, 142
Ceramics manufacturing, 174–175
César, Francisco, 30, 36
Cerro Tusa, 15, 82
Chambas, 132
Chamí Indians, 84, 112
Chardon, Carlos, 119
Chayote, 117
Chibcha Indians, 10, 31
Chicha, 112

Chinchiná, 21, 73–76 *passim*, 98
Chinchiná river, 72, 73, 75, 166
Chocó (department), 16, 37, 74, 84, 85, 154, 166, 172
Chocó Indians, 30, 39, 42, 49, 52, 91, 95, 154
Cieza de León, Pedro, 26, 28, 34, 50, 199
Circasia, 13, 35, 80
Cisneros, 21, 160, 169
Cisneros, Francisco J., 138, 167
Climate, 17–23, 192
Clothing: trade in, 124–125, 158–159, 206; manufacture, 174 f., 210
Coal beds, 14
Coca, 118
Coffee, 1, 15, 16, 19–20, 23, 24, 77, 80, 89, 90, 97, 103, 106, 110–111, 193, 207–208; systems of cultivation, 137–154, 207
Coffee sacks, 126
Colonization, agricultural: colonial period, 60 ff.; modern period, 69 ff., 203, 212
Coltejer, 132, 175, 176, 180, 182, 183
Colombian coffee in world markets, 145
Comía, 83–84, 98, 201
Comino (*Aniba* sp.), 25
Commerce, 7–8, 109–111, 124, 154 ff., 162 ff., 178
Concepción, 139
Concordia, 83, 138
Congress of Cúcuta (1821), 51
Cornish stamp mill. See Stamp mill
Cocacabana, 14, 26, 61, 138
Codesarrollo planning group, 211
Contraband trade, 154, 208
Córdoba (department), 130
Cotton, 24, 110, 111, 124–125, 182
Cotton textile industry, 125–126, 179–183, 211
Credit, agricultural, 8
Cucurbits, 117
Cúcuta, 137, 173
Cundinamarca, 137, 140, 141, 142

Dabeiba, 91, 92, 125
Dabeybe, 33, 36
Dairying, 128–129, 206
Darién (Valle), 31, 87
Decentralization, political, 187–188, 212
De la Roche, Manuel Vicente, 126
d'Elúyar, Juan José, 55
Demography, 102–107
Diet, 8, 119

Index

Don Matías, 47, 66–67, 128
Dredging, gold, 57–58
Dress, 8

Earthquakes, 74
Ebéjico, 38, 48, 49, 125, 139
Ecclesiastical jurisdiction, colonial, 41, 195
Echavarría, Alejandro, 180
Economic development, 175, 178–179, 211
Economic plants, relationship to climate, 22–23
Ecuador, 6, 10
Ejidos (common lands), 64
El Bagre, 21, 57, 58, 173
El Cairo, 87
El Peñol, 13, 49, 116, 163, 211
El Poblado, 60, 186
El Retiro, 163
Emancipation of slaves, 51, 52
Empresas Públicas de Medellín, 21, 185, 186, 192, 207
Encomienda, Indian, 42, 44, 45, 47, 48
Enka de Colombia, 183
Entrerríos, 13
Envigado, 60, 82, 84, 163, 180, 186
Escuela de Minas, 14
Exfoliation domes, 13
Escobar, Jerónimo de, 85
Espeletia, 23

Fabricato, 175, 176, 180, 182, 185
Family size, 102, 104
Feininger, Tomas, 21
Feria de Medellín, 131, 132, 207
Ferrocarril de Amagá, 100, 169
Ferrocarril de Antioquia, 14, 100, 141, 160, 167–169, 170, 171, 210
Ferrocarril del Atlántico, 170
Filadelfia, 72, 202
Filandia, 79
Finestrad, Padre Joaquín de, 55
Finzenú, 31
Fique. See Cabuya
Florencia (Caquetá), 6
Food supply for mines, 51, 60, 65, 85, 128, 130
Forest clearing, 21, 25–30 *passim*, 85–95 *passim*
Foundries, 175
Fredonia, 6, 15, 82–83, 85, 140–141, 144, 151, 152

Fresno, 87, 98
Frontiers of settlement, 6, 8, 80, 90, 95, 101
Frontino, 16, 21, 38, 91, 92
Frontino Gold Mines, Ltd., 58, 59, 211

Garment industry, 181
Génova, 80, 81
Geology. *See* Topography
Geomorphology. *See* Topography
Giraldo, 122
Gobernación de Antioquia, 39 f.
Gold mining, 1–2, 19, 33, 41–59, 69, 74, 78, 85, 86, 179
González Salazar y Cía, 68, 72–73, 75, 98
Granitic batholith. *See* Batholith, Antioquia
Grasses. *See* Pasture grasses
Guaca, valley of, 36, 194
Grosse, Emil, 11, 14, 57, 191
Gravels, auriferous, 14, 19, 41 ff., 53, 57, 69, 74
Graves, Indian. *See* Guacas
Guacas, 29, 33–34, 64, 78, 80, 85
Guadua, 24, 25, 34, 77
Guamacó, 41, 44, 48, 63
Guarne, 14, 47, 53, 56, 64, 126, 127
Guatapé, 29, 163, 186
Guatemala, 139
Gühl, Ernesto, 93
Guinea grass. *See* India grass
Gutiérrez González, Gregorio, 9, 62
Gynerium. See Cañabrava

Hagen, Everett E., 178, 211
Hats, Panamá, 43, 174
Health conditions, 103, 105–106, 204
Heliconia, 25, 37
Heredia, Pedro de, 36 ff.
Herrera y Campuzano, Oidor Francisco, 48, 49, 60
Herveo (páramo), 23, 74
Herveo (province), 37
Herveo (road), 87, 158, 161
Herveo (town), 87, 89, 98
Hettner, Alfred, 11
Hogs, 66, 73, 79, 89, 165
Homesteading. *See* Frontiers of settlement
Honda, 155, 157, 159, 160
Humboldt, Alexander von, 22, 159, 161
Human carriers, 163
Hydroelectric power, 185–186

Ibagué, 21, 90, 98, 170
Instituto para el Desarrollo de Antioquia (IDEA), 171, 187
Immigration, 3, 6, 53, 61–62, 65, 102, 203–204
Imperial grass, 128, 136
INCORA, 8, 95
India grass, 23, 24, 131–133
Indians: agriculture, 5, 25, 31, 34–35, 109; population, 4, 29–31, 35, 37–38, 46, 48–50, 51, 84, 86, 193–194, 197; reservations (*resguardos*), 25, 49–50, 92, 99; distribution of, 32; uprisings, 38, 39, 42; mining activity, 41, 48; use of tobacco, 124; as source of mine labor, 2, 42 ff.
Indigo, 110, 111, 121
Industrial development. See Manufacturing
Infant mortality, 62
International Mining Corporation, 57, 198
Intestinal parasitism, 106, 204
Islitas. See Nare
Itagüí, 61, 173, 180
Italian immigrants, 3
Ituango, 95, 98

Jaraguá grass, 134
Jaramillo, José María, 138
Jardín, 84, 85
Jericó, 15, 85
Jews. See Semitic origins, legend of
Juntas road, 155–156, 158, 209

La Estrella, 25, 49, 50, 126
La Manuelita, 21
La Miel river, 45, 71
Landforms. See Topography
Land grants, 3, 6–7, 60, 66, 68 ff., 83, 89, 97 ff.
Land holdings, size of, 19, 109, 111, 144, 204, 207
Land Reform Institute. See INCORA
La Pintada, 15, 85, 169
La Quiebra pass, 160, 169
Lava flows, 12, 13, 14
La Vieja river, 75, 77
León river, 154
Líbano, 87, 98, 144, 147
Livestock, 1, 23, 28, 46, 58, 60, 77, 85, 94–95, 98, 127–132, 206
López, Fermín, 76, 77, 200

Mafafa, 115–116

Magangué, 166
Magdalena river valley, 3, 7, 10, 23, 27, 43, 45, 65, 74, 91, 94, 131, 132, 147, 160
Maize, 9, 24, 34, 64, 66, 73, 78, 89, 93, 109–114, 140, 150, 205
Malaria, 91, 94, 107, 204
Manizales, 7, 13, 19, 21, 72–73, 74, 77, 81, 86, 87, 116, 121, 131, 139, 147, 148, 159, 166, 170, 173, 184
Manufacturing, 7, 94, 174–188, 210
Manzanares, 16, 89, 98
Marinilla, 40, 41, 49, 51, 52, 64, 65, 69, 157, 169
Mariquita, 13, 39, 41, 45, 55, 64, 71, 86, 87, 123, 158
Marmato mines, 11, 15, 30, 41, 56, 59, 71, 74, 85, 86, 159
Marriage, 4, 102
Marsella, 77, 151
Marulanda, 89, 98, 116
Mazamorreros, 53 ff.
Medellín; as Antioqueño culture hearth, 1, 7; population growth, 7, 93, 94; population composition, 52, 62, 84; transport links, 16, 155–173 *passim*; climate, 19, 21; first settlement, 42, 47–49, 60–62, 66; manufacturing, 125, 147, 175 ff., 211; *valorización*, 211–212
Medellín valley, 10, 13, 14, 26, 37, 38, 46, 60, 62, 66, 127, 175 ff.
Mellizos, Altos de, 15, 16, 142
Mestizos, 4, 49, 61
Metallurgy, Indian, 33
Micay grass, 24, 135
Mining, 2, 3, 7, 11, 14, 16, 28, 36–59, 86, 196, 203
Molasses grass, 23, 24, 33, 134–135, 152
Mompox, Province of, 39, 45, 155, 157, 160
Montenegro, 34, 80
Montería, 95, 131, 173
Montoya, Francisco, 79
Mon y Velarde, Oidor Juan Antonio, 5, 25, 42, 49, 64–66, 71, 82, 120, 122, 123, 155, 191, 193
Moore, Tyrell, 100
Moreno, Walker y Cía, 75
Mosca. See Guarne
Mulattos, 4, 23, 49, 52–53, 75
Mulberry, 110, 111, 126
Mule transport, 58, 65, 147, 157, 162 f., 209

Index

Murindó, 98

Nare, 65, 94, 98, 155, 157, 159, 163, 173, 184, 209
Nare river, 46, 158, 186
Nare road, 124, 138, 155–157, 205
National Federation of Coffee Growers, 144, 148
National Planning Association, 175, 210
Natural vegetation. *See* Vegetation
Nechí river, 28, 41, 43, 44, 46, 53, 57, 59
Negro river valley, 64, 69, 127, 160
Negroes, 2, 23; as mine labor, 42 ff.; numbers, 49, 52, 86; as slaves, 50 ff.; disease and population decline, 51
Neira, 72–73, 98
New towns, 5, 7, 66 ff., 98, 110
Nore valley, 38, 39
Nus river, 45, 94, 131, 148, 155, 157, 158, 167
Nutibara, *Cacique*, 30, 36

Oca, 115
Occidente of Antioquia, 6, 33, 53, 84 ff., 91–93
Oil palm, African, 93
Old fields, Indian, 32, 34–35, 194
Orchids, 27
Oriente of Antioquia, 47, 53, 63–67, 170, 184, 211
Ospina, Captain Francisco, 45
Ospina, Mariano, 83, 139, 148
Ospina, Pedro Nel, 179
Ospina, Tulio, 29, 138, 148, 191, 193
Ospina Vásquez, Luis, 178, 210
Otú, 58, 173
Oxen as carriers, 163

Pácora, 72, 85
Palagua road, 155–157
Palestina, 76, 98
Palomino land grant, 81
Panela, 118–120
Panzenú, 31
Pará grass, 23, 24, 131, 132, 133
Paramillo, 16, 23
Passes, mountain, 11, 16, 90, 160–161, 202
Pasture grasses, 23, 24, 93, 132–136
Pasture lands, 35, 60, 89, 127, 128
Pato Mines, 17, 21, 57, 59, 166
Pato Consolidated Gold Dredging, Ltd., 57

Pavarandocito, 92
Pedroso, Francisco Nuñez, 45, 60
Pensilvania, 16, 87, 90, 202
Pepalfa, Textiles, 184
Perales, 94
Pereira, 7, 57, 77–78, 98, 147, 166, 173, 184, 201
Petroleum, 94; pipelines, 166, 170
Physiographic regions, 12
Pijao, 80, 81, 90
Pipintá, legend of, 78
Place names, Biblical, 8
Placer mining techniques, 53 ff.
Plant geography, 22–28
Pleneta Rica, 173
Plantains, 24, 79, 85, 93, 109, 120, 150
Popayán (province), 11, 39, 41, 52, 71, 81, 86, 159
Population: aboriginal, 29–31, 35, 37–38, 46, 48, 193–194; Antioqueño, racial composition of, 49–50, 52–53; growth 93, 94, 102–107, 183, 184
Porce river, 10, 13, 26, 43, 53, 155, 191
Potatoes, 24, 35, 60, 90, 115–116
Public land policy, 96 ff.
Pueblorico, 86, 121
Puerto Antioquia, 165
Puerto Berrío, 93, 94, 131, 133, 158, 166–173 *passim*
Puerto Espíritu Santo, 3, 155–156, 165, 208
Puerto Valdivia, 10, 165
Pumps, mining, 42

Quercus, 27
Quibdó, 91, 172, 173
Quimbaya Indians, 25, 31, 37, 78
Quinchía, 86
Quindío area, 1, 20, 29, 33, 75, 77–82, 141–142, 153
Quindío road (pass), 28, 78, 81, 156, 159–161, 170
Quindío (volcano), 11, 13, 15, 16
Quito, Audiencia of, 39

Racial composition of Antioqueños, 3–4, 49–50, 52–53
Railroads, 81, 138, 141, 145, 147, 160, 165–171, 216. *See also Ferrocarril* entries
Railroad land grants, 100
Rainfall, 17–21
Raza Antioqueña, 3

Reichel-Dolmatoff, Reichel, 114
Remedios, 26, 38, 40, 41, 63, 94, 127, 155; mining at, 42–58 *passim*
Resguardos, Indian. *See* Indians
Restrepo, José Maruel, 55, 110, 112, 120, 137
Restrepo (town), 1, 31, 33, 34, 87
Restrepo, Vicente, 59, 196
Rice, 24, 93, 122–123, 205
Ridged fields. *See* Old fields, Indian
Rionegro, 6, 40, 47–49, 51, 52, 63–64, 65, 66, 69, 116, 126, 155–159 *passim*, 169, 180
Riosucio, 21, 30, 86, 202
Risaralda (department), 1, 77
Risaralda (river), 15, 81
Rivers, 10, 13, 15–16, 198; as transport routes, 145, 147, 155, 158, 165–166, 170–171, 179
Rivet, Paul, 30
Roads, 8, 16, 58–59, 67, 69, 74, 76, 81, 85, 87, 90, 91, 94, 95, 100, 130, 145, 154–163, 171–172, 210
Robledo, Emilio, 62
Robledo, Mariscal Jorge, 3, 31, 37 ff., 60, 65, 77
Rodas, Governor Gaspar de, 39, 43, 60, 64
Rodriguez, Jorge, 104
Roncesvalles, 1, 90
Root crops, 115–117
Rosellón, textile mill, 180, 211
Rosenblatt, Angel, 29
Rubber: Castilla, 27, 78; Hevea, 93
Ruiz (volcano), 10, 11, 13, 74, 122

Sabanalarga, 49, 50, 72
Safford, Frank, 179, 211
San Andrés, Valley of, 67
San Carlos, 66, 138, 157
San Jerónimo, 26, 123
San Jerónimo del Monte, 48, 63
San Jorge river, 35, 48, 95
San Juan river (Antioquia), 14, 15, 84
San Marcos, 35
San Pedro, 47, 56
San Sebastián de Urabá, 36, 38
San Vicente, 64, 126
Santa Barbara, 28, 82, 85, 139
Santo Domingo, 47, 56, 126, 158
Santa Fe Antioquia: physical setting, 3, 10, 17, 22; founding of, 38–39, 63; *vecinos* of, 42, 43, 51, 61; population, 52–53; suit against Rionegro for meadow lands, 6, 64; cacao-growing, 74, 120–121; cattle, 127, 154
Santa Rosa de Cabal, 76, 77, 98, 116, 147, 200
Santa Rosa de Osos, 5, 14, 22, 27, 42, 46, 52–56, 66, 100, 155
Salamina, 26, 72, 74, 76, 86, 152, 197
Salento, 78, 79, 98
Salt production, 25, 37
Samaná river, 158, 159
Santuario, 86
Sardela, Juan Bautista, 63
Sauer, Carl O., 113
Schenck, Ferdinand von, 11, 74, 77, 85, 191
Segovia, 57–58
Semitic origins, legend of, 2, 62–63, 211
Sericulture, 111, 125–126, 206
Sevilla, 80–82 *passim*, 148
Silver, occurrence of, 15
Silvestre, Governor Francisco, 5, 42, 52, 64, 124, 130, 191
Simití, 44
Simón, Fray Pedro, 44, 45, 48, 50, 51, 123
Sinú Indians, 31, 36, 203
Sinú valley, 2, 7, 41, 93, 95, 131
Slaves, 2, 42 ff., 50 ff., 196, 197
Smallpox epidemics, 44, 46, 51, 196, 197
Soil erosion, 26, 89, 132, 134, 135, 152, 153, 203, 208
Soils, volcanic, 6, 11, 13, 35, 77, 142
Sonsón, 6, 13, 21, 69–71, 73, 74, 85–89, 152, 172, 199–200
Sopetrán, 11, 26, 48, 49, 50, 74, 121, 122, 123
Spanish conquest, 33, 36 ff.
Speech, 8–9
Squatters, land, 6, 72
Stamp mills, 56
Stockraising. *See* Livestock
Sugar cane, 24, 109, 118–120, 205
Supía, 59, 85, 86
Surnames, Antioqueño, 2–3, 63, 65
Sweet potatoes, 115–116
Syphilis, 51

Támesis, 85
Tebaida, 80
Temperatures, 17, 192; vertical distribution of, 22–24
Tenerife, 43

Index

Tertiary zone of Antioquia, 14–16, 47, 142
Textile manufacturing. *See* Cotton textiles
Timminś-Ochalí Mining Co., 58
Titiribí, 15, 37, 42, 56–59, 82–83, 138
Tobacco, 24, 124, 179
Tolima (department), 6, 7, 20, 53, 83, 87–89, 98, 142, 144, 153
Toloma (volcano), 10, 11, 13, 192
Tonusco river, 16, 32
Topography 10–16; relationship to climate, 22
Trade routes, 16, 28, 65, 79, 91, 154 ff.
Trails, pack, 160–161, 209
Transportation, 7–8, 79, 91, 131–132, 141, 154–173
Tranvía del Oriente, 169, 172
Trucking, 131, 145, 147, 166, 172
Trujillo, 87
Tuberculosis, 107
Tumbaga, 33
Turbo, 93, 95, 98, 172, 173
Turgurios, 187
Typhoid, 107

Úbeda, 39
Ulluco, 35, 115
United Fruit Company, 93
Universidad de Antioquia, 187, 212
Urabá area, 7, 16, 30, 36, 39, 91, 93, 123, 131, 154, 172
Urban slums. *See Turgurios*
Urbanization, 7, 184 ff.
Uré, 51
Urrao, 30, 91, 154, 173

Vagrancy laws, 5
Valdivia, 39, 100, 123
Valdivia, Andrés de, 39
Valle del Cauca (department), 74, 77, 80, 82, 87, 191. *See also* Cauca valley.

Valorización, 211–212
Valparaíso, 85
Vanilla, 78, 11, 121
Vásquez de Espinosa, Antonio, 44, 60
Vegetation, 17, 25–28, 193
Vein gold, 42 ff.; mining methods, 56–57
Vélez Escobar, Ignacio, 171
Venecia, 15, 152
Venereal disease, 107
Versalles, 87
Vertical zonation: temperature, 22–23; economic plants, 24, 193
Victoria, 45–46, 98, 196
Villa Arteaga, 93
Villahermosa, 89
Villamaría, 75, 78, 98, 116, 156
Villegas, Felipe, 69, 71
Villegas land grant, 68, 69, 70, 71
Villegas road, 89, 156, 161
Violencia, 90, 206
Volcanism, 11–16 *passim*

Wax palm. *See Ceroxylon*
Wheat, 24, 110
White, Juan Enrique, 25, 30, 92
Women: immigration of, 3; in industrial labor force, 182
Work, tradition of, 2, 5

Yaraguá gordura. See Molasses grass
Yarumal, 5, 21, 58, 59, 66, 138
Yarumo. *See Cecropia*
Yolombó, 5, 29, 45, 138, 155, 157, 160
Yuca, 24, 35, 109, 115, 140, 150

Zancudo mine, 56
Zaragoza, 3, 26, 39–57 *passim*, 63, 94, 155, 166, 196
Zarzal, 81, 82
Zenufaná Indians, 29, 37
Zenufaná, province of, 31

PLATES

PLATE 1

a, Medellín, with bridge over Río Medellín (Río Aburrá) in foreground, looking towards the Oriente highlands. Ríonegro and Guarne lie beyond the treeless, serpentinized horizon on a plateau 1,000 meters above the city. (Foto Carvajal)

b, The Valley of Aburrá looking southwest. The urbanized area of metropolitan Medellín covers virtually all of the flat land. (Foto Carvajal)

PLATE 2

Aerial photography looking eastward from Río Cauca toward Fredonia and Amagá. (U.S. Army Air Forces photo, 91 PMS-4M-Proj. 2016 w; 2-212L62; May 12, 1943)

PLATE 3

a, Plaza of Envigado with characteristic colonial-style architecture.

b, Aerial view of Itagüí plant of Coltejer with town of Itagüí lying beyond, in middle foreground.

PLATE 4

a, *Mazamorreras* working gold-bearing gravels of Río Porce near Gómez Plata with wooden *bateas*. Scars from former hydraulic mining activities on slopes across river. (Foto Carvajal)

b, Carolina, a typical country town of highland Antioquia. Central plaza, dominated by Catholic church, and the white stucco dwellings with red tile roofs are characteristic of all Antioqueño settlements of this type.

PLATE 5

a, Typical Antioqueño campesinos at San Pedro.

b, Blanco oreji-negro cattle standing in Pará grass pasture near Yolombó.

PLATE 6

a, El Peñol, a giant exfoliation dome rising from granitic highland surface of Oriente near Guatapé. With completion of Río Nare project reservoir waters will rise sufficiently high to make it an island. (Foto Carvajal)

b, Río Cauca looking upstream towards old bridge and gorge from new bridge at Puerto Valdivia on Medellín-Cartagena highway. In colonial days cargo-laden *canoas* were able to reach a few miles farther upstream, to Puerto Espiritu Santo, where they were met by mule trains. (*Foto Carvajal*)

PLATE 7

a, Mud slide (*volcán*) on the Carretera al Mar near Dabeiba.

b, Winding mountain road linking upper Valley of Aburrá with Amagá, Fredonia and Bolombolo. View is westward towards Tertiary slopes between Amagá and Titiribí.

Plate 1, *a*.

Plate 1, *b*.

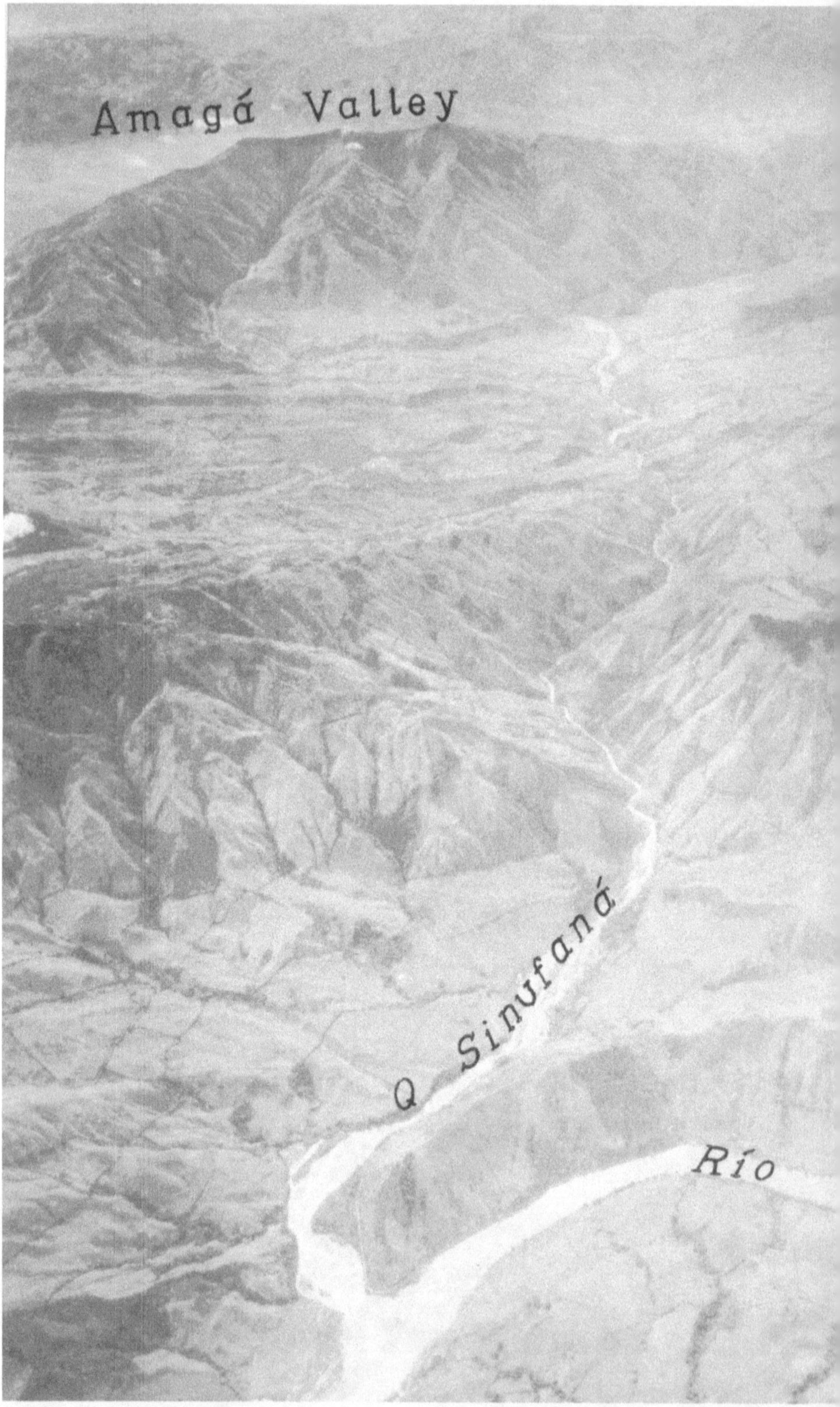
Amagá Valley
Q Sinifaná
Río

Cerro Bravo

Cerro Tusa

auca   Bolombolo

Plate 3, *a*.

Plate 3, *b*.

Plate 4, *a*.

Plate 4, *b*.

Plate 7, *a*.

Plate 7, *b*.

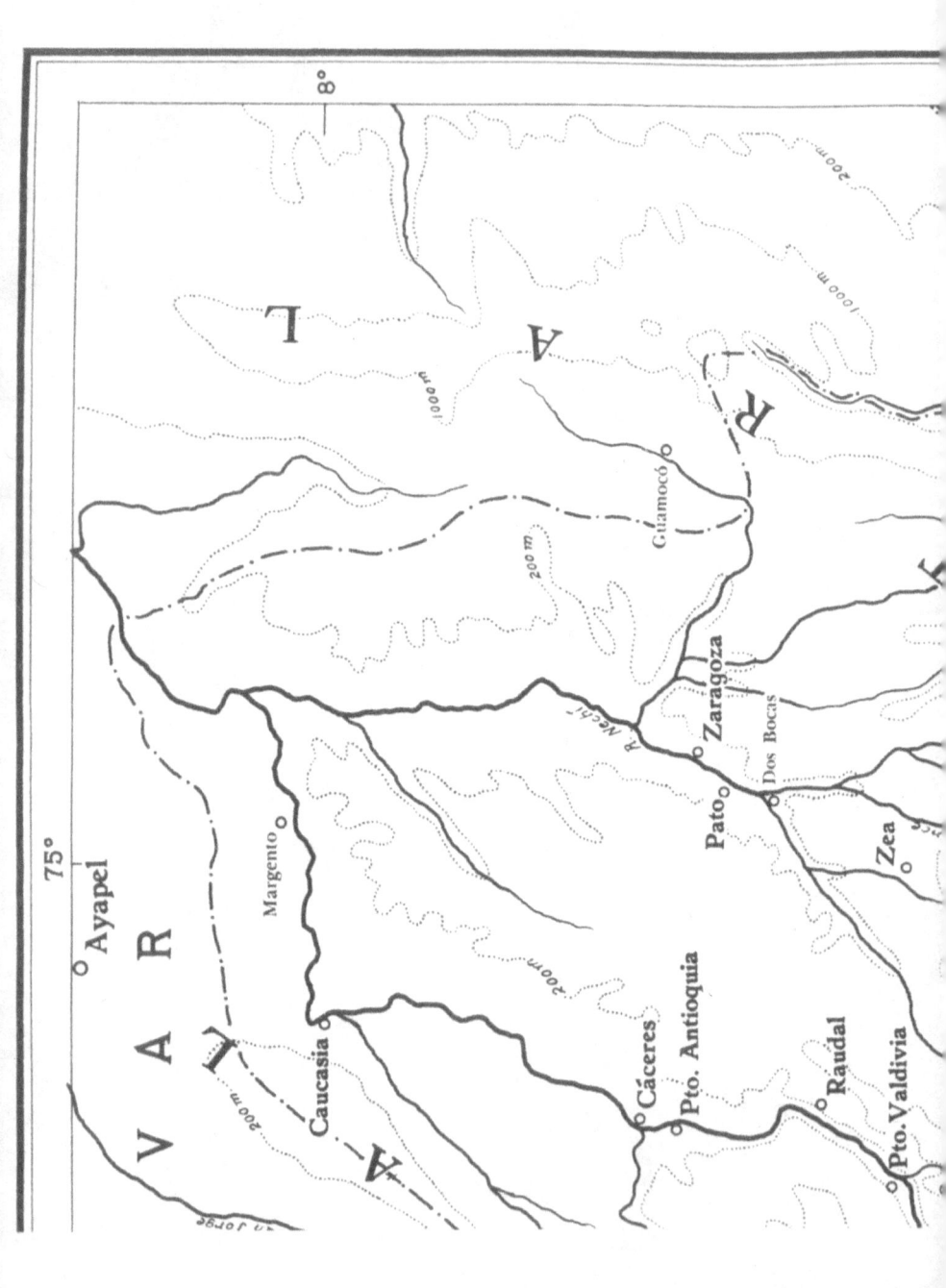

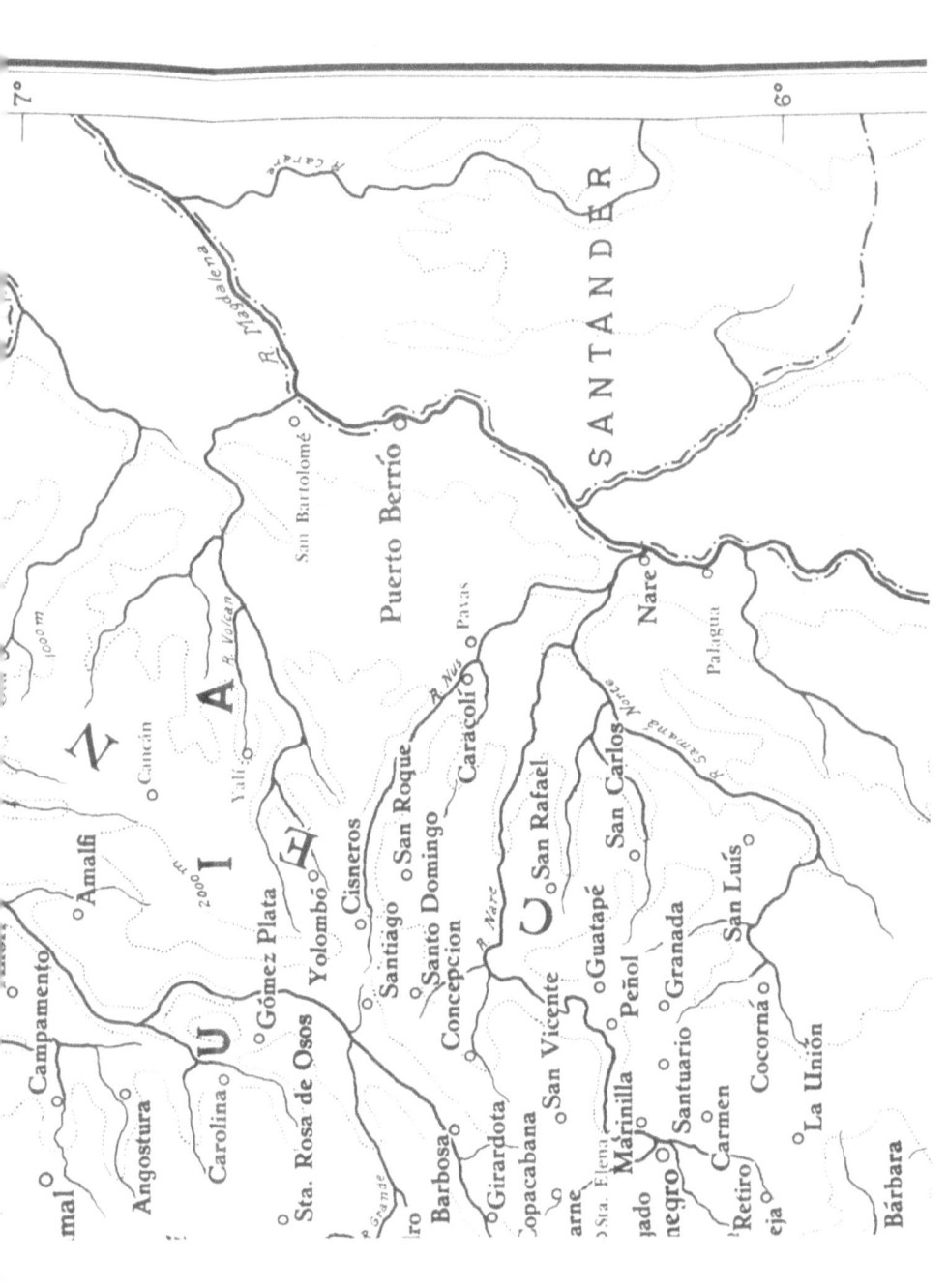

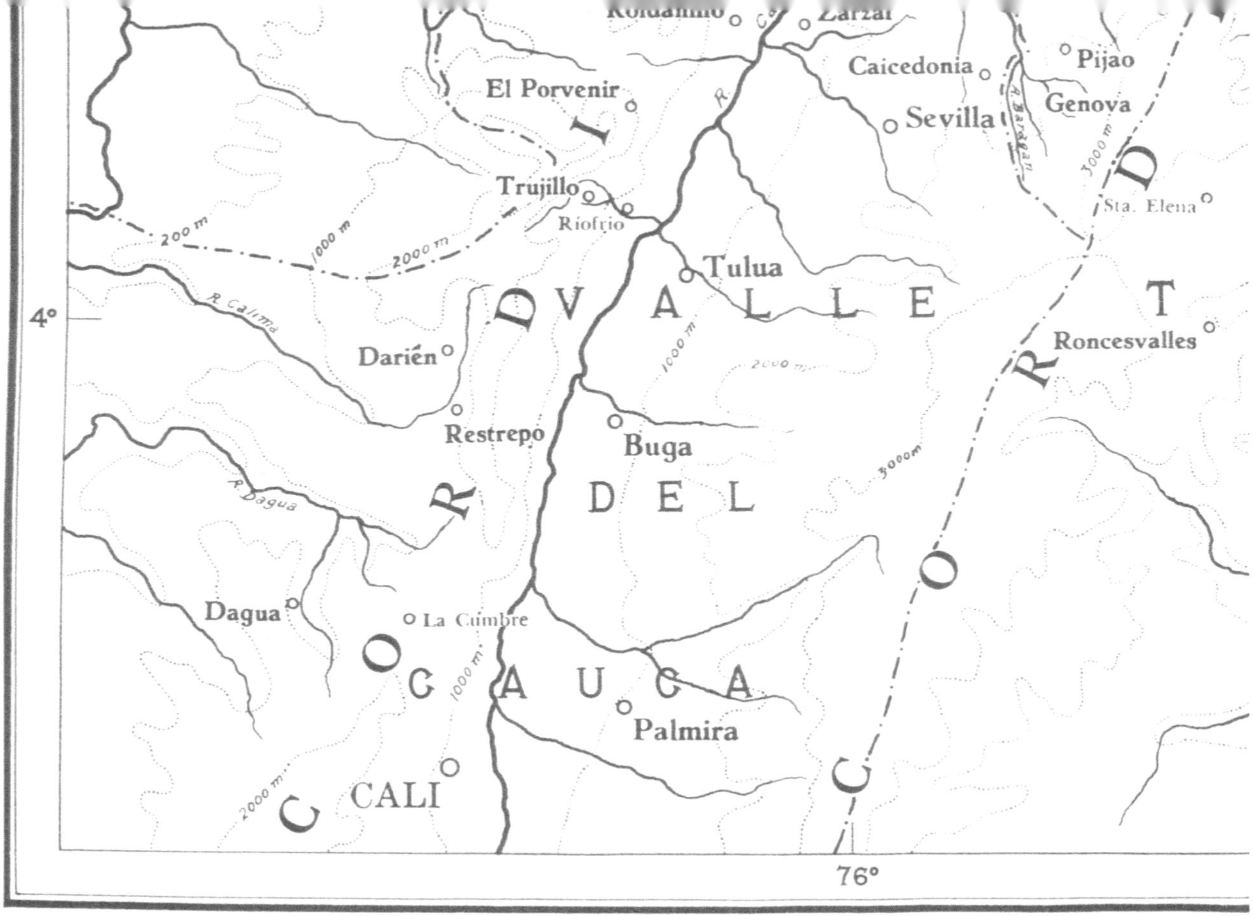
El Porvenir
Caicedonia
Pijao
Genova
Sevilla
R. Bargan
Trujillo
Riofrio
Sta. Elena
Tulua
VALLE
Roncesvalles
Darién
Restrepo
Buga
DEL
R. Calima
R. Dagua
Dagua
La Cumbre
CAUCA
Palmira
CALI
200 m
1000 m
2000 m
3000 m
4°
76°

Map

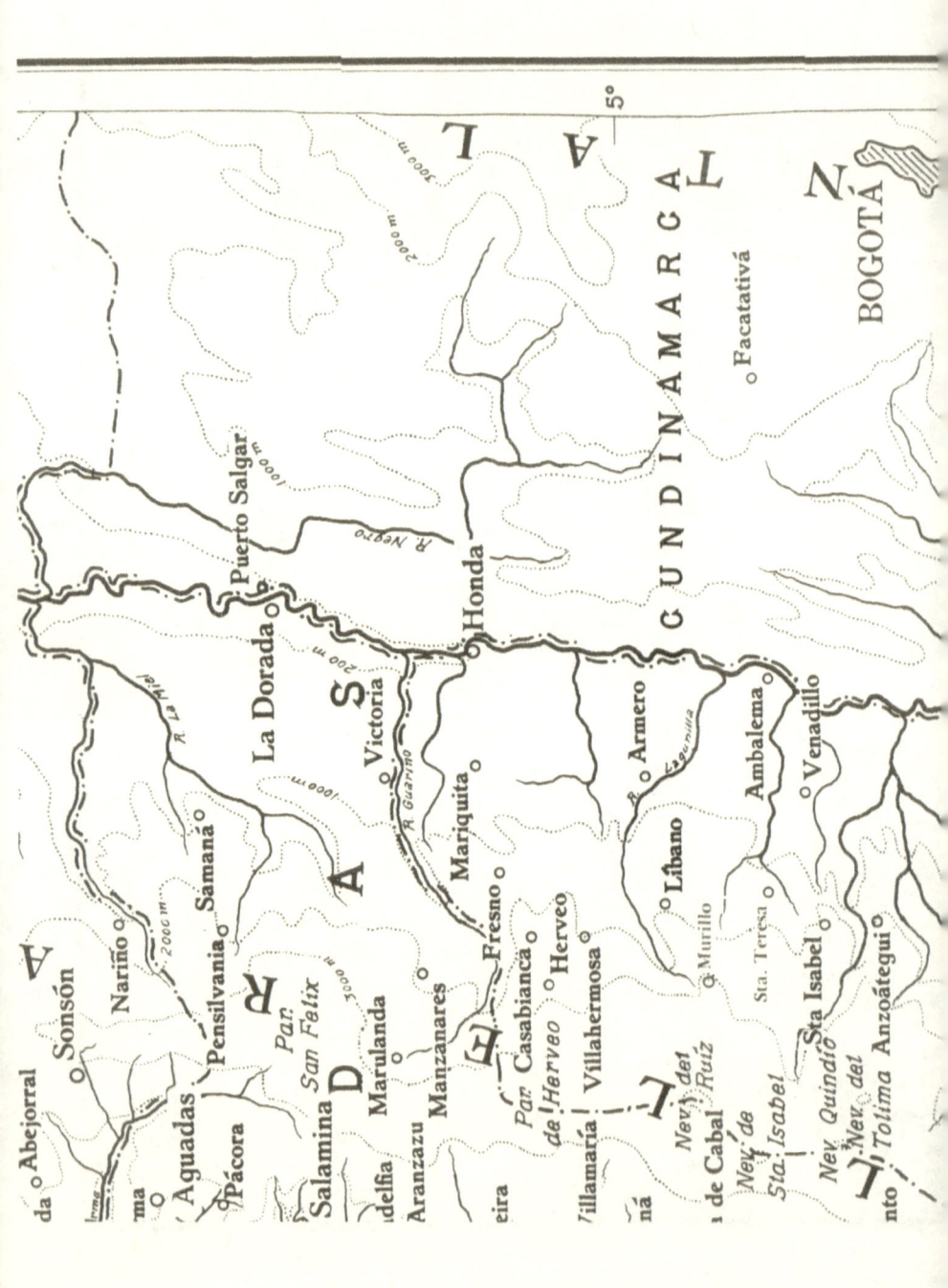

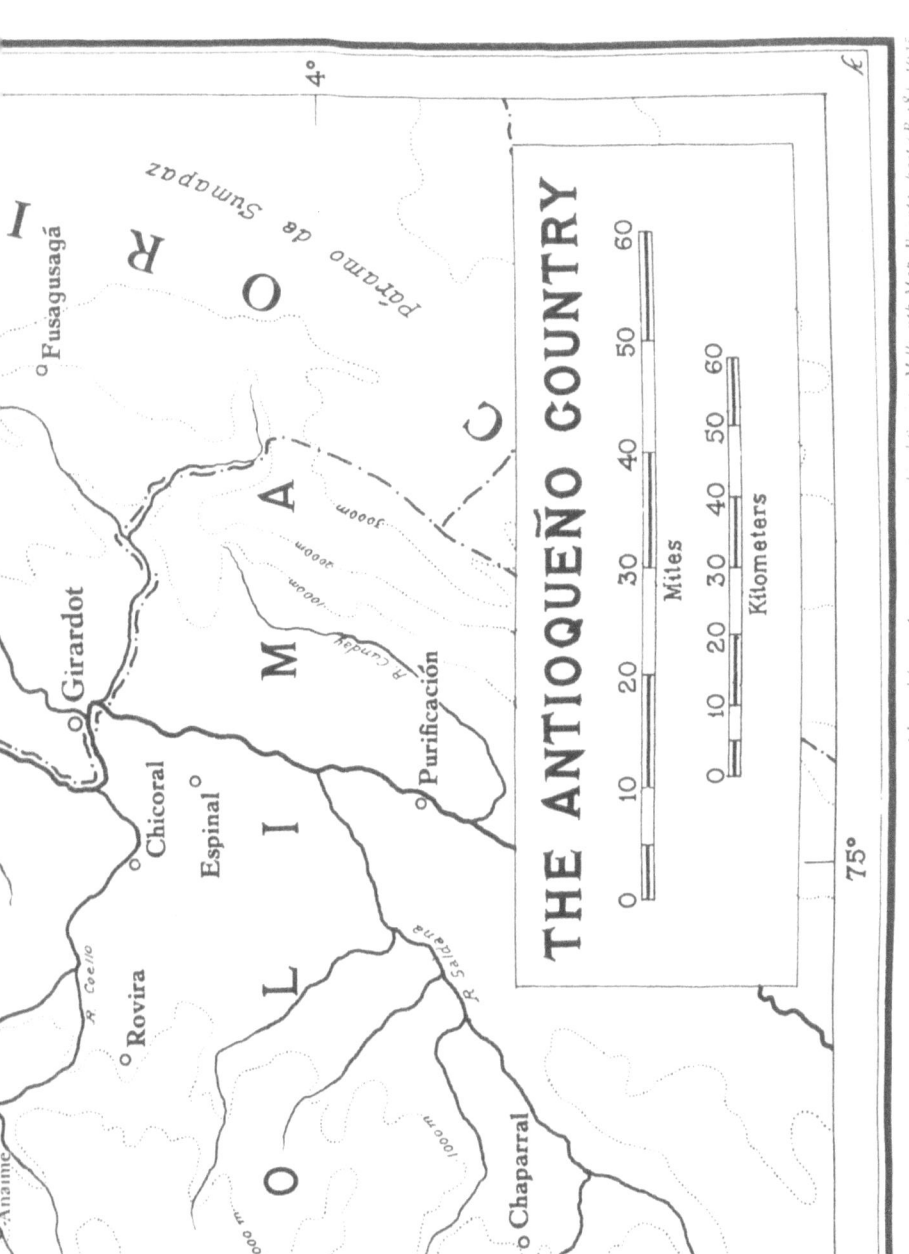

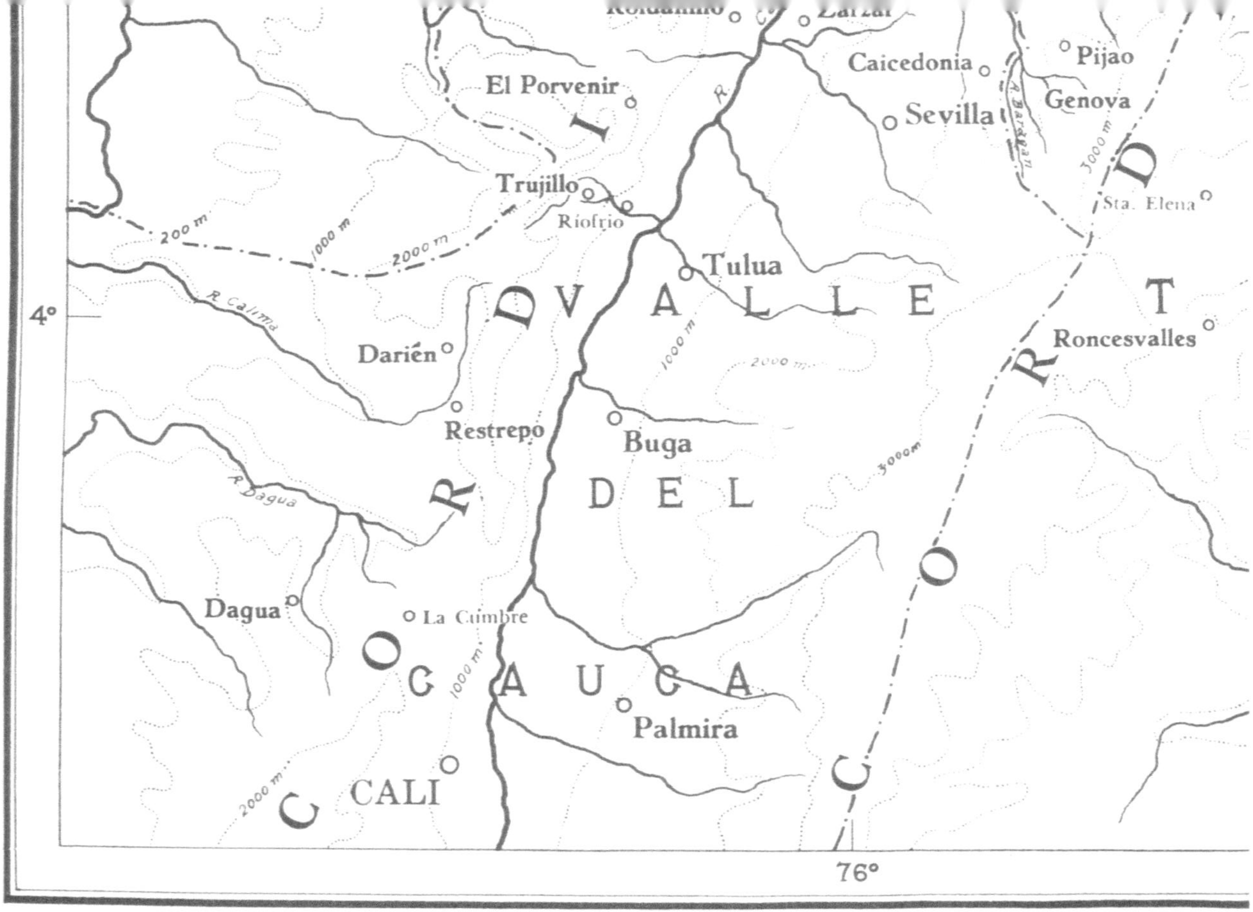

El Porvenir
Trujillo
Riofrio
Tulua
Caicedonia
Sevilla
Pijao
Genova
R. Bargan
Sta. Elena
Roncesvalles
Darién
Restrepo
Buga
R. Calima
R. Dagua
Dagua
La Cumbre
Palmira
CALI
VALLE DEL CAUCA
CORDILLERA
CORDILLERA
200 m
1000 m
2000 m
3000 m
4°
76°

Map

www.ingramcontent.com/pod-product-compliance
Lightning Source LLC
Chambersburg PA
CBHW021700230426
43668CB00008B/682